In the Name of Entrepreneurship?

The Logic and Effects of Special Regulatory Treatment for Small Business

Susan M. Gates, Kristin J. Leuschner
Editors

Supported by the Ewing Marion Kauffman Foundation

KAUFFMAN-RAND INSTITUTE FOR
ENTREPRENEURSHIP PUBLIC POLICY

The research described in this monograph was conducted by the Kauffman-RAND Institute for Entrepreneurship Public Policy (KRI), which is housed within the RAND Institute for Civil Justice (ICJ). KRI's work is supported by a grant from the Ewing Marion Kauffman Foundation.

Library of Congress Cataloging-in-Publication Data

In the name of entrepreneurship? : the logic and effects of special regulatory treatment for small business / Susan M. Gates, Kristin J. Leuschner, editors.
   p. cm.
   ISBN 978-0-8330-4204-0 (pbk. : alk. paper)
   1. Small business—Government policy—United States. 2. Small business—Law and legislation—United States. I. Gates, Susan M., 1968– II. Leuschner, Kristin.

HD2346.U5I546 2007
338.6'420973—dc22

          2007030590

The RAND Corporation is a nonprofit research organization providing objective analysis and effective solutions that address the challenges facing the public and private sectors around the world. RAND's publications do not necessarily reflect the opinions of its research clients and sponsors.

RAND® is a registered trademark.

Cover design by Eileen Delson La Russo

Published 2007 by the RAND Corporation
1776 Main Street, P.O. Box 2138, Santa Monica, CA 90407-2138
1200 South Hayes Street, Arlington, VA 22202-5050
4570 Fifth Avenue, Suite 600, Pittsburgh, PA 15213-2665
RAND URL: http://www.rand.org/
To order RAND documents or to obtain additional information, contact
Distribution Services: Telephone: (310) 451-7002;
Fax: (310) 451-6915; Email: order@rand.org

Preface

The Kauffman-RAND Institute for Entrepreneurship Public Policy (KRI) was established in 2004 (as the Kauffman-RAND Center for Regulation and Small Business) to respond to the need to understand the impact of policy and regulation on small businesses. KRI's initial objective was to evaluate and inform legal and regulatory policymaking related to small businesses and entrepreneurship through objective, rigorous, empirically based research. For the past three years, KRI activities have been devoted to improving understanding of business responses to regulatory policymaking. Our initial research efforts over the past three years have focused on three broad questions:

- What insights can be drawn from existing research on the impact of regulation and litigation on small businesses and entrepreneurship?
- What data are available to support research on the impact of regulation and policy on small businesses, and what additional data are needed?
- What do focused studies in selected policy areas reveal about the differential effects of regulation and policy on small businesses?

KRI has supported a number of research studies on different topics. Specific topics were chosen to leverage existing RAND expertise, utilize readily available data sources, and develop new data sources. This book highlights some of the key findings from research efforts supported by KRI and describes a road map for future work.

The RAND Institute for Civil Justice

The RAND Institute for Civil Justice (ICJ) is an independent research program within the RAND Corporation. The mission of ICJ, a division of the RAND Corporation, is to improve private and public decisionmaking on civil legal issues by supplying policymakers and the public with the results of objective, empirically based, analytic research. ICJ facilitates change in the civil justice system by analyzing trends and outcomes, identifying and evaluating policy options, and bringing together representatives of different interests to debate alternative solutions to policy problems. ICJ builds on a long tradition of RAND research characterized by an interdisciplinary, empirical approach to public policy issues and rigorous standards of quality, objectivity, and independence.

ICJ research is supported by pooled grants from corporations, trade and professional associations, and individuals; by government grants and contracts; and by private foundations. ICJ disseminates its work widely to the legal, business, and research communities and to the public. In accordance with RAND policy, all ICJ research products are subject to peer review before publication. ICJ publications do not necessarily reflect the opinions or policies of the research sponsors or of the ICJ Board of Overseers.

The Kauffman-RAND Institute for Entrepreneurship Public Policy (KRI), which is housed within ICJ, is dedicated to assessing and improving legal and regulatory policymaking as it relates to small businesses and entrepreneurship in a wide range of settings, including corporate governance, employment law, consumer law, securities regulation, and business ethics. KRI's work is supported by a grant from the Ewing Marion Kauffman Foundation.

For additional information on ICJ or KRI, please contact the directors:

Robert Reville, Director
RAND Institute for Civil
Justice
1776 Main Street
P.O. Box 2138
Santa Monica, CA 90407-2138
310-393-0411 x6786
Fax: 310-451-6979
Robert_Reville@rand.org

Susan Gates, Director
Kauffman-RAND Institute for
Entrepreneurship Public Policy
1776 Main Street
P.O. Box 2138
Santa Monica, CA 90407-2138
310-393-0411 x7452
Fax: 310-451-6979
Susan_Gates@rand.org

Contents

CHAPTER FOUR

Small Businesses and Workplace Fatality Risk: An Exploratory Analysis
*John Mendeloff, Christopher Nelson, Kilkon Ko, and
Amelia Haviland*

CHAPTER FIVE

Sarbanes-Oxley's Effects on Small Firms: What Is the Evidence?.... 143
Ehud Kamar, Pinar Karaca-Mandic, and Eric Talley

Figures

Tables

Acknowledgments

Many people both within and outside RAND contributed to this book. We are grateful for the input of the numerous experts on small business and public policy who participated in the Kauffman-RAND symposia in fall 2004 and fall 2005, contributing to the research agenda for KRI. We are particularly indebted to John Graham, who reviewed the entire book manuscript and provided extensive comments and suggestions that have dramatically improved the book. We are also grateful for the comments and feedback received from Robert Litan of the Kauffman Foundation and Robert Reville of RAND on earlier versions of the book manuscript.

In addition to the review of the entire book, at least two people, both internal and external to RAND, also reviewed each substantive chapter. We wish to thank all of these individuals, whose reviews improved each study. At RAND, these reviewers included Anthony Bower (now at Amgen), Richard Buddin, Debra Knopman, John Russer, Michael Greenberg, Carole Gresenz, Pinar Karaca-Mandic, Jacob Klerman (now at Abt Associates), and Darius Lakdawalla. External reviewers included Scott Baker of the University of North Carolina at Chapel Hill, R. Preston McAfee of Yahoo! Research, Larry Ribstein of the University of Illinois College of Law, and Mark Showalter of Brigham Young University. Of course, we are responsible for the final volume.

All authors would like to thank our RAND colleagues, especially Donna White, who pulled together the final manuscript and managed to keep track of each chapter through the writing and review process.

Nancy Good, Michelle Platt, and Donna White provided administrative support, Lisa Bernard carefully edited the report, and James Torr proofread the final copy.

This book would not have been possible without generous support from the Ewing Marion Kauffman Foundation. We are especially grateful to Carl Schramm and to our project monitor, Robert Litan, for their insightful input to the activities of KRI leading up to this book and for their commitment to research on issues related to entrepreneurship public policy.

Abbreviations

ADA	Americans with Disabilities Act of 1990
ADEA	Age Discrimination in Employment Act of 1967
AHIP	America's Health Insurance Plans
AHRQ	Agency for Healthcare Research and Quality
BAPCPA	Bankruptcy Abuse Prevention and Consumer Protection Act of 2005
BED	Business Employment Dynamics
BITS	Business Information Tracking System
BLS	U.S. Bureau of Labor Statistics
BR	Business Register
CBO	Characteristics of Business Owners
CBP	county business pattern
CDC	Centers for Disease Control and Prevention
CDHP	consumer-directed health plan
CERCLA	Comprehensive Environmental Response, Compensation, and Liability Act
CES	Current Employment Statistics
CESQG	conditionally exempt small-quantity generators

CFN	census file number
CFOI	National Census of Fatal Occupational Injuries
COBRA	Consolidated Omnibus Budget Reconciliation Act of 1985
COS	Company Organization Survey
CPS	Current Population Survey
CSI	Common Sense Initiative
D&B	Dun and Bradstreet
DMI	DUNS® Market Identifier
DOL	U.S. Department of Labor
EC	Economic Census
EEOC	U.S. Equal Employment Opportunity Commission
EIN	employer identification number
EPA	U.S. Environmental Protection Agency
ERISA	Employee Retirement and Income Security Act of 1974
FAT/CAT	fatality/catastrophe
FDA	U.S. Food and Drug Administration
FEI	Financial Executives International
FIFRA	Federal Insecticide, Fungicide, and Rodenticide Act
FSA	flexible spending account
GAO	U.S. Government Accountability Office
GP	general partnership
HC	household component

HDHP	high-deductible health plan
HDHP/SO	high-deductible health plan with a savings option
HI	health insurance
HIPAA	Health Insurance Portability and Accountability Act
HRA	health reimbursement arrangement
HRET	Health Research and Educational Trust
HSA	health savings account
HSE	health and safety executive
IC	insurance component
ILBD	Integrated Longitudinal Business Database
IMIS	Integrated Management Information System
KFF	Henry J. Kaiser Family Foundation
KFS	Kauffman Firm Survey
KRI	Kauffman-RAND Institute for Entrepreneurship Public Policy
LBD	Longitudinal Business Database
LEEM	Longitudinal Establishment and Enterprise Microdata
LEHD	Longitudinal Employer-Household Dynamics
MEPS	Medical Expenditures Panel Survey
MH	Martindale-Hubbell
MHPA	Mental Health Parity Act of 1996
MPC	medical-provider component
MSA	medical savings account

MSD	musculoskeletal disorder
NAICS	North American Industrial Classification System
NCS	National Compensation Survey
NEHIS	National Employer Health Insurance Survey
NEPA	National Environmental Policy Act
NFIB	National Federation of Independent Businesses
NHC	nursing-home component
NLRA	National Labor Relations Act of 1935
NLRB	National Labor Relations Board
NMHPA	Newborns' and Mothers' Health Protection Act of 1996
OLS	ordinary least squares
OSH	Occupational Safety and Health
PA	professional association
PC	professional corporation
PCAOB	Public Company Accounting Oversight Board
PCV	piercing the corporate veil
PDA	Pregnancy Discrimination Act of 1978
PLC	professional limited company
PPN	permanent plant number
PRA	Paperwork Reduction Act of 1995
QCEW	Quarterly Census of Employment and Wages
RCRA	Resource Recovery and Conservation Act
RDC	Research Data Center

RFA	Regulatory Flexibility Act of 1980
S&P	Standard and Poor's
SARA	Superfund Amendments and Reauthorization Act
SBA	U.S. Small Business Administration
SBIR	Small Business Innovation Research
SBO	Survey of Business Owners
SBPRA	Small Business Paperwork Relief Act of 2002
SBREFA	Small Business Regulatory Enforcement Fairness Act of 1996
SDWA	Safe Drinking Water Act
SEC	U.S. Securities and Exchange Commission
SESA-ID	state employment security agency identification number
SIC	standard industrial classification
SIPP	Survey of Income and Program Participation
SMOBE	Survey of Minority-Owned Business Enterprises
SOI	Statistics of Income
SOX	Sarbanes-Oxley Act
SP	sole proprietorship
SSBF	Survey of Small Business Finances
SSEL	Standard Statistical Establishment Listing
SWOBE	Survey of Women-Owned Business Enterprises
TAMRA	Technical and Miscellaneous Revenue Act of 1988
TSCA	Toxic Substances Control Act

UCFE	Unemployment Compensation for Federal Employees
UI	unemployment insurance
WARN	Worker Adjustment and Retraining Notification
WC	workers' compensation
WHCRA	Women's Health and Cancer Rights Act of 1998
WIRS	Workplace Industrial Relations Survey

CHAPTER ONE

Introduction

Small businesses are an important feature of the U.S. political and economic landscape. Small businesses (defined as firms with fewer than 500 employees) account for almost half of all gross revenues generated by U.S. businesses, employ half of all private-sector workers, and generate between 60 and 80 percent of net new jobs. Entrepreneurship is generally viewed as an engine of technological progress and economic growth. It is also an important element of the American dream: a means for those who have little more than ambition and a good idea to improve their lot in life. Not surprisingly, the interests of small businesses and entrepreneurs are frequently mentioned in policy debates.

Every day, policymakers at the federal, state, and local levels make decisions that have important implications for the livelihoods of entrepreneurs and small-business owners. There is ongoing concern that some regulations, rules, and government policies place a disproportionate burden on small businesses. For example, there is empirical evidence that some regulations place higher costs of compliance on small businesses than on other entities, since many of these costs do not vary by firm size and are incurred on an ongoing (rather than one-time) basis (Bradford, 2004). The tort system can affect small businesses differently as well, though the precise nature of that effect is less clear: In some cases, customers, employees, and government agencies might be *less* likely to punish or sue small businesses, because the perceived payoff is low; on the other hand, customers or employees might be likelier to sue a small business if they perceive that it cannot afford to mount an effective legal defense.

For both economic and political reasons, policymakers at the local, state, and federal levels have an interest in promoting, or at least not getting in the way of, small businesses and entrepreneurs. As a result, the special concerns of small businesses often receive prominent attention in the laws, regulations, requirements, and programs that result from those decisions. For example, food producers with *fewer than 100 full-time–equivalent employees* are exempt from the U.S. Food and Drug Administration's (FDA's) nutrition-labeling requirements *on food products that have U.S. sales of fewer than 100,000 units per year* (FDA, 1999). The Massachusetts Health Care Reform Plan requires all employers *with more than 10 employees* either to provide health-insurance (HI) coverage or to pay into a statewide fund (Commonwealth of Massachusetts, 2006, section 188[b]). Small public companies, *those with a market capitalization of $75 million or less*, have been granted four extensions to the compliance deadline, now December 15, 2007, for section 404 of the Sarbanes-Oxley Act (SOX) (P.L. 107-204). This section of the act requires firms to issue a report assessing the effectiveness of internal controls on financial reporting. These are but a few of the countless examples of special regulatory treatment received by small businesses.

The desire to support small businesses can come into conflict with the desire to address the other social concerns that led to regulation in the first place. This can occur, for example, when the cost of compliance places an excessive burden on small businesses or when regulation is ineffective in attaining its purpose due to exemptions made for small businesses. Other questions arise with regard to the effect of special regulatory treatment designed to help small businesses. Why and under what circumstances does special regulatory treatment for small businesses occur? Why does it take the specific form it takes? What objectives is it designed to serve, and how effective is it in achieving these aims?

The goal of this book is to begin to shed light on the ways in which the legal and regulatory environments affect small businesses— both in terms of any differential effect of regulation and policy on small businesses compared to large ones and in terms of the impact of the special regulatory treatment afforded to small businesses. We summarize findings from the first three years of research effort within the Kauffman-RAND Institute for Entrepreneurship Public Policy (KRI). KRI's research focus to date has been on describing the legal and regulatory environments to examine the effects of specific policies and regulations on small businesses. This introduction sets the stage for the book by describing the role of regulation in managing the relationship between business and society, illustrating how small businesses fit into that landscape, and emphasizing the limitations in our knowledge of the ways in which regulation affects small businesses.

Managing the Relationship Between Business and Society

We begin with a brief discussion of the evolution of business regulation and policy in the United States. Although regulations and the litigation system were typically designed with large businesses in mind, they nevertheless affect small businesses in both direct and indirect ways. To understand their effects on small businesses, it is necessary to understand the general approaches for managing the relationship between business and society and how those approaches have evolved over time.

The perceived need to manage or shape the relationship between business and society stems primarily from concerns about the effects of large businesses on society: high or predatory prices charged by monopolists, pollution emitted by large manufacturers, unfair labor practices exercised by large employers, or large manufacturers' ability to subvert the tort system designed to protect consumers. Government regulation and private litigation provide two important mechanisms for shaping the relationship between businesses and society in the United States. These mechanisms are used to address two overriding public objectives: (1) to promote market competition and control large firms' market power over customers and smaller firms and (2) to mitigate or prevent the adverse effects of business activity (negative externalities) on individuals, organizations, and the environment. The first objective is addressed through federal and state antitrust regulation and litigation over anticompetitive practices. The second objective is tackled through an expansive array of environmental, securities, employment, health, and safety regulation and the tort system.

Regulation assumed an important role in the U.S. economic landscape during the Progressive Era of the late 1800s and early 1900s with the passage of legislation such as the Sherman Act (26 Stat. 209), the Interstate Commerce Act (P.L. 49-41), and the Pure Food and Drug Act (P.L. 59-384) and the establishment of federal regulatory agencies such as the FDA (P.L. 59-384), the Interstate Commerce Commission (P.L. 49-41), and FTC (38 Stat. 717). Prior to this, private litigation was the primary means of resolving conflicts involving businesses, and the government had little capacity to intervene in such conflicts. Glaeser and Shleifer (2003) attribute the ascendance of government regulation in the Progressive Era to economic industrialization and the ensuing concentration of economic wealth in the hands of large firms. They argue that large, wealthy firms have much to lose in legal contests and that the cost of influencing the process through bribery and intimidation was relatively low. In other words, large firms had both a strong incentive and the ability to subvert the legal system for their own benefit. Although, as we discuss below, the regulatory system is not immune to such influence either, it may be less vulnerable than the legal system is. By this argument, regulation emerged from societal frustration with the legal system's ability to control the behavior of large businesses and from a sense that regulation could do a better job—at least in some spheres. Regulations targeted large firms, and little consideration was given to the fact that smaller firms might be affected.

Since the Progressive Era, the regulatory environment facing businesses has grown infinitely more complex. Typically, new regulations and regulatory agencies are added to what already exists, although occasionally regulations are repealed, deregulation occurs, and regulatory agencies close down. At the federal level, new waves of regulation have typically corresponded to heightened public concerns about wide-ranging social, consumer product, health, HI, safety, and environmental issues. The Securities Act of 1933 (P.L. 73-22) and the Securities Exchange Act of 1934 (P.L. 73-291) established disclosure requirements designed to protect investors in the wake of the stock-market collapse and the Great Depression. The Securities Exchange Act led to the establishment of the U.S. Securities and Exchange Commission (SEC), which has responsibility for enforcing federal securities laws and regulating the industry. The Fair Labor Standards Act of 1938 (P.L. 75-718), which came into effect at the end of the Great Depression, guaranteed a minimum wage and regulated the use of child labor and overtime pay. The Great Society Era saw the introduction of the Civil Rights Act of 1964 (P.L. 88-352) and several other antidiscrimination laws that regulated the employment relationship and established the U.S. Equal Employment Opportunity Commission (EEOC) (42 U.S.C. 2000e). That era also set the stage for a wave of federal environmental and safety regulation, starting with the Air Quality Act of 1967 (P.L. 90-148) and the establishment of the U.S. Environmental Protection Agency (EPA) (Nixon, 1970) and OSHA (P.L. 91-596) in 1970. In the 1980s and 1990s, regulations on employer-sponsored HI emerged in response to rising HI costs and concerns about access to group coverage; these included parts of the Consolidated Omnibus Budget Reconciliation Act of 1985 (COBRA) (P.L. 99-272) and the Health Insurance Portability and Accountability Act (HIPAA) (P.L. 104-191). HI regulation, and even the idea of a national, universal, health-care system, remains a subject of consideration well into the new millennium. Finally, in response to the corporate scandals of the late 1990s and early 2000s, SOX created the Public Company Accounting Oversight Board (PCAOB) and introduced additional auditing and documentation requirements for publicly traded firms.

The complexity of the regulatory environment stems not only from the addition of new regulations and regulatory agencies on top of old ones but also from the absence of mechanisms capable of coordinating regulation across substantive areas at the federal level. The situation is further complicated by the layering of federal, state, and local regulations, as well as by a lack of coordination across governmental levels and across regulatory areas. While some federal regulations, such as the Employment Retirement and Income Security Act of 1974 (ERISA) (P.L. 93-406), preempt state regulations in the same regulatory area, in other areas, it is not uncommon for state and even local governments to impose regulations that are more stringent or broader than the federal regulation. For example, many states and cities have established minimum-wage laws that set a higher wage than the federal minimum wage. In addition, state and local government can impose regulations in areas that the federal government does not regulate. Thus, a single business operating in several states and localities might need to keep abreast of thousands of regulations.

A 1996 report by the U.S. General Accounting Office highlighted the day-to-day implications of the complex regulatory environment and the fragmented nature of information on regulatory responsibilities. In the study, the office attempted to thoroughly document the federal regulatory burden faced by 15 U.S. companies. Many firms that were contacted to participate in the study declined because they did not have the type of information for which the office was looking. Even those that did agree to participate could not provide the office with a complete list of all federal regulations that applied to them. In particular, firms had trouble separating federal regulations from state and local ones. Further, the office found that federal regulatory agencies themselves could often not determine whether a regulation would apply to a particular firm. The study found great concern among firms about the lack of coordination across agencies and across government jurisdictions.

It is important to recognize that this regulatory complexity is further layered atop the risk of litigation. The risk of private litigation typically remains in spite of government laws. Government can choose to play an active role in enforcing laws that govern business behavior—for example, by establishing an agency with the power to monitor and impose sanctions. However, governments can also rely on the legal system for enforcement. Particularly in the absence of formal regulatory enforcement, government laws can increase a firm's legal exposure.

This brief summary of the roles of regulation and litigation in managing the relationship between business and society highlights several potentially salient issues for small businesses. First, most of the regulation that applies to small businesses was developed with larger businesses in mind. Secondly, the legal and regulatory environments that have emerged over the past century are extremely complex. The number of laws and the variation in how they are applied make it difficult for small businesses to comply. Finally, the fragmented nature of regulation, with a lack of coordination across substantive areas and across jurisdictions, contributes to the difficulty in complying.

The Politics of the Legal and Regulatory Environments

The regulatory landscape for businesses is made more complex due to its politicization. Large businesses, in particular, are an important and potentially powerful interest group. Politicization has different implications for large businesses and small businesses. The "iron triangle" theory of policymaking and the theory of "regulatory capture" (Stigler, 1971; Peltzman, 1976) suggest that the firms in a regulated industry will use whatever means available (e.g., lobbying; provision of electoral support, information, and expertise) to influence the regulatory design for their own benefit.[1]

Firms use their influence to make sure that legislators and bureaucrats take their objectives into account in the design of regulation. In certain contexts, firms might actually prefer a regulated environment, because government regulation enhances firms' ability to coordinate with one another to fix prices, deter the entry of new firms, and reap targeted benefits from government (Kolko, 1970). Influence can extend beyond the features of the regulation itself to include procedural rules for the regulatory agency in charge of implementing the regulation (McCubbins, Noll, and Weingast, 1987, 1989). These rules are often designed to prevent "regulatory drift" by limiting the discretion that regulatory agencies might otherwise exercise in implementing the regulation. Firms in the regulated industry may have deeper understanding of practical implications of these rules ex ante and their ultimate implications for regulatory outcomes. In the end, regulatory agencies can be substantially affected and constrained by the political influence

---

[1] *Iron triangle* is a term used to describe the relationships among interest groups, the U.S. Congress, and the bureaucracy (i.e., federal agencies) in the policymaking process. *Regulatory capture* refers to a phenomenon in which the targets of regulation can influence or direct the actions of the government agencies that are responsible for enforcing the regulation.

of interest groups (Wilson, 1989) and by information asymmetries and the knowledge that firms in the regulated industry possess (Laffont and Tirole, 1991).

As we mentioned earlier, it has been argued that regulation emerged, in part, out of societal frustration with the legal system's ability to control the behavior of large businesses and out of a sense that regulation could do a better job—at least in some spheres. This section has illustrated that the regulatory system is open also to influence from interest groups. A relevant question, then, is whether larger firms would be in a better position than smaller firms are to exert that type of influence over the regulatory environment. We turn to that question next.

Small Businesses and the Legal and Regulatory Environments

As described in the preceding section, most regulations were put in place in response to concerns about the effects of businesses—primarily large businesses—on society. Given the importance of small businesses in society, it is crucial to consider how the legal and regulatory environments influence small businesses and the ways in which those influences differ from those on large businesses.

The public concerns that generate demand for regulation or legal reform are usually significant ones, and there are many interest groups representing various sides of these issues. As a practical matter, the specific concerns of small businesses add rarely more than a footnote to the legislative history of reform. However, that is not to say that the concerns of small businesses are ignored.

Small businesses do receive a variety of special considerations—particularly in the regulatory context. This approach is often referred to as *tiering*. As will be described more fully in Chapter Two of this book, these special considerations vary tremendously across specific regulations. In some cases, small businesses receive a complete exemption from regulations. In other instances, small businesses receive special consideration in regulatory enforcement, support programs designed to assist them in complying, or delays in the application of new regulations. The definition of a small business can vary dramatically by regulatory context—typically ranging from two to 500 or more employees. Regulations can also use other measures of firm size, however, such as gross receipts. Regulatory thresholds inherent in a tiering approach should logically create incentives for firms that are near the threshold to restrain their growth because, if they go above the threshold, they will suddenly be subject to a regulation from which they used to be exempt. If regulatory compliance is costly and something to be avoided, then such thresholds should have behavioral effects. This is an issue we discuss in greater detail in this book.

The theory of collective action (Olson, 1965) suggests that large firms would be likeliest to exert influence over the regulatory and legal process. Not only do they have greater financial and political resources available than do small businesses, but they also may have more to gain or lose from the regulatory process. On the one hand, small firms might benefit from the activities of larger firms. To the extent that the interests of small firms are well aligned with the interests of larger firms in an industry, the small firms can "free ride" on the influence or activities of the larger firms. Smaller firms can also benefit from whatever compromises the larger firms can win in the political process—for example, in terms of the stringency of the regulation or delays in adoption. However, the interests of small firms may also differ from those of larger firms in important ways. For example, a major concern of small businesses is that compliance with regulations can impose substantial fixed costs of operation that create barriers to new entry or increase the minimum efficient scale in an industry. Large firms are unlikely to be as concerned about such issues, and, indeed, might view such costs or entry barriers as advantageous in the long run, because they reduce potential competitors' ability to enter the market.

The small-business community long ago recognized a need to represent its interests in a coordinated way across industries. The National Federation of Independent Businesses (NFIB) was founded in 1943, and other trade associations subsequently emerged to represent the common interests of small businesses in the political process. Today, the small-business lobby is an important player on the political landscape. Initially, this lobby was focused on small-business assistance programs and initiatives to ensure that small businesses received a fair share of government contracts (e.g., the Small Business Act of 1953 [P.L. 83-163]). However, interest in regulatory issues increased significantly with the proliferation of regulation in the 1960s and 1970s, coupled with federal agencies' tendency to adopt a one-size-fits-all approach to regulation that often involved extensive reporting requirements or arbitrary and piecemeal regulatory tiering.

The small-business lobby sought a greater voice for small businesses in the regulatory rulemaking process and a reduction in reporting burdens across the board, as well as assistance with regulatory compliance. As early as 1974, legislation that would ultimately lead to the Regulatory Flexibility Act of 1980 (RFA) (P.L. 96-354) was being introduced in Congress.[2] The RFA requires federal agencies to consider carefully whether proposed rules will have a "significant economic impact on a substantial number of small entities." Unless the agency certifies that a rule will not have such an impact, it must conduct a regulatory-flexibility analysis. The regulatory-flexibility analysis focuses on the expected effects of a proposed rule on small entities and requires a public commentary period, a description of alternatives considered, and a justification for the final rule that was adopted.

Tiering is just one of several approaches that agencies can consider for mitigating the effect of a regulation on small businesses. Also passed in 1980, the Paperwork Reduction Act (PRA) (P.L. 96-511), which was designed to reduce reporting requirements and improve the management of information provided to the federal government by centralizing authority over information collection to the Office of Management and Budget of the Executive Office of the President of the United States of America (OMB).

Although the RFA was considered to be a step in the right direction in terms of providing small businesses with a voice in the regulatory process, its limitations were quickly recognized. For example, it was fairly easy for government agencies to simply ignore the act or to certify that a rule would not substantially influence small entities (Verkuil,

---

2   See Verkuil (1982) for a detailed legislative history and description of the RFA.

1982; Holman, 2006). The Small Business Regulatory Enforcement Fairness Act of 1996 (SBREFA) (P.L. 104-121) amended the RFA to impose specific requirements on federal agencies in the interest of improving compliance with the act. Executive Order 13272 (signed in August 2002) (Bush, 2002) requires federal regulatory agencies to develop written procedures for implementing the RFA. The NFIB legal foundation remains active in efforts to ensure that federal agencies live up to RFA requirements and in promoting RFA-type legislation at the state (MRP, 2002) and local levels.

In response to a growing wave of government regulation at the federal, state, and local levels, small-business interests have organized to represent their interests in the policymaking process. The prevalence of regulatory tiering, as well as legislation such as RFA (P.L. 96-354), suggest that small businesses have had some influence over regulatory policymaking. Nevertheless, questions remain as to the effectiveness of that influence.

Improved Understanding of the Impact of Regulation on Small Businesses Is Needed

Figure 1.1 provides a conceptual model of the regulatory and legal reform process as discussed in this chapter. As shown in the figure, regulation or legal reform originates with public concern regarding the impact of some business action on employees, customers, other individuals or organizations, or the physical environment or ecological resources. A new regulatory environment is then created or the existing legal or regulatory environment is modified to address these concerns. This environment, which includes regulations, laws, and enforcement mechanisms, may affect different firms in different ways, whether intentionally or unintentionally. These business responses to the legal and regulatory environments lead to economic and other outcomes (e.g., social, environmental). Once this chain of events has played out,

Figure 1.1
Conceptual Model of the Regulatory and Legal Reform Process

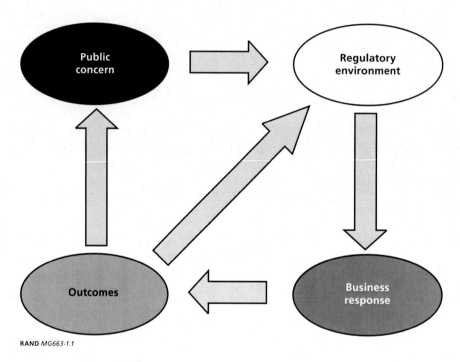

the outcomes may feed into new public concerns and lead to additional changes in the regulatory environment as part of an ongoing cycle.

With RFA (P.L. 96-354), SBREFA (P.L. 104-121), and similar laws at the state level, policymakers have clearly recognized a need to consider the effect of regulation on small businesses. However, the information required to make this assessment and to develop reasonable policy alternatives appropriate to small businesses is sorely lacking. Unfortunately, there is little quantitative evidence to demonstrate the specific impacts of policies and regulations on small businesses; nor has there been much evidence showing whether rules and exemptions designed to benefit small businesses actually have that effect. Additionally, there is little evidence that small-business exemptions are crafted in a way that appropriately balances the costs and benefits of regulation. We currently know little about exactly when and under what circumstances it makes sense for policymakers to institute differential legal treatment—or wholesale retrenchment from regulatory intervention—based on firm size.

Much of what we know about the interactions among regulation, litigation, and business stems from research that looks at the implications of regulations for large firms. The greater emphasis given in research to the impact of regulations on larger firms is understandable. Larger firms tend to receive the most public exposure, both in the popular press and by word of mouth. Moreover, the policy goal of mitigating the adverse effects of business activity on other individuals or organizations is geared specifically toward perceived problems generated by large firms, since the capability of inflicting economic and social harms typically increases with firm size. And finally, because larger businesses are more frequently subject to reporting and disclosure requirements, they are a much more fertile harvesting ground for empirical data. However, the importance of large businesses does not negate the need to understand the impact of regulation on smaller businesses. Excluding such a significant component of economic activity from the landscape of informed policy debate is both risky and imprudent.

This book takes an important step in the direction of improving our understanding of how the legal and regulatory environments affect small firms. It summarizes results from the first three years of effort within KRI. KRI's initial objective was to evaluate and inform legal and regulatory policymaking related to small businesses and entrepreneurship through objective, rigorous, empirically based research. Our initial research efforts over the past three years have focused on three broad questions:

- What insights can be drawn from existing research on the impact of regulation and litigation on small businesses and entrepreneurship?
- What data are available to support research on the impact of regulation and policy on small businesses, and what additional data are needed?
- What do focused studies in selected policy areas reveal about the differential effects of regulation and policy on small businesses?

KRI has supported a number of research studies on different topics designed to address these questions.

Overview of the Book

This book highlights some of the key findings from research efforts supported by KRI and describes a road map for future work. Specific topics were chosen to leverage existing RAND expertise, utilize readily available data sources, and develop new data sources.

Chapter Two describes the regulatory and legal environments in four key areas in which government regulation and private litigation both play a role in controlling the relationship between business and society and in which the regulatory and legal systems might be expected to have a different effect on small businesses: corporate and securities law, environmental law, employment law, and HI regulation.[3] This chapter provides a review of previous research and summarizes what we know about the relationship between regulation and small businesses. In reviewing the regulatory environment, the chapter describes the exemption thresholds and other approaches to adjusting the regulatory environment for small businesses. The chapter emphasizes the importance of considering whether regulations or programs designed to benefit small businesses are meeting their objectives, whether they are well targeted, and whether they have unintended consequences that interfere with intended aims. The chapter concludes with some general observations on the way in which the regulatory and legal environments are adjusted to address small-business concerns and a summary of what we know about the effectiveness of these approaches.

This overview sets the stage for four research studies presented in Chapters Three through Six of this book. These focused analyses

---

[3]   Although these four areas cover a significant slice of government regulation, our review does not provide a comprehensive summary of the effect of government policy on small businesses. In particular, we do not consider the effects of taxation and tax policy. While tax policy may not always be viewed as regulatory in nature, government actions and policies related to taxation have an enormous effect on business decisions.

contribute to our knowledge about the effect of public policy on small businesses and the role of research in policy assessment.

Chapter Three provides an assessment of recent policies designed to improve the HI market that small businesses face. In so doing, it considers the more general issue of the effect of regulatory thresholds on the behavior of small businesses. The study reviews evidence that state-level regulation of HI did not result in the intended benefits for small businesses. Although HI regulations have been designed and implemented by nearly all states with the purpose of improving access to HI among employees of small businesses, research suggests that the regulations have had no impact on the propensity of small firms to offer HI. Moreover, the study suggests that these regulations had unintended effects. Specifically, the analysis provides evidence that firms that were close to the threshold for inclusion in small-group HI reforms actually hired more employees in order to avoid being subject to the regulation.

Chapter Four summarizes results from a recent study on the relationship between firm size and workplace fatalities. The study separates out the effects of firm size and establishment size on safety risk and discusses the implications for health and safety policy. The distinction between firm size and establishment size and its implications for public policy arises in many settings. This study found that the smallest establishments within a firm have the highest fatality rates. Surprisingly, the risk associated with small establishments depends on the size of the firm of which they are a part. The research found that, for establishments in size categories with fewer than 100 workers, those in the smallest firms had the lowest fatality rates. Smaller establishments in larger firms were the riskiest, while small, single-establishment firms were among the safest. The findings point to several issues that should be considered in developing policy options to address health and safety problems at small establishments or firms.

Chapter Five provides an overview of the regulatory regime created by SOX (P.L. 107-204) and its implications for small firms. The authors review the available evidence on SOX's effects on compliance costs, market reactions, and firm deregistrations. This chapter points out the challenges involved in comparing the findings from different research studies due to variation in the definition used of *small business*. Nevertheless, the chapter finds evidence that SOX increased the auditing and accounting costs for public firms and that the cost burden on small firms relative to large firms grew. The review also suggests that SOX adversely affected the market value of small but not large firms and made small public firms likelier than large ones to be acquired by private providers.

Beginning in the 1990s, states permitted law firms (and other professional service firms) to organize as LLPs and LLCs. These organizational forms preserve many of the attractive features of a partnership while shielding each of a firm's owners from liability for the malpractice of other owners. Chapter Six examines how the availability of these new business forms affected the organization of law firms. The authors find that smaller firms were much less likely than larger firms to reorganize but that small partnerships that reorganized grew faster than those that did not. Limited liability appears to be modestly beneficial to the owners of small law firms.

Chapter Seven turns to a consideration of the availability of data for investigating small-business policy issues. We describe key data sources, highlighting the pros and cons of each source. We also discuss the limitations of existing data. This discussion will be of particular interest to researchers as well as policymakers who would like to commission research to inform the policy debate.

The book concludes with an assessment of our efforts to date and some suggestions for future research. This research represents a first step in a larger research and policy agenda designed to better understand how government actions affect small firms and how policies could be better designed to promote entrepreneurship.

CHAPTER TWO

The Impact of Regulation and Litigation on Small Businesses and Entrepreneurship: An Overview

Lloyd Dixon, Susan M. Gates, Kanika Kapur, Seth A. Seabury, and Eric Talley

This chapter summarizes key differences between large and small firms in the way the legal and regulatory environments affect them. These differences stem from variations in laws and regulations by firm size, in implementation, and in business response. The chapter examines the regulatory and policy environments in four key areas: corporate and securities law, environmental law, employment law and regulation, and HI regulation. These four areas cover a significant slice of regulatory activity that is important to small business and entrepreneurship. HI is the number-one concern of small businesses today, and HI regulations are designed to address these concerns. Policymakers and other stakeholders have long-standing concerns regarding whether regulations in the environmental and employment areas place an unfair burden on small firms compared to that placed on larger ones due to the financial, personnel, and resource costs required for compliance. Although corporate and securities law has not traditionally garnered much attention from the small-business community, that changed in 2002, when SOX was passed. More generally, it provides an interesting area of focus for understanding issues related to the growth of small firms and their transformation into large firms.

This discussion builds on the view of the regulatory reform process shown in Figure 1.1 in Chapter One. As noted in Chapter One, most regulation tends to originate from concern about large businesses or about business in general rather than because of concern about small businesses per se. However, the regulatory environment that is created to address public concerns sometimes focuses specifically on small businesses by, for example, exempting certain types of businesses from the regulation or applying different enforcement mechanisms to different types of firms.

The distinction between large and small businesses is reflected in the extent to which we find different responses to the regulatory environment due to firm size. Such differences may or may not be evident depending on the regulatory issue in question. For example, the cost of implementing a complicated pollution-abatement technology may be so large as to invoke the same responses from a firm with 10 employees and from a firm with 100 employees (i.e., to close down). Meanwhile, the cost associated with a labor-reporting requirement may be a great burden on the firm with 10 employees but not on the firm with 100 employees.

In this chapter, we use a flexible definition of *small business* that is appropriate to the contextual application, the form of legal regulation, and the underlying social policy rationale being discussed. Perhaps the most often-cited definition of *small business* is that provided by the Small Business Act: "One that is independently owned and operated and [that] is not dominant in its field of operation" (P.L. 83-163). Note that this definition does not require the size of a business to be viewed through a unique lens, such as employee ranks, gross receipts, ownership structure, or market presence.

The remainder of this chapter focuses on the four areas of corporate and securities law, environmental law, employment law and regulation, and HI regulation. For each topic, we attempt to answer two questions:

- What are the key features of the regulatory and policy environments, and in what ways does the regulatory environment distinguish between large and small businesses?
- How have the regulatory policy and legal environments affected small businesses, and, in particular, in what ways has the small-business response to these environments differed from those of larger firms?

To tackle these questions, we begin with a review of the major laws and rules governing business behavior as well as any regulatory provisions focusing specifically on small businesses. Then we consider how the effects of and the small-business response to the regulatory and policy environments differ or might be expected to differ from those for large businesses. In this discussion, we draw on insights from existing research when available.

Corporate and Securities Law

We first consider the role that business-organization law and securities regulation can play in the formation, growth, and transition of small, entrepreneurial businesses. Corporate and securities law and regulations have real implications for the future growth potential of businesses and are thus relevant to the issue of entrepreneurship. Many small firms are formed with at least a partial eye toward becoming large firms, and the road to doing so almost always involves consideration of business form and capital structure. At critical junctures, the role of corporate and securities law is paramount. Consequently, these areas of law are likely to loom large to entrepreneurs even at the very inception of a business plan.

We should note that the definition of *small business* used in corporate and securities law is not generally based on conventional measures of operational size (such as employees, revenues, or market power), as is the case for most other regulatory spheres. Instead, corporate and securities law typically conceives of size in terms of either the distribution or the value of ownership in the firm. Privately held firms are generally considered small for the purposes of securities regulation; they are largely exempt from the mandates of federal securities law as long as they maintain their existing ownership form. While privately held firms would also usually be classified as small according to more typical measures (e.g., number of employees, gross receipts), there are exceptions. For example, privately held Cargill does business in the agricultural, food-distribution and -export, and industrial sectors; employs more than 100,000 people in 59 countries; and generates annual sales of approximately $60 billion, making it among the world's largest companies.

Regulatory Environment

There are three key decisions in the area of corporate and securities law that influence a business's size, or how it is affected by the regulatory environment: the decision to incorporate, the choice of organizational form, and the decision to be publicly as opposed to privately held.

Incorporation. Incorporation creates a legal distinction between a firm and its owners. Unincorporated firms can incur business-liability risks that have the potential to imperil the assets of the firm's owners. Incorporation is available to firms of all sizes—even those owned by sole proprietors.

The primary benefit of incorporation is to limit the liability of the firm's owners for the firm's debts and obligations. Other advantages include an unlimited life span (the corporation can continue even after the owner dies), transferability of shares, and the ability to raise capital. The major disadvantages associated with incorporation stem from the administrative paperwork burden and taxation.

Because the debts and obligations of unincorporated businesses are frequently indistinguishable from those of the owners, in the event of a business failure, personal bankruptcy law may affect the owners of unincorporated businesses. The Bankruptcy Abuse Prevention and Consumer Protection Act of 2005 (BAPCPA) (P.L. 109-8) was designed to reform some aspects of U.S. personal bankruptcy law, and (in part) to stem a perceived crisis in consumer credit that had culminated in record numbers of personal bankruptcy filings (see U.S. House of Representatives, 2005, p. 3).

One of the key reforms implemented by the law involves a personal-income threshold for access to Chapter 7 (liquidation) bankruptcy proceedings, the effect of which will likely be to force many would-be bankruptcy petitioners to file under Chapter 13 (reorganization) instead. As a practical matter, traditional Chapter 7 proceedings involved partial liquidation of a debtor's assets and legal termination of most debts without lien against a debtor's future income. By contrast, proceedings under the revised Chapter 13 are more burdensome, and primarily involve scheduled repayment of debts out of future income rather than a dismissal of debts in return for a liquidation of assets. The result is a new bankruptcy regime that is far less friendly to personal debtors, one that will focus more on restructuring and enforcing debt payments than on dismissing them. Several other changes implemented by the recent legislation likewise serve to make personal-bankruptcy laws more favorable to creditors and less protective of debtors. These changes include a longer schedule of mandatory repayments for some debtors under Chapter 13, more limitations on the categories of debt subject to Chapter 13 proceedings, and new statutory provisions designed to prevent debtor forum-shopping for favorable state property exemptions (see, e.g., Walker, 2005; see also Compact Library Publishers, undated).

Organizational Structure. Organizational choices are broader than the decision of whether to incorporate, and the options available to firm owners have grown substantially over the past 20 years. Table 2.1 summarizes these options. Organizational options do sometimes take firm size into account (e.g., S-corporation status is limited to firms with fewer than 75 shareholders).

The traditional general partnership[1] allows for comanagement as well as profit- and loss-sharing and allows governance to be tailored to a firm's individual needs. Partnerships receive pass-through treatment for tax purposes, allowing the owners to avoid entity-level taxation of their partnership income. A key disadvantage of partnerships is that all general partners are jointly and severally liable for the professional misconduct of other partners and are jointly liable for all other obligations of the firm.

The state-chartered corporation provides a more formalized structure than a partnership. Corporate status confers limited liability on its owners, so that they risk only the value of the shares they own. On the downside, corporate status is generally perceived as more

---

[1] This continues to be the default legal relationship for multiperson firms; however, *default* does not mean "dominant." Rather, if a business organization comes into being without complying with statutory formalities for forming, for example, a corporation, it will be considered a general partnership by default.

Table 2.1
Options for Business Organizational Structure

Organizational Form	Key Characteristics
General partnership	Allows for comanagement, profit-sharing, and loss-sharing, with governance tailored to the firm's individual needs. Receives pass-through treatment for tax purposes, allowing the owners to avoid entity-level taxation of their partnership income. Holds all partners jointly and severally liable for torts of other partners.
State-chartered corporation	Provides more formalized structure than partnership. Confers limited liability on its owners. Governance is largely regulated by statutes that are difficult to overturn.
S corporation	Allows professional corporations to take advantage of pass-through taxation under subchapter S of the Internal Revenue Code. Limited to companies with fewer than 75 shareholders, who must be U.S. citizens. Allowed to have only one class of stocks.
LLC and LLP	Combines the flexibility and pass-through taxation attributes of partnerships with a form of limited liability akin to that accorded to corporate status. LLCs and LLPs are required to have a limited life span and typically must carry a minimum amount of insurance against claims of third-party creditors.

cumbersome and inflexible, as governance procedures are largely regulated by statutes that, while allowing participants to opt out, are nonetheless perceived as difficult to overturn. Moreover, corporate status generally implies double taxation, in which the firm is taxed at the entity level and distributions to shareholders are once again taxed at the individual level.

About 25 years ago, both state business-recognizing bodies and state and federal taxation authorities began to implement significant reforms to their company-law statutes in a way that eroded the distinction between corporate and partnership status. During the early 1980s, federal taxation authorities began to allow professional corporations to take advantage of pass-through taxation by electing tax treatment under subchapter S of the Internal Revenue Code. For some firms, this option has proven extraordinarily beneficial. Nevertheless, S-corporation status still imposes a few important constraints on firms choosing this form. First, subchapter S applies only to companies with fewer than 75 shareholders, all of whom must be U.S. citizens. Second, while enjoying pass-through taxation, S corporations often cannot deduct the full expenses of many employee-benefit plans (which C corporations can) and are generally unable to use basic strategies to reduce or avoid tax liabilities on a sale of assets or share redemption, such as a step-up in the tax basis of an asset. In addition, S corporations are allowed to have only one class of stock.

Meanwhile, state legislatures have passed statutes authorizing the LLC and LLP forms, which many professional firms have adopted. LLCs and LLPs combine the flexibility and pass-through taxation attributes of partnerships, while according their owners a form of limited liability akin to corporate status. These novel business forms were adopted either jointly or individually within every state and the District of Columbia between 1977 and 1996.

Publicly Held Status. Firms that choose a corporate organizational status may also choose to be publicly held. Generally speaking, a publicly held corporation is one with shares held by a large number of people. The value of the assets and the number of shareholders determine whether the corporation is considered private in the sense that the SEC governs its activities. Although few entrepreneurs choose public status at the inception of a small business, the issue becomes increasingly germane as the firm grows and requires access to additional capital. Securities regulations are a central consideration for smaller firms seeking to make the transition to publicly traded status or to sustain and expand that status.

Federal securities regulations require firms to file an Exchange Act registration statement if they have more than $10 million in assets and a class of equity securities with more than 500 shareholders of record or list securities on an exchange. Firms that do not meet these criteria may, but are not required, to register. Registered firms face a variety of reporting requirements and restrictions outlined in the Securities Act of 1933 (P.L. 73-222) and the Securities Exchange Act of 1934 (P.L. 73-291). These regulations are designed to protect investors' interests by requiring the disclosure of pertinent information.[2]

---

[2] For details on these federal requirements, see SEC (2006b).

Federal securities regulations have simplified registration procedures for small businesses, allowing them to use streamlined processes either to begin offering securities for sale to the public or to expand their current offerings. In particular, the SEC allows an enterprise to use a special form SB-1 (SEC, 2007a) or SB-2 (SEC, 2007b) to register as a small-business issuer if (1) the business is a U.S. or Canadian issuer that had less than $25 million in revenues in its last fiscal year and (2) the business's outstanding, publicly held stock is worth no more than $25 million. Registration with the SEC using the SB-1 or SB-2 forms still requires the submission of audited financial statements. The SEC also allows small businesses (there are some exceptions) to do Regulation A offerings (SEC, 2001), which allow for public offerings of stock not to exceed $5 million in any 12-month period. The Regulation A option was created to allow a small business to "test the waters" for interest in its securities before going through the expense of filing with the SEC. Even though Regulation A offerings still require the submission of financial statements, the statements are simpler and do not need to be audited.

SOX (P.L. 107-204) imposes additional requirements on publicly traded firms. These requirements have major implications for the governance, accounting, auditing, and executive-compensation environment for publicly traded firms. For example, the act requires senior executives to personally certify financial statements; requires firm-auditing committees, nomination committees, and compensation committees to be completely independent; and requires the board of directors to be majority independent.[3]

The SOX legislative language does not single out small businesses for special or different treatment. However, in its rulemaking process, the SEC has delayed the start dates for compliance with key elements of section 404 of the act for nonaccelerated filers[4] and foreign firms and

---

[3] Companies that are majority owned by a single shareholder or unified group, however, are exempt from the some of these requirements.

[4] *Accelerated filers* are firms with a minimum float of $75 million and at least one year's worth of financial reporting.

is also debating further guidance regarding small-business compliance with the act.

Effects of Corporate and Securities Law on Small Businesses and the Small-Business Response

We now consider the effects of the regulatory and policy environments in corporate and securities law on small businesses and the ways in which small businesses have responded to these environments.

Effect on the Decision to Incorporate. In business-organization law, one of the most salient differences between firms lies in the degree to which their respective owners bear personal liability for business risks. This difference in liability exposure can have important implications for firm behavior. Unincorporated firms (or those that have not sought refuge in other statutory forms) can incur business-liability risks that could imperil the firm's owners' assets. This is true even if a sole proprietor owns the firm. Existing research (see, e.g., Ribstein, 2004) indicates that unincorporated business owners[5] are less likely to take risks, are often less innovative, and have distinct (often slower) growth trajectories than their corporate counterparts.

The different legal and regulatory environments facing unincorporated firms from those facing incorporated ones may also have significant implications for the initiation and growth of small businesses. The threat of financial liability for a firm's obligations might loom large for entrepreneurs and influence their ability to innovate, grow, or even begin operations in the first place. Previous research (Fan and White, 2003) finds evidence of a "chilling effect" of strict personal-bankruptcy laws on entrepreneurship. Changes to the personal-bankruptcy law following from BAPCPA (P.L. 109-8) may have a significant impact on small businesses and entrepreneurs. There is broad concern that BAPCPA, which makes it much harder for individuals to obtain a fresh start, will exacerbate the distinction between incorporated and unincorporated firms in terms of the level of financial risk borne by the owners and further chill entrepreneurship.

---

[5] These findings apply to business owners who engage in the business on a full-time basis.

Although incorporation is an organizational choice that is available to firms of all sizes, small businesses (measured in terms of number of employees or gross receipts) are much likelier than larger businesses to be unincorporated. More than 75 percent of all small businesses in the United States (measured in terms of annual sales receipts) have no payroll employees at all, and a majority of those are unincorporated (U.S. Census Bureau, 2007b). There are important reasons that small firms may find incorporation less attractive than their larger counterparts do. First, the formalities required to incorporate (involving not only the initial paperwork, but also creation and management of governance bodies) involve fixed costs that smaller firms may be less likely to be in a position to bear. Second, incorporation does not necessarily eliminate the risk of personal liability for shareholders, particularly for closely held companies. In many circumstances, courts can (and do) disregard the veil of limited liability that ostensibly protects shareholders of a corporation, using a doctrine known as "piercing the corporate veil" (or PCV). When PCV doctrine is invoked, shareholders of an incorporated entity are held liable for the firm's debts and liabilities as if the firm were an unincorporated business entity. Although PCV doctrine differs slightly across jurisdictions, a factor that is common to all is whether there is unity of ownership and interest between the corporation and its shareholders, an inquiry that generally turns on determining whether there is sufficient separation between the firm and its owners. The only successful PCV cases that have *ever*, to our knowledge, been asserted have been against closely held corporations and not against publicly traded firms (although wholly owned subsidiaries of publicly traded firms, which are technically closely held firms, are also common targets). Thus, incorporation is unlikely to be a complete liability-risk panacea for firms whose ownership is closely held.

Effect on Choice of Organizational Form. The characteristics of the LLC and LLP forms might make them of particular interest to small entrepreneurial firms; however, little is currently known about the take-up of these forms among smaller firms (see Chapter Six). The LLC and LLP organizational forms were intended to allow owners of firms to share the best attributes of partnerships and corporations in terms of both flexibility and pass-through taxation as well as limited liability. Most states have permitted firms to organize as either LLCs or LLPs (sometimes both) without the cumbersome constraints that frequently attend corporate status.

However, LLC and LLP forms also come with a few costs that could affect their take-up among small or large firms. First, unlike corporations (and even partnerships), LLCs and LLPs are required to have a limited life span (frequently in the neighborhood of 35 years). Although firms are allowed to re-form at the end of this period, the terminal period itself can create both tax and strategic problems for a firm. In addition, enabling statutes typically require that LLCs and LLPs carry a minimum amount of insurance against claims of third-party creditors. Moreover, even within a state, there is frequently some variation in the nature and extent of liability protection that these new business forms afford. For example, the LLP form frequently provides only a partial shield against liability[6] and imposes larger fiduciary duties on its members than the LLC form does but is also significantly more flexible than the LLC form.

The Public-Private Divide. As entrepreneurial firms grow larger and require access to additional capital, they face a choice as to whether the benefits of publicly traded status are worth the costs associated with regulatory requirements. Securities and exchange laws have long imposed reporting and other requirements on firms that register with the SEC; however, by all accounts, SOX legislation (P.L. 107-204) (as well as related regulations) has changed the landscape of securities law for firms that are publicly traded. There is no consensus regarding how SOX rules affect the interests, prospects, and growth trajectories of companies that are not listed on a national exchange (and thus not subject to federal securities regulations).

On the one hand, some argue that SOX (P.L. 107-204) changes make it *easier* for closely held businesses to make the transition to pub-

---

[6] Most notably, a number of states provide partners in an LLP only partial liability shields against third-party creditors (most notably, tort claimants alleging malpractice by other partners). These "partial shield" states still allow for liability as to the LLP's general debts and include Alaska, Arkansas, District of Columbia, Hawaii, Illinois, Kansas, Kentucky, Louisiana, Maine, Michigan, Nevada, New Hampshire, New Jersey, North Carolina, Ohio, Pennsylvania, South Carolina, Tennessee, Texas, Utah, and West Virginia.

licly traded status—because the additional reports and assessments they must produce help convince prospective investors that good internal controls are already in place, thereby making small-business investments safer than they have tended to be in the past.[7] Many critics, however, have pointed out that the requirements will simply impose a compliance cost for doing business as a public company. If such costs are high enough, privately held firms will eschew registration or, if they are already registered, might delist because of the increase in recurring expenses and other effects that the new SOX rules will impose. If the SOX regulatory innovations create a situation in which only large businesses can afford to go or remain public, small businesses may face differential difficulties in accessing capital, with potentially far-reaching effects for the markets and economic growth in general.[8] Chapter Five explores these issues further.

Section Conclusion

This brief review suggests several ways in which the regulatory environment surrounding corporate and securities law might affect small businesses differently from the way it affects larger ones. However, while there is ample theoretical justification for this hypothesis, empirical evidence regarding the differential effect of corporate and securities law on small businesses is lacking. Key questions remain to be addressed empirically, including the extent to which the new regulatory requirements have affected small firms' willingness to go into (or stay within) the public capital markets, how well alternative sources of capital (e.g., private-equity markets) substitute for the benefits of public capital, and

---

[7]   The PCAOB chief auditor, Douglas Carmichael, has expressed the view that "small companies may actually benefit from the new [SOX reporting] requirements, because fraud tends to be more prevalent among small companies, making access to capital markets harder. The new requirements should reduce uncertainty and therefore improve access" (Solomon and Bryan-Low, 2004).

[8]   Quantitative estimates have already begun to appear on the costs associated with SOX (P.L. 107-204) compliance. Solomon and Bryan-Low (2004), for example, cite a study released by Financial Executives International estimating that firms with annual revenues of less than $25 million will incur first-year SOX-compliance costs of $0.28 million and 1,996 hours.

whether the viability of these alternative sources differ according to firm size. Chapters Five and Six in this book will, respectively, examine the regulatory regime surrounding SOX (P.L. 107-204) and its effect on small firms and consider the benefits of limited-liability organizational forms among small law firms.

Environmental Protection

We now look at the regulatory environment surrounding environmental protection. There are several reasons to expect firm size to be an important consideration in formulating and evaluating environmental policy. From the regulator's perspective, it may be more cost-effective to focus regulation and enforcement on large sources, which are usually large firms. Liability-based approaches may be more effective for firms that have deep pockets. In addition, regulatory approaches that require firms to provide information may succeed better with firms concerned about their public image, which again may tend to be larger. At the same time, it may be easier for larger firms to comply with environmental regulations; as a result, regulations might increase the minimum efficient scale of production, putting small firms at a competitive disadvantage.

Regulatory Environment

There are three main components to the regulatory environment surrounding environmental protection: the regulations, government mechanisms for enforcing the regulations, and liability or citizen enforcement mechanisms.

Regulations. Environmental regulations attempt to reduce the negative effects of manufacturing and other business operations on the environment and people's health. Firms frequently do not bear the full environmental or public-health costs of their operations. Thus, they do not have appropriate incentives to control emissions. The purpose of environmental regulations is, at least in part, to correct these so-called negative externalities.

In the United States, federal environmental laws initially focused on large sources of pollution and on large firms. These laws were implicitly designed with large firms in mind—firms that could afford in-house environmental-compliance offices and that had engineering expertise. Over time, as large sources increasingly came under control, the EPA, state environmental agencies, and environmentalists gradually turned their attention to midsize sources of pollution and to smaller firms. While the emissions of any one small firm might not be large, the large number of small firms in many industries made the cumulative emissions of all small firms a source of concern. As attention has shifted toward smaller sources, the question arises whether regulatory approaches that were initially developed with large firms in mind are appropriate for small firms. Table 2.2 lists major federal environmental laws.[9]

Many environmental regulations impose different requirements on firms of different sizes. Varying the requirements of environmental regulations by firm size became common starting in 1985 (Hopkins, 1995, p. 8). This tiering means that small firms are exempted from certain requirements or are required to meet less stringent emission- or treatment-technology standards. According to the U.S. Small Business Administration (SBA) Office of Advocacy, the EPA has tiered more than 50 different regulations based on either firm size or the amount of pollution released (SBA, 1995, p. 5).

Governmental and Private-Sector Enforcement Mechanisms. The implementation and enforcement of environmental regulations occurs through a variety of mechanisms that differ according to the regulation, industry, and firm in question. State agencies frequently play the lead role in this process. Firms are often required to collect substantial data on emissions and the use of hazardous substances and to document the plans and procedures that they have put in place to comply with regulations. These data and plans are then submitted to various local, state, and federal agencies. When firms are found to be out of compliance, they may be subject to fines and required to take

---

[9]   Several states have also have enacted their own environmental laws and regulations that are stricter than the federal laws.

Table 2.2
Major Federal Environmental Laws

Law	Year Enacted or Amended	Focus
Federal Insecticide, Fungicide, and Rodenticide Act (FIFRA) (P.L. 80-104)	Enacted in 1947, but amended with major changes in 1972	Regulates pesticides and particular chemicals
Clean Air Act (P.L. 91-604)	Enacted in 1967 as the Air Quality Act (P.L. 90-148) and amended in 1970, 1977, and 1990	Regulates air emissions
National Environmental Policy Act (NEPA) (P.L. 91-190)	1969	Addresses general environmental policy and practice
Federal Water Pollution Control Act Amendments of 1972 (Clean Water Act) (P.L. 92-500)	Enacted in 1972 and amended in 1977 and 1987	Regulates discharges into bodies of water
Safe Drinking Water Act (SDWA) (P.L. 93-523)	1974	Sets standards for drinking water and discharges into sources of drinking water
Resource Recovery and Conservation Act (RCRA) (P.L. 94-580)	Enacted in 1976 and significantly amended in 1984	Focuses on waste disposal into landfills
Toxic Substances Control Act (TSCA) (P.L. 94-469)	1976	Regulates chemical use and disposal in general
Comprehensive Environmental Response, Compensation, and Liability Act (CERCLA) (P.L. 96-510)	1980	Addresses cleanup of abandoned or inactive hazardous-waste sites
Superfund Amendments and Reauthorization Act (SARA) (P.L. 99-499)	1986	Amended CERCLA and established the Toxic Release Inventory
Pollution Prevention Act (P.L. 101-508)	1990	Addresses general environmental policy and practice

action to remedy the problem. The federal statutes listed in Table 2.2 were adopted or substantially amended between the late 1960s and 1990. During the 1990s, efforts were made to integrate and streamline the fragmented air, water, and waste laws and programs. We briefly review some of these here.

Voluntary Agreements. Voluntary agreements can be classified into three types: public-voluntary, unilateral, and negotiated agreements (OECD, 1998). Public-voluntary agreements are nonmandatory rules developed by EPA or other government regulators. For example, the EPA's 33/50 program, which concluded in 1995, encouraged manufacturers to voluntarily reduce emissions of 17 target chemicals by 50 percent (EPA, 1999). Unilateral agreements are made by industry for industry. An example is the American Chemistry Council's Responsible Care® program, which encouraged member companies to adopt environmental management principles (American Chemistry Council, undated). Negotiated agreements are contracts between public authorities and industry. The two most visible examples have been EPA's Project XL (EPA, 2006a) and its Common Sense Initiative (CSI), both designed in response to complaints from the regulated community regarding the growing complexity of federal environmental laws (OECD, 1998).[10] All these types of agreements were largely abandoned when the George W. Bush administration came into office in 2001. The main exception is EPA's National Environmental Performance Track program, a voluntary partnership program that recognizes and rewards private and public facilities that demonstrate strong environmental performance beyond current requirements (EPA, 2007).

Government Programs. Several government programs were adopted over the past 10 years in an attempt to improve the regulatory system's performance for small businesses. SBREFA (P.L. 104-121) directs the SBA to establish a regulatory-enforcement ombudsman and regulatory-fairness boards in 10 regional cities. SBREFA allows a small business to file a grievance in court if it believes that the business has been "adversely affected or aggrieved" by a regulatory ruling. The courts can rule that the regulations should not be enforced against a small firm ("Small Business Not So Small," 2002). To monitor agency efforts to reduce regulatory burden, the Small Business Paperwork Relief Act of 2002 (SBPRA) (P.L. 107-198) requires agencies to report to Congress

---

[10] See Coglianese and Allen (2003) for a review of EPA's Common Sense Initiative.

and the Small Business and Agricultural Regulatory Ombudsman on their enforcement actions against small businesses and the penalty reductions in such actions. The PRA (P.L. 104-13) also requires federal agencies to review the impact of their regulations on small businesses and to consider less costly alternatives for accomplishing public policy goals ("Small Business Not So Small," 2002). EPA's Small Business Compliance Policy (EPA, 2000) promotes environmental compliance among businesses with 100 or fewer employees by providing incentives to discover and correct environmental problems. EPA eliminates or significantly reduces penalties for small businesses that voluntarily discover violations of environmental law and promptly disclose and correct them (EPA, 2006b).

SBREFA (P.L. 104-121) provides new avenues for small businesses to participate in the federal regulatory process. In response, EPA has set up panels to facilitate greater small-business participation in the regulatory process (SBA, undated[b]). This initiative responds to concerns that greater large-firm participation in the regulatory and political process has resulted in regulations that are tailored to the experiences and capabilities of larger firms. There do not appear to be studies on the use and effectiveness of this or similar programs.

Environmental Management Systems. In recent years, government and industry have been exploring standards and guidelines for the management of a firm's activities related to environmental performance. Environmental management systems do not specify particular emission standards, but they provide guidelines for management structures. For example, EPA has adopted management-based regulations aimed at preventing accidents involving hazardous chemicals. These regulations require facilities to conduct risk assessments of their operations, develop procedures to prevent accidents, and seek to make continuous improvement in the management of their operations (Coglianese and Nash, 2006, p. 6).

Liability and Citizen-Enforcement Mechanisms. The tort system is an alternative to active regulatory oversight. Firms often face liability for the release of pollutants into the environment. The highest-profile example is probably the federal Superfund program (part of CERCLA implementation, P.L. 96-510), which imposes strict, joint and several, and retroactive liability for the cleanup of hazardous-waste sites. Small firms accounted for the majority of businesses potentially liable for cleanup, but for a more moderate share of the total waste sent to the site (Dixon, 2000).

Environmental and toxic-tort claims can also cause firms to incur costs and requirements to change their business practices. The use of class-action lawsuits for environmental and toxic-tort claims has been a topic of ongoing debate. From 1980 to the mid-1990s, the trend was toward more widespread usage of class-action suits for environmental and toxic-tort claims. In the mid-1990s, however, a series of federal appellate court decisions reversed class certifications in pending class-action tort cases (Schwartz and Sutherland, 1997).

A third dimension of environmental liability is the impact of recent court decisions on large firms' exposure to liability claims. In the 1990s, the U.S. Supreme Court first considered the question of whether large, multinational firms could shield themselves from CERCLA liability through a parent-subsidiary relationship. In *United States v. Bestfoods* (1998), the court held that a corporate parent could be held vicariously liable for its subsidiary's environmental damage if the parent's right of control over the subsidiary's business was sufficiently large to convert the parent into an "operator" under CERCLA (P.L. 96-510). If these events enhanced large firms' exposure to vicarious liability, the predicted effect would be to induce them to contract out much of their high-risk work to smaller, less liquid firms, working substantially independently.

Citizen enforcement can provide another form of oversight. The federal Clean Water Act (P.L. 95-217) and several other federal environmental laws allow citizens to bring enforcement actions. Private enforcement of environment-related regulations is also allowed under California's Safe Drinking Water and Toxic Enforcement Act of 1986 (Proposition 65). Proposition 65 prohibits businesses from knowingly discharging listed chemicals into sources of drinking water and requires warnings before otherwise exposing someone to a listed chemical.[11]

---

[11] Citizen suits have also been allowed under California's Unfair Competition Law (California Business and Professions Code, §17200). Citizen suits brought under this law were com-

There is a great deal of controversy about the social value of citizen-suit provisions. Supporters contend that empowering "private attorneys general" is an appropriate and effective way to augment the limited resources of public enforcement agencies. Critics contend that citizen suits are often used to pursue narrow private interests, generate legal fees while focusing on permit violations that cause little environmental harm, and restrict the socially useful discretion of public enforcement agencies. Citizen-suit provisions have now been in place for more than 25 years, but there is little systematic, empirical information about them. There has been a good deal of legal analysis of the various statutes and court cases (see Leonard, 1995; Austin, 1986–1987; James Thompson, 1987), but little data have been collected on the frequency, costs, and outcomes of these cases.

Effects of Environmental Regulations on Small Businesses and the Small-Business Response

There has been ongoing debate over whether environmental regulations put small firms at a disadvantage relative to larger ones. Environmental regulations may more heavily impact small firms because of variation in statutes, compliance, or enforcement (Dean, Brown, and Stango, 2000, p. 58). We discuss each in turn.

Statutory Variation. While the tiering of environmental regulations obviously works to the advantage of small businesses, two factors work to reduce this advantage. First, environmental regulations often contain grandfathering provisions that allow older, and perhaps larger, firms to postpone compliance with new regulations or to meet less stringent standards. For example, under new federal source-review guidelines, existing firms are not required to upgrade pollution-control equipment until they modify their existing plants by making nonroutine physical or operational changes that result in a significant increase in emissions of a regulated pollutant. Second, as Shaller, McNulty, and Chinander (1998) observed, large firms are usually much more active in the regulatory process than smaller firms, with the result that regu-

---

monly referred to as Section 17200 suits. The passage of Proposition 64 on the California state ballot in November 2004, however, narrowed these citizen-suit provisions.

lations are tailored to the experiences and capabilities of large firms. The result may be that the advantages given to small firms under the regulations may not be as large as they might first appear.

Compliance Variation. Compliance with environmental regulations can induce responses by firms along several dimensions. Compliance might involve installation of pollution-control equipment that removes pollution produced in the production process (so-called *end-of-the-pipe treatment*) or installation of production equipment that generates less pollution. Compliance can also require firms to monitor waste streams or releases of pollutants into the environment and to report results to government agencies. Finally, compliance can have internal, organizational implications for firms by, for example, requiring them to designate points of contact for government agencies or to develop an emergency-response plan for the release of hazardous substances.

Complying with environmental regulations can potentially put small firms at a disadvantage vis-à-vis large firms. Pollution equipment can increase the minimum efficient scale of production. There can also be economies of scale in discovering and understanding environmental regulations and in completing required paperwork. The result is that environmental regulations may cause costs per unit of output to increase more for small firms than they do for larger ones.

Studies have found evidence of compliance asymmetries. Pittman (1981) found that emission-control technologies required in the pulp and paper industries increased the minimum efficient size of a plant. Not all studies agree, however. Using data on manufacturing firms from between 1978 and 1981, Evans (1985) did not find strong evidence that there were substantial economies of scale in complying with EPA and OSHA regulations. More recent analyses of the impact of environmental regulations also raise questions about the economies-of-scale argument. Dean, Brown, and Stango (2000) believe that a small but growing body of evidence indicates that firms have found ways to convert environmental regulations into a competitive advantage. For example, there is evidence that, when reducing emissions, some firms have found ways to save enough inputs so that unit-production cost declines. Weakening the link between environmental compliance and cost might also weaken arguments that regulation gives large firms advantages over smaller firms, although it could still be that large firms are better at finding cost savings than smaller firms are.

Even if there are not substantial economies of scale in complying with environmental regulations, environmental regulations may still make it more difficult for new firms to enter the industry. Existing firms may have gradually learned the cheapest and most effective way to comply with environmental regulations over time. Thus, compliance costs may be initially higher for potential entrants, discouraging entry. To the extent that entrants tend to be smaller firms, environmental regulations would disadvantage smaller firms.

Enforcement Variation. Asymmetries in enforcement result when government or private parties enforce regulations more vigorously against firms in one size range than they do in another. Charles Brown, Hamilton, and Medoff (1990, p. 84) found that government enforcement practices serve to reduce the regulatory burden placed on smaller firms and that the preferential treatment more than offsets any disadvantages for small firms created due to economies of scale in complying with environmental regulations. Finto (1990) concluded that limited enforcement budgets cause EPA to focus enforcement efforts on larger firms. There are contrary views, however. Several studies have concluded that enforcement is less stringent against larger firms than it is against smaller ones. For example, Bartel and Thomas (1987) suggested that large producers face less stringent EPA and OSHA enforcement. Some argue that larger firms often escape stringent enforcement because they are more politically influential than smaller firms are and can directly or indirectly influence enforcement priorities.

Even if regulations are enforced equally for large and smaller firms, the ultimate impact of regulations on large firms may be less if they are more successful in defending themselves. Yeager (1987) found that, because larger firms have more resources, they are more successful in defending themselves against enforcement actions. Larger firms must bear the costs of such defenses, but the cost is presumably less than the expected cost of compliance, thus reducing the difference in the cost of environmental regulations between large and small firms from what it would otherwise be.

Research has shown that enforcement actions by private parties tend to focus on larger firms. Greve (1989) found that environmental groups were more like to pursue enforcement actions against larger firms under the Clean Water Act (P.L. 95-217) even when these firms were not the largest polluters. Dean, Brown, and Stango (2000, p. 59) argued that private groups are likelier to target large firms than small firms because large firms are more concerned about their reputations and thus more prone to settle.

Combined Effects. The net advantage or disadvantage for small firms created by variations in statutes, compliance, or enforcement policies is difficult to determine and undoubtedly varies by industry as well as environmental regulation. For example, compliance asymmetries that disadvantage small firms may be offset by statutory and enforcement asymmetries that favor them. Empirical studies that attempt to evaluate the combined effects of environmental regulations on small firms relative to large ones have come to mixed conclusions.

Before environmental tiering became widespread, Pashigian (1984) found that environmental laws placed greater burdens on smaller manufacturing plants, resulting in increased market share for larger firms. Pashigian (1984) and Bartel and Thomas (1987) concluded that, while regulations can impose significant burdens on larger manufacturing firms, decreased competition from smaller firms might mean that, on the whole, large firms are better off with environmental regulations than without them.

Dean, Brown, and Stango (2000) found that higher pollution-abatement costs resulted in fewer small firms entering into the industries examined, but not in fewer large firms entering. They concluded that, on the whole, environmental regulations put small firms at a unit-cost disadvantage relative to large firms. Dean, Brown, and Stango also concluded that the disadvantages faced by small firms were not a temporary phenomenon that disappeared as firms learned to cope with regulations or as organizations evolved to aid small firms in abatement efforts (2000, p. 61). It should be noted, however, that their conclusions are based on data only through 1987 and may not reflect conditions today.

Other studies suggest that environmental regulations do not put small firms at a significant disadvantage. Hopkins (1995, p. 61) found that environmental regulations accounted for a smaller share of the overall regulatory burden on small firms than that for large firms and that tax- and payroll-related burdens, not environmental regulation, were the main concerns for smaller firms. A 1994 survey by Arthur Andersen and National Small Business United came to similar conclusions. In addition, the study found that firms with fewer than 20 employees were more than twice as likely as larger firms to report that they faced no major regulatory burden of any kind (including environmental regulations) (Arthur Andersen and Company and National Small Business United, 1994, p. 25, quoted in Hopkins, 1995, p. 9).

Researchers have found that the presence of environmental regulations can increase the number of small firms in some circumstances. For example, Ringleb and Wiggins (1990) argued that concerns about liability have induced larger firms to shed operations involving hazardous substances. Becker and Henderson (1997) found a proliferation of small firms in four high-polluting industries. These findings are consistent with arguments by Ringleb and Wiggins (1990) that concerns about liability have induced larger firms to shed operations involving hazardous substances. The 1998 *United States v. Bestfoods* Supreme Court decision would reinforce such concerns.

It is difficult to judge the success of efforts over the past 10 or 15 years to make it easier for small firms to comply with environmental regulations. EPA's Office of Enforcement and Compliance Assurance does not keep records on the number of small businesses participating in the agency's self-audit program—although data may be available at regional offices. Reed (1999, p. 324) found increasing large-corporation participation in EPA's self-audit program, and she speculated that small firms might not want to participate in the program because they feared potentially high costs of correcting violations. Small firms may also have little incentive to participate in the program if they think the probability of direct government enforcement is low. Some states also have adopted audit programs, although coordination between EPA and the states has not been good (Meason, 1998). Under Illinois's Clean Break program, businesses agree to come into compliance within a reasonable time in exchange for amnesty for past violations. In spite of Clean Break and EPA's small-business programs, the audit rate in the Illinois small-business community is almost zero (Meason, 1998, p. 510).

Section Conclusion

This review of research to date suggests that there are no easy answers to the question of how environmental regulations have affected small firms relative to how they have affected larger ones. Moreover, many of the key studies rely on data that are now quite dated. Rapid evolution in environmental regulations and policy may mean that findings of past studies do not reflect today's regulatory environment.

Environmental policymaking must balance competing objectives. Ultimately, it is up to policymakers to determine the balance between the benefits of regulatory compliance and the costs associated with regulation. Better information would allow policymakers to make more informed decisions, particularly as they related to the impact of regulation on small firms. While the existing body of research on environmental protection in the business context is extensive, further research is needed to better understand how recent trends in environmental regulation, enforcement, and liability are affecting businesses of different sizes. Better information is also needed concerning which aspects of environmental regulatory and liability policy cause the greatest problems for small firms. Information needs to be synthesized on the environmental damage caused by small firms and the benefits of reducing this damage.

Major environmental initiatives have traditionally focused on large firms, and there is clear evidence that the regulations were formulated with large firms in mind. There is a need to understand whether a different approach to source control, pollution prevention, compliance assistance, and enforcement is needed to deal with the operations of small firms.

There also needs to be a more thorough evaluation of how small firms have used different initiatives, such as the Common Sense Initiative and self-auditing programs, and what types of modifications to these programs would make them more attractive to small firms. Large firms are motivated to participate in environmental initiatives partly by concerns about their image in the communities in which they operate or their image with consumers. More research is needed to determine the types of concerns that would motivate small businesses to address their operations' effects on the environment.

Employment Law and Regulation

We now examine the ways in which policies regulating the contractual relationships between employers and employees might have a differential impact on small businesses and entrepreneurship.[12] A variety of regulations, rules, and policies at the federal, state, and local levels influence or restrict the ways in which businesses interact with prospective, current, and former employees. Such regulations and policies recognize that various factors can alter the balance of power between employer and employee and are designed to address concerns that one party (usually, but not always, the employer) might intentionally or unintentionally impose harm on the other. Harm may result from an employer's intentional or unintentional discrimination against certain groups of current or potential employees that denies them access to jobs or fair wages; the establishment of a hostile or unsafe work environment; the exercise of market power to drive down wages; or lost wages due to job loss, workplace injury, or, on the employee's side, from the theft of intellectual property or a client base from an employer.

Employment laws, regulations, and policies can protect or benefit one party (usually employees) from such harms but typically impose some cost on the other party. Thus, in striving to strike a balance between costs and benefits, policymakers often adjust the application of or enforcement of employment-related regulations according to firm size due to the belief that a given regulation or regulatory policy will impose a greater relative cost on a smaller firm.

---

[12] In many cases, the regulations imposed on employers are designed to influence the health and safety environment for workers.

Regulatory Environment

We can categorize employment-related regulations, rules, or policies under three broad headings: (1) regulations and rules governing employer and employee behavior; (2) workers' compensation (WC), an administrative compensation program that dictates the remuneration provided to individuals who are injured at or become sick because of their work; and (3) unemployment insurance (UI), a social insurance program that compensates individuals who lose their jobs and are, at least temporarily, unable to find new work. We will also discuss mechanisms used to enforce these regulations.[13]

Regulations. Key regulations and rules limiting employer and employee behavior fall into two broad categories: government regulations and restrictions on contractual form.

Government Regulations. Many federal statutes have been put in place over the past 40 years that protect individuals against discrimination or a hostile or unsafe environment in the workplace and that prevent employers from terminating employees in certain protected classes for specific reasons. Many of these regulations are applied according to size thresholds such that businesses with a small number of employees are not covered. Appendix A provides a summary of such thresholds.

Thresholds based on the number of employees in a firm are particularly common in employment regulation. These size thresholds can be quite low, as in the case of the Fair Labor Standards Act of 1938 (P.L. 75-718), which applies to businesses with two or more employees. The act guarantees a minimum wage and 1.5 times the regular rate of pay for hours worked over 40 hours per week. It also restricts the use of child labor and imposes recordkeeping provisions on employers (DOL, undated[a]). Another regulation with a low employment threshold is the Immigration Reform and Control Act (P.L. 99-603), which restricts employers with four or more employees from discrimi-

---

[13] It is worth noting one important class of employment regulation that we are explicitly not discussing here: law governing unions and union membership, to which we loosely refer as *labor law*. There are two main reasons we do not consider it here. The first is that fewer workers in the United States are union members than have been in the past, particularly in the private sector. A second, related point is that very few workers in small firms are unionized.

nating against U.S. citizens, nationals, or authorized aliens on the basis of national origin in hiring, discharge, or referrals.

The core federal antidiscrimination acts apply to employers with 15 or more employees. These include Title VII of the Civil Rights Act of 1964 (discrimination in hiring, employment, or termination based on race, color, religion, sex, or national origin; sexual harassment) (P.L. 88-352), the Pregnancy Discrimination Act of 1978 (PDA) (P.L. 95-555), the Equal Pay Act of 1963 (P.L. 88-38), and the Americans with Disabilities Act of 1990 (ADA) (P.L. 101-336). Employers of 20 or more employees must comply with the Age Discrimination in Employment Act of 1967 (ADEA) (P.L. 90-202), which prohibits discrimination against individuals age 40 or over. Employers of this size are also required under COBRA (P.L. 99-272) to provide employees and their families with the opportunity to temporarily extend their healthcare coverage under group heath-care benefit plans (if any) sponsored by the employer in certain cases in which the coverage would otherwise end (e.g., death of the employee, termination, divorce). The Family and Medical Leave Act (P.L. 103-3) requires employers with 50 or more employees to allow employees 12 weeks of unpaid leave for specific reasons such as the birth or adoption of a child or to care for a seriously ill immediate family member.

The federal Occupational Safety and Health Act (OSH Act) (P.L. 91-596), administered by OSHA within the U.S. Department of Labor (DOL), regulates safety and health conditions in most private-industry workplaces. In general, federal health and safety regulations apply to all firms, regardless of size, but enforcement practices vary depending on the size of the employer.[14]

In addition to these federal regulations, 49 of the 50 states plus the District of Columbia and Puerto Rico have their own versions of anti-

---

[14] Existing research on health and safety issues has suggested that fatality rates are higher at smaller establishments (work sites) across all major industry sectors (Mendeloff and Kagey, 1990; Peek-Asa, Erickson, and Krauss, 1999; Bennett and Passmore, 1985). However, recent research described in this book (specifically, Mendeloff et al., 2006) reveals that the relationships among firm size, establishment size, and fatality risk are significantly more complicated. That research shows that, after controlling for the size of the establishment (work site), small firms actually have lower fatality rates than midsized firms have.

discrimination statutes. In many cases, these statutes are more stringent than the federal regulations, either in terms of the size threshold
used to determine the applicability of the antidiscrimination statute or
in terms of the type of discrimination covered by the statute.

Restrictions on Contractual Form. Employer behavior is also cir-
cumscribed by restrictions on contractual form that create exceptions
to the employment-at-will doctrine. As a general premise, employment in the United States constitutes an at-will contract between an
employer and an employee. An employer can terminate an employee
for no reason, just as an employee can leave a job for any reason. The
employment-at-will doctrine does not (necessarily) apply if an individual works under a contract, including a union contract. In that case,
the contract may dictate terms under which an employer may terminate an employment contract. Either party may be subject to a breach
of contract claim if the party does not live up to the terms of the contract. Generally, there is no threshold that determines whether a firm is
subject to a lawsuit or claim for violating an employment contract.

Businesses can also be influenced by restrictions on contractual
form that address employee behavior. A noncompete agreement is one
common type of restriction that may be included in the employment
contract. These agreements may prohibit an employee from competing or assisting competitors with the employer by engaging in a related
business as an employee, contractor, owner, or investor both while
employed and often for some period after employment ends. Similarly,
trade-secret rules prevent individuals from making use of information or trade secrets that they acquire on the job to compete with the
employer. There is no size threshold of which we are aware that limits
an employer's ability to sue an employee for a similar breach.

Workers' Compensation. Since the early twentieth century, virtually all private-sector employers in the United States have been required
to pay WC benefits to employees who are injured at work. WC makes
employers liable for medical costs and partial income replacement for
workers injured at or because of their jobs. WC functions as a "carve-
out" of the tort system and acts as more of a social insurance system
than as a regulatory program. WC benefits cover some portion of lost
wages, as well as direct costs associated with the injury itself. While

state WC programs have frequently been subject to reform over the years, there have been few wholesale changes. Moreover, WC programs make relatively few distinctions among employers with different characteristics. Thus, the coverage offered by one firm will be very similar, if not identical, to that offered by another, regardless of important differences such as industry, the level of risk, or firm size.[15] Fourteen states have established thresholds, ranging from one to five, that exempt very small firms from having to provide WC coverage (DOL, undated[b]). Employers are required either to purchase insurance to cover potential WC losses or to demonstrate sufficient financial resources to self-insure. For employers who purchase insurance, the market for such insurance is characterized by an experience rating, a tool used by insurers to adjust premiums based on previous claim history and the implementation of specific safety measures.

Unemployment Insurance. UI systems are social insurance programs that provide income-replacement benefits to individuals who are unemployed through no fault of their own. Each state administers a separate program, though federal law has established guidelines. Benefits are paid from taxes on employer payrolls. There are very low size thresholds for employers to be liable for the UI payroll taxes. Generally, employers are required to pay taxes if they pay wages of $1,500 or more in any quarter of a calendar year or if they had at least one employee on any day of a week during 20 weeks in a calendar year. The standards are higher for agriculture employers, with the wage requirement of $20,000 or more or at least 10 employees.

While both UI and WC are forms of social insurance and provide partial income-replacement benefits, there are some differences, particularly in the finance mechanisms for the programs, which are important for thinking of how they influence small businesses. Unlike WC, which is structured and financed as an insurance program (with firms paying premiums calculated using experience ratings), UI benefits are

---

[15] In addition to the size thresholds, some public employees, most notably public-safety employees, receive different coverage. The coverage afforded to agricultural employees varies significantly across states, with only 14 states covering agricultural employees the same way as other employees (as of 2006).

paid out of a government fund collected as part of a payroll tax. There is no size threshold for participation in the system, and essentially any business that maintains at least one employee is responsible for paying the tax. There are federal and state payroll taxes. The federal tax is equal to 6.2 percent of the first $7,000 in wages paid to each employee during the calendar year. The state taxes vary both in the taxation rate and the wage base.

In the event that a worker loses his or her job due to lack of work at the place of employment or for some other eligible cause, he or she receives a payment from the government until the worker either finds a job, violates some aspect of the state eligibility criteria, or exceeds the maximum benefit duration. The payment amount varies by state and typically depends on the worker's earnings prior to job loss up to some maximum amount. The duration of benefits also varies by state but is typically 26 weeks. The duration of benefits is often extended during times of high unemployment.

Enforcement Mechanisms. We will now discuss administrative enforcement and court enforcement mechanisms.

Administrative Enforcement of Government Regulations. Several of the regulations or statutes have employer size thresholds that determine the coverage of the regulation. Employers that fall below the threshold cannot be sued, fined, charged, or otherwise reprimanded under the aegis of the law. In addition, these employers are not subject to the recordkeeping requirements associated with these laws. For example, EEOC requires that employers keep all personnel and employment records for one year, and ADEA requires employers to retain payroll records for three years. As part of antidiscrimination enforcement, EEOC requires employers with 100 or more employees (or 50 or more employees and federal contracts totaling more than $50,000) to file an Employer Information Report EEO-1 that characterizes the workforce by race and gender.

EEOC has the legal standing to investigate employee complaints against firms in the area of antidiscrimination to determine whether there has been a violation of the law. If the government investigation establishes a violation of the law, EEOC may offer mediation to the disputing parties or attempt to settle with the employer. If these attempts fail, then EEOC may choose to sue the employer. Punitive damages beyond a remedy may also be sought if the violation is deemed to be intentional, malicious, or recklessly indifferent.

OSHA regulates safety and health. Safety standards cover hazards such as falls, explosions, fires, and cave-ins, as well as machine and vehicle operation and maintenance. Health standards regulate exposure to a variety of health hazards through engineering controls, the use of personal protective equipment (e.g., respirators, hearing protection), and work practices. Employers covered by the OSH Act (P.L. 91-596) are required to maintain safe and healthful workplaces. These employers must become familiar with job safety and health standards applicable to their establishments, comply with the standards, and eliminate hazardous conditions, to the extent possible. Where OSHA has not set forth a specific standard, employers are responsible for complying with the OSH Act's "general duty" clause, which states that each employer "shall furnish . . . a place of employment [that] is free from recognized hazards that are causing or are likely to cause death or serious physical harm to [its] employees." The act assigns OSHA two regulatory functions: setting standards and conducting inspections to ensure that employers are providing safe and healthful workplaces.

OSHA regulations cover such items as recordkeeping, reporting, and posting. OSHA covers every employer with more than 10 employees (with *employer* defined as an establishment or workplace rather than as a firm), except for employers in certain low-hazard industries in the retail, finance, insurance, real estate, and service sectors. These employers must therefore maintain three types of OSHA-specified records of job-related injuries and illnesses. In addition, every employer, regardless of industry category or the number of its employees, must advise the nearest OSHA office of any accident that results in one or more fatalities or the hospitalization of three or more employees.

Although small firms are not exempt from health and safety regulations, OSHA has developed a special consultation program that is available to firms with fewer than 500 employees (DOL, 2007). The program is confidential and separate from the inspection process and is designed to help small firms identify and correct potential workplace hazards, thereby complying with regulations. OSHA considers the employing firm's size, among other factors, when determining the penalty to be proposed for any violation. Penalties are generally reduced by 60 percent if an employer has 25 or fewer employees, 40 percent if the employer has 26 to 100 employees, and 20 percent if the employer has 101 to 250 employees.

While OSHA does engage in regulatory enforcement, it also encourages states to develop and operate their own safety and health programs.[16] These plans are subject to OSHA approval. In 2007, 24 states have OSHA-approved state plans.[17] OSHA is responsible for enforcement in the remaining states. The state entities enforce their own safety and health standards, which are at least as strict as federal OSHA requirements, but may have different or additional requirements. Many states offer additional programs of assistance to small businesses.

Litigation and Court Enforcement of Employer and Employee Behavior. An employee who believes that his or her employer has intentionally harmed him or her has the right to file a civil suit and seek damages from the employer. The threat of such legal action exists for all employers on a wide range of matters. Similarly, an employer of any size may use the court system to enforce an employment agreement if an employee fails to live up to the terms of a contract. Federal regulations, as well as the parallel regulations at the state and local levels, create additional avenues through which firms may be punished for specific types of harms. In general terms, this is accomplished through the establishment of a government entity that is given the legal authority to monitor business activities on specific employment-related matters and to investigate or respond to complaints. The government entity may also have the authority to sue firms, impose fines, or promote mediation between employers and employees.

---

[16] State plans are authorized under section 18 of the OSH Act (P.L. 91-596).

[17] OSHA (2006). Alaska, Arizona, California, Connecticut, Hawaii, Indiana, Iowa, Kentucky, Maryland, Michigan, Minnesota, Nevada, New Jersey, New Mexico, New York, North Carolina, Oregon, South Carolina, Tennessee, Utah, Vermont, Virginia, Washington, and Wyoming have OSHA-approved state plans, although the Connecticut, New Jersey, and New York plans cover only state and local government employers.

An employer of any size may be subject to a civil suit brought by an employee who claims that the employer has harmed him or her. Firms over specific size thresholds may also face criminal suits, civil suits brought by a government agency, or fines for alleged regulatory violations of specific types. Restrictions on contractual form that limit the behavior of either the employer or the employee (e.g., noncompete agreements, exceptions to the employment-at-will doctrine) are remedied through the court system, which may or may not find these agreements to be legal or binding. States vary substantially in terms of their willingness to enforce such contract terms.

Effects of Employment Regulations on Small Businesses and the Small-Business Response

Enforcement Variation. Two kinds of enforcement are relevant to the discussion of the small-business response: administrative enforcement of regulations and court enforcement policies.

Administrative Enforcement of Regulations. A firm of any size is potentially at risk of a civil action in response to a claim that the firm's actions have harmed an employee. However, federal, state, and local regulations increase the risk by giving a government agency the authority to investigate firm behavior and take legal action. This implies that very small firms falling below the employment threshold for a regulation may face a lower risk of legal action in this area.

The benefits of staying below a certain size threshold might induce some firms to limit growth. For example, in the antidiscrimination arena, in which the regulations are fairly vague and therefore the risk associated with legal action may be higher, it is plausible that very small businesses might consider the employment threshold stipulated by the regulation and limit growth to avoid the reporting requirements and the threat of fines or legal action. In addition to the legal risk, administrative enforcement imposes information-gathering burdens (such as the requirement to file an EEO-1 report) on firms larger than a certain size threshold. Some firms might also try to remain smaller than the reporting threshold to avoid the costs of gathering, reporting, and maintaining required information.

Existing research suggests that, in some industries, large, unionized firms are more efficient in implementing health and safety programs, in the sense that the per-worker cost of such programs is lower (Bartel and Thomas, 1987). This research shows that, as a result of regulation, large, unionized firms are more profitable at the expense of small, nonunionized firms. This is consistent with a hypothesis that there are substantial fixed costs involved in complying with health and safety regulations.

Court Enforcement Policies and Regulations. Although court enforcement does not explicitly consider firm size, one of the key differences between small and large firms is the level of resources available to spend on litigation, either as plaintiffs or defendants. There are several means through which these resources might influence the prospects of larger firms in the tort system.

For actions that would be initiated by employees (e.g., discrimination, wrongful discharge, violation of the employment contract), employees (or, more realistically, lawyers) might be likelier to go after large firms with deep pockets. On the other hand, large firms with deep pockets might have a stronger incentive to spend substantial resources aggressively defending any one suit to deter future suits. This threat of deterrence might make employees less likely to go after large firms because they perceive a lower chance of winning.

For legal actions that would be initiated by firms (e.g., violation of a noncompete agreement, trade-secret suit) and for which the firm seeks redress from employees, large firms can spend more resources litigating against employees who violate these agreements and may have a stronger incentive to do so to deter other employees from violating these contract clauses in the future. Small firms are, by nature of their size, likelier to face bankruptcy due to a costly legal action. Of course, small firms may be more vulnerable to breach of a noncompete agreement or violation of trade-secret rules as the entire business may depend on that trade secret. As a result, they may be likelier to prosecute, in spite of the costs and the risks of bankruptcy.

It is currently difficult to assess whether restrictions on the contractual form that employers use to restrict employee behavior affect small businesses differently from how they affect large ones. Nor is there any indication that small businesses are prevented from using noncompete agreements. However, because the agreements can be enforced only through litigation, a small business may face a greater burden in enforcing such a clause. On the other hand, these businesses may also have more to lose in the event that such an agreement is violated. Moreover, noncompete agreements may impact labor supply in a way that has a particularly strong impact on entrepreneurship or small businesses. For example, the natural labor pool for start-ups may include individuals who recently worked for a larger company in the same industry. Noncompete agreements might prevent current employees from leaving a company to start their own businesses but might also hinder employers' ability to hire individuals who had worked for a competitor.

Overall, economic theory points to conflicting forces regarding the question of whether the threat of or use of lawsuits places a greater burden on small businesses than on large businesses. In the end, it is difficult to determine who bears a heavier burden from legal costs. A recent study by Pendell and Hinton (2007) suggests that the legal costs per dollar of revenue are substantially greater for small businesses than they are for large businesses. Small businesses, which Pendell and Hinton define as those with less than $10 million in annual revenue and at least one employee in addition to the owner, account for 19 percent of business revenue but 69 percent of tort-liability costs. Very small businesses, defined as those with less than $1 million in annual revenue, account for 6 percent of business revenue and 21 percent of tort-liability costs. The authors find that the tort-liability costs per $1,000 in revenue decline steadily as the revenue category increases. For firms with revenue less than $1 million, the cost per $1,000 in revenue is $20.84; for firms with revenue greater than $50 million, that figure is $1.33.

Impact of the Workers' Compensation System. Despite the relative uniformity of coverage, there are good reasons to believe that WC might have a differential impact on different-sized firms. Employers are required either to purchase insurance to cover potential WC losses or to demonstrate sufficient financial resources to self-insure. Large firms typically have a greater ability to self-insure their benefit payments because they are better able to bear the risks involved in a WC claim, which could require a large payout in one period. An ability to self-insure can reduce the expected costs of WC by allowing firms to bypass an insurance system with two possible sources of inefficiency. First, many argue that the WC-insurance market is not perfectly competitive and therefore that premiums exceed the expected value of insurance payouts. Second, experience rating, a tool used by insurers to adjust premiums based on previous claim history and the implementation of specific safety measures, is imperfectly applied. This imperfect application of experience rating tends to work to the relative disadvantage of smaller firms, resulting in less reliable experience on which to base premiums. Experience rating is a potentially important tool because it allows insured firms to reap some benefits from investments in safety. Absent any bias in the application of experience rating, smaller firms might still find it costlier to promote safety measures if the implementation of those measures involves substantial fixed costs because there will be fewer workers over whom to spread the fixed costs. If smaller firms are imperfectly experience rated, this further reduces the incentive to promote workplace safety. All of this suggests that WC insurance will be costlier for smaller employers than for larger ones.

In addition to the higher costs, we might also expect that the outcomes for the injured workers are worse at smaller firms. If, as suggested, smaller firms have fewer incentives or less ability to implement effective safety measures, then we might expect workers to suffer injuries with greater frequency and perhaps greater severity at small firms. Large firms are also likelier to be able to accommodate injured workers with modified work, and return to work is a critically important predictor of the long-term impact of disability (as shown in Peterson et al., 1998, and Reville et al., 2001).

All of this suggests that WC in particular, and occupational health and safety programs more generally, might lead to significantly different costs for employers and workers depending on employer size. Specifically, there are reasons to believe that employers will face higher WC costs, while workers will face worse potential outcomes from job-related injures at smaller firms. Given that WC premiums represent approximately 2 percent of all payroll costs nationwide, this could have substantial implications for the operating costs of small businesses.

Impact of the Unemployment Insurance System. Since the UI system covers all employers and there is no opportunity to self-insure, we do not expect the business response to the UI system to vary dramatically by firm size. In principle, the taxes that an employer pays should be proportional to the number of people it employs, reducing any disparities between firms of different sizes.

In reality, an employer is experience rated, in the sense that the tax rate it pays depends on its past experience with unemployment. New employers are assigned a flat rate, and, over time, their rates will change based on the stability of their labor force and the number of layoffs they experience. In California in 2002, for example, the base rate for new employers was 3.4 percent, while the minimum rate was 0.7 percent and the maximum rate 5.4 percent. This has the potential to benefit large firms more than it might small ones, because large firms are probably more flexible in response to changing economic conditions and may be able to avoid some layoffs that would increase their payroll taxes. Smaller firms might not be able to absorb the cost of a worker when faced with lower demand or higher costs and will bear the full brunt of unemployment taxes. Just how strong this effect would be is an empirical matter.

Section Conclusion

This section has discussed a number of ways that policy instruments designed to regulate aspects of the employee-employer relationship might have intended and unintended consequences that impose higher costs on small businesses than it does on larger businesses. Overall, there is little empirical research that documents the effects of workplace regulations in general and the effects on small firms in particular. As noted, there are many federal statutes that protect individuals against discrimination or a hostile or unsafe environment in the workplace and that prevent employers from terminating employees in certain protected classes for specific reasons. Many of these federal rules are applied using size thresholds such that the regulation does not cover businesses with a small number of employees. Similar laws that exist at the state and local levels supplement these federal statutes. Because these regulations increase the risk of legal action by establishing a government agency with the authority to investigate firm behavior and take legal action, the very small firms that fall below the employment threshold for a regulation may face a lower risk of legal action in this area. There is little empirical research examining the effectiveness of the exemption thresholds that do exist. In general, more careful consideration of unintended consequences and of the benefits of policy and regulation in the workplace setting is warranted.

Health-Insurance Regulations

Firms face myriad regulations governing the HI coverage that they offer to their employees. However, HI regulations are often targeted to companies that sell group HI products to firms rather than toward the firms that offer HI to their employees.

Although HI regulation has emerged in response to a general concern about the cost of access to HI, there is particular concern about access for individuals who are employed by small businesses. Nearly three-fourths of employed Americans obtain HI through an employer. However, while 79 percent of workers in large firms have employer-provided HI, only 36 percent of workers in small firms have such coverage. This difference stems mostly from the fact that small firms are substantially less likely to offer HI coverage than large firms are. In particular, only 40 percent of firms with fewer than 10 workers offer HI, compared to 99 percent of firms with more than 500 workers (authors' calculations from AHRQ, 2000).

The difficulties that small firms face in obtaining and maintaining HI for their employees have been widely documented (Charles Brown, Hamilton, and Medoff, 1990; McLaughlin, 1993; Fronstin and Helman, 2000). Among small firms that offer coverage, HI is routinely cited as the most salient area of concern (NFIB, undated). The low proportion of small firms offering HI coverage has been attributed, in part, to the high cost of HI for small firms, the low demand for HI among workers in these firms, and insurers' unwillingness to take on small-firm risks (McLaughlin, 1993; Fronstin and Helman, 2000; Monheit and Vistnes, 1999).

Regulatory Environment

Regulation. The intention of small-firm HI regulation has consistently been to make HI more accessible and affordable for small-firm employees. Several goals have dominated the policy landscape (Blumberg and Nichols, 1995). Because small firms may be disadvantaged relative to large firms, reforms have aimed to extend economies of size to small firms. Small firms are disadvantaged relative to large firms in two ways: First, HI companies face substantially higher administrative costs in insuring small firms than they do in insuring large ones, which has led to higher premium levels for small firms; second, small firms have limited opportunities to share health-care risks with other individuals or groups, which can threaten access to HI for some small firms, especially those with employees with potentially higher health expenses.

Policy reforms have also aimed to promote competition in the private HI market. A competitive HI market is likely to lead to more efficient delivery of health services, higher service quality, and decreases in average premium levels. The more informed the purchasers of services are, the more that providers of services will compete on quality and cost. Therefore, an important goal of policy is to promote various avenues for small firms to obtain HI.

Policymakers have had to balance insurers' concerns against small firms' needs. Insurers have resisted stringent regulations on premiums and underwriting and have stopped doing business in some states that have had excessively restrictive regulations (Epstein, 1996). As a result, in many cases, HI regulation has been weak and ineffective. In other cases, as discussed later in this section, regulations have had unintended consequences on labor-market outcomes and possibly on business size.

Table 2.3 lists major federal regulations related to HI. We discuss these regulations in relation to three topics: HI access, small-group HI, and HI benefits.

Health Insurance Access. Many federal and state regulations aim to increase access to HI for firms and individuals.[18]

---

[18] For another source of information on HI, see U.S. General Accounting Office (2003a).

ERISA preempts state regulation of self-insured health plans. Essentially, this implies that firms can avoid potentially burdensome state HI regulations by choosing to self-insure rather than purchasing coverage from an HI company.

COBRA (P.L. 99-272) provides continuation of group health coverage that otherwise would be terminated when an employee leaves a job. COBRA applies to firms that employ more than 20 workers. COBRA contains provisions giving certain former employees, retirees, spouses, and dependent children the right to temporary continuation of health coverage at group rates. Job leavers are entitled to continue purchasing group coverage from their former employers for up to 18

Table 2.3
Major Federal Regulations Governing Health Insurance

Law	Main Purpose or Relevance for HI
ERISA (P.L. 93-406)	Preempts state regulation of self-insured health plans, thus implying that firms can choose to self-insure rather than purchasing coverage from an HI company. Sets uniform, minimum standards to ensure that employee-benefit plans are established and maintained in a fair and financially sound manner.
COBRA (P.L. 99-272)	Provides continuation of group health coverage that would otherwise be terminated when an employee leaves a job.
HIPAA (P.L. 104-191)	Adds provisions to ERISA that are designed to provide participants and beneficiaries of group health plans with improved portability and continuity of HI coverage. Limits scope and length of exclusion periods for people with preexisting conditions in group health plans and prohibits cancellation of health coverage due to illness.
ADA (P.L. 101-336)	Prohibits employers from discriminating against individuals with disabilities in the provision of HI but allows medical underwriting.
Mental Health Parity Act of 1996 (MHPA) (P.L. 104-204)	Stipulates that, if mental-health coverage is offered, dollar limits on mental-health benefits have to be equal to dollar limits on medical benefits.
PDA (P.L. 95-555)	Requires businesses with 15 or more employees to cover expenses for pregnancy and medical conditions related to pregnancy on the same basis as it does for other medical conditions.

months after a separation at a maximum of 102 percent of the employer's average group rate.

Many states have continuation-coverage laws. These laws specify that employees and their families may continue coverage for a specified length of time after job termination. Unlike COBRA, state continuation-coverage laws apply to all firms that are not exempt from state regulation by ERISA. The majority of states (39) extended the federal COBRA requirements to individuals covered by group HI provided by businesses with fewer than 20 employees (U.S. General Accounting Office, 2003a).

HIPAA (P.L. 104-191) added several provisions to ERISA that are designed to provide participants and beneficiaries of group health plans with improved portability and continuity of HI coverage. The HIPAA portability provisions relating to group health plans and HI coverage offered in connection with group health plans are designed to improve access to HI and protect against discrimination on the basis of health status.[19] HIPAA also prohibits a person's health coverage from being canceled because of sickness. Moreover, HIPAA requires that HI coverage be guaranteed issue and renewable for small employers (2 to 50 employees). HIPAA also prohibits any employer-sponsored health coverage from charging employees a higher premium based on health-related factors. However, it is important to note that these requirements regulate only the premium charged to employees, not the premium faced by employers.

ADA (P.L. 101-336) is a federal law focusing on employment and other rights for the disabled, including several provisions that apply to employer-provided HI. ADA prohibits employers from discriminating against individuals with disabilities in the provision of HI; however, ADA explicitly allows medical underwriting.[20] An employer who treats individuals with disabilities differently from others under an HI or benefit plan because the people who are disabled represent increased risks or costs is not in violation of the ADA if the employer treats the disabilities in the same manner as other conditions of the same risks or

---

[19] For further details on HIPAA, see HHS (2007).

[20] See DOJ (2005) for details on ADA.

costs. While an employer must provide people with disabilities equal access to the HI coverage provided to all employees, the employer may offer a policy that limits the number of treatments or excludes certain conditions from coverage that are not disability based. ADA applies only to businesses with more than 15 employees.

Small Group HI. During the 1990s, most states passed laws regulating the terms and conditions of HI provided to small firms (Monheit and Cantor, 2004). States have tended to pass these reforms in packages that generally contain the following provisions:

- *Guaranteed-issue and -renewal laws.* Every state (except Georgia) that has passed small-group HI reform has included guaranteed-renewal reform in its package. This reform requires insurers to renew coverage for all groups, except in cases of nonpayment of premium or fraud. Guaranteed-issue legislation, on the other hand, is excluded from the reform packages of eight states that have passed guaranteed renewal laws. These laws have now been preempted by the federal HIPAA.
- *Preexisting-condition exclusion laws.* Health plans often impose waiting periods for coverage generally or coverage for preexisting health conditions. In some instances, health plans permanently exclude coverage for specific health conditions. State reforms limit the length of time for which preexisting health conditions can be excluded from coverage. HIPAA reinforces preexisting-condition exclusion limitations.
- *Portability reforms.* Portability reforms ensure that an individual who is covered by HI on a previous job does not face any new preexisting-condition exclusions or waiting periods as a result of changing jobs. However, portability reforms do not place any restrictions on either premiums that HI companies charge small firms or premium contributions that firms charge workers.
- *Premium rating reforms.* State reforms have placed restrictions on the factors that can be used to set HI premiums and have limited the rate variations to specified ranges. The reforms restrict the variation in premiums that an insurer can charge to firms within each of a set number of classes and restrict the variation

allowed between business classes. Most states allow nine business classes, with about 15 to 30 percent premium variation within and between classes. The use of factors such as group size, family type, age, and other demographic variables to set premiums is generally allowable.

- *Reinsurance provisions.* An administered reinsurance mechanism allows individual insurers to reinsure any firms that are expected to generate costs exceeding the prices of HI. Reinsurance allows insurers to pass their highest-risk clients over to an industry-funded reinsurance pool. This outlet encourages insurers to accept all clients, making it less risky for insurers with small market shares to remain in a market with guaranteed issue.

HI Benefits. Another set of federal regulations place restrictions on the package of benefits offered by health insurers. MHPA (P.L. 104-204), which took effect in January 1998, stipulates that, if mental-health coverage is offered, the dollar limits on mental-health benefits have to be equal to dollar limits on medical benefits. The parity legislation exempts businesses with fewer than 50 employees. PDA (P.L. 95-555) requires businesses with 15 or more employees to cover expenses for pregnancy and medical conditions related to pregnancy on the same basis as coverage for other medical conditions.[21]

State-mandated HI benefit laws regulate the services that insurers must cover to sell HI in a state. While all states have mandated that certain benefits be covered by HI policies, the number, type, and scope of the states' requirements vary substantially. According to a survey published in 2002, the total number of mandated benefits varied among states from fewer than 10 in five states to more than 30 in seven states. The two most commonly mandated benefits, required by 43 or more states, were mammography screening and diabetic supplies. States also have provider mandates that specify that insurers must

---

[21] The Newborns' and Mothers' Health Protection Act of 1996 (NMHPA) (P.L. 104-204) mandates a minimum length of stay after childbirth; however, this legislation applies equally to businesses of all sizes that offer HI. Similarly, the Women's Health and Cancer Rights Act of 1998 (WHCRA) (P.L. 105-277) requires that employer-sponsored HI cover reconstructive surgery after mastectomies—this regulation also applies to firms of all sizes.

cover the services of certain providers, such as chiropractors, psychologists, and optometrists. Most states allow the sale of bare-bones policies that do not need to comply with benefit mandates (U.S. General Accounting Office, 2003a).

Policies to Assist Businesses in Providing Insurance. In addition to these regulations, several policies have been developed to aid businesses, particularly small businesses, in providing HI.

Premium Assistance Programs for Small Businesses. Tax incentives are often used as a tool for encouraging access to HI for small businesses. A common strategy is for small businesses to receive transitional tax credits when they insure for the first time. More than 10 states offer some form of tax incentives. Another form of premium assistance relies on direct subsidies to small businesses. Several states have implemented programs to subsidize premiums using public dollars under HIPAA. In some states, the employee is subsidized directly, while, in others, the subsidy goes through the employer (U.S. General Accounting Office, 2003a; Williams, 2003).

Purchasing Pools. Some state small-group HI reforms have included provisions to establish a publicly sponsored purchasing pool for small employers. In a purchasing cooperative, firms join together to purchase HI in larger volumes at more affordable prices, thereby aiming to diversify risk and reduce administrative costs. Most purchasing cooperatives are private, but a few states have public cooperatives. By one estimate, almost one-third of small firms purchase their HI through some form of cooperative purchasing arrangement (Long and Marquis, 1999).

Health and Medical Savings Accounts. Health savings accounts (HSAs) or medical savings accounts (MSAs) are tax-free savings accounts for medical expenses.[22] In 2007, taxpayers with high-deductible health plans (HDHPs) can contribute up to $2,850 per year ($5,650 for families) into an HSA. Both employers and employees may contribute to these accounts. While HSAs are not explicitly targeted to

---

[22] The MSA was a precursor of the HSA, was authorized as a demonstration project in 1996, and was not reauthorized when the demonstration period ended.

small businesses, it is yet to be seen whether small businesses are more or less attracted than large businesses are to HDHPs.

Patient and Provider Protections. Federal and state laws have also established a number of laws and standards to protect the interests of patients and providers.

ERISA (P.L. 93-406) lays out administrators' fiduciary standards (to administer the plan in the best interests of beneficiaries) and provides for internal review of denied claims, requirements for plan descriptions to be given to enrollees, and reporting to the federal government. ERISA sets uniform, minimum standards to ensure that employee-benefit plans are established and maintained in a fair and financially sound manner. ERISA also sets out requirements for managing and administering private pension and welfare plans.

Most states have enacted laws to regulate the nature of the provider panels created by managed-care firms and the administration of managed-care benefits. The extent to which ERISA (P.L. 93-406) preempts these laws is still unknown. These laws can generally be grouped into three categories:

- *Any willing provider.* These laws require managed-care plans to allow any provider to be included in the network if he or she is willing to abide by the network contract's terms and conditions.
- *Freedom of choice.* These laws require that a managed-care subscriber be allowed to obtain services outside the network from any licensed provider as long as the subscriber pays more out of pocket than would be necessary to pay for an in-network provider.
- *Review of denied claims.* States have stipulated a process for the internal review of denied claims, although considerable variation exists among these processes, including determining which claims are eligible for review. Most states have also mandated an external review process that requires an independent, external review of denials by managed-care companies.

Many states have enacted patient-protection laws to protect consumers through means such as the availability of a point-of-service option. Most states also have patient protections that allow patients direct access (without prior approval) to certain health-care providers and services, such as emergency services and obstetricians and gynecologists. Most states also prohibit gag clauses in insurers' contracts with health-care providers. These laws allow a provider to inform a patient about treatments that are not covered by his or her HI policy. States have also regulated utilization review by requiring registration and accreditation. In addition, states have instituted solvency requirements and reporting requirements. Many of these regulations are more stringent than ERISA. Most states require health insurers to maintain a certain minimum level of reserves (Charette, 1995).

Effects of Health-Insurance Regulations on Small Businesses and the Small-Business Response

The regulations reviewed in this section might lead small businesses to respond differently from larger businesses to maximize the benefit and minimize the negative impact of regulation. We consider the effect of the regulatory environment on small businesses in four areas: HI offering, premiums, labor-market outcomes, and business size.

Effect on HI Coverage and Premiums. HI regulations that affect small firms differently from how they affect large firms might be expected to impact the likelihood that small firms will offer HI coverage or lead to changes in HI premiums. Furthermore, the cost of state regulation might influence a small firm's decision on whether to self-insure.

Self-insurance is an attractive option for larger firms that are able to diversify variations in worker medical costs internally. However, small firms are less able to do this and therefore are usually unable to self-insure. A recent survey found that 10 percent of covered workers in all small firms (3–199 workers) are in self-insured plans, compared to 50 percent of workers in midsized firms (200–999 workers) and 79 percent of workers in jumbo firms (5,000 or more workers) (KFF/ HRET, 2003). As a result, small firms are likelier than large firms are to face the burden of state HI regulations even if there are no explicit size thresholds in the state legislation.

Research examining the effect of state insurance mandates on HI coverage, firms' propensity to offer coverage, and HI premiums generally has shown a small effect or no effect on small firms' propensity to offer HI or on employees' insurance coverage (Sloan and Conover, 1998; Jensen and Morrissey, 1999; Zuckerman and Rajan, 1999; Monheit and Schone, 2004; Buchmueller and DiNardo, 2002; Marquis and Long, 2001). A few studies do find modest effects of the reforms on insurance offer rates and insurance coverage; however, the direction of the effects varies among the studies (Uccello, 1996; Hing and Jensen, 1999; Simon, 2005; Buchmueller and Jensen, 1997). The Health Insurance Association of America estimates that guaranteed-issue provisions have a small impact on premiums, equal to about 2 to 4 percent.

Another line of research has examined the effects of mandated benefits on HI costs and offerings. Two studies have estimated that the additional costs associated with state-mandated benefits represented about 3 to 5 percent of total premium costs (Gruber, 1994a, 1994b). Another study finds little effect of mandated benefits on HI coverage among employees in small firms, primarily because most firms offer comprehensive benefits even in the absence of the mandates (U.S. General Accounting Office, 2003a).

In general, it appears that HI regulations have had little effect on premiums or HI coverage. Proponents of small-group HI reforms are likely to find these results disappointing. The lack of realizable effect on HI may be due to the lack of effective price controls. In most states, limitations on premium increases and premium rating factors are weak. As a result, guaranteed-issue provisions mandating coverage for small groups or continuation-coverage laws mandating all employees to be offered coverage have a muted effect, since the available coverage is too expensive for small firms. Without stronger and more effective premium regulation, we are unlikely to see the HI changes that policymakers had envisioned. Nonprice factors such as the relative ineffectiveness of small-firm purchasing alliances and the lack of information on HI alternatives may also be partly responsible.

Effect on Workforce Composition. HI can be thought of as a fixed cost associated with hiring someone. HI regulation can affect this cost, and businesses might respond to regulation by changing their hiring practices. For small firms, regulation might affect an employer's choice of hiring full-time versus part-time workers. If a firm offers

HI, it must be offered to full-time employees, but the offering is not required for part-time employees. In addition, small firms may prefer to hire personnel with demographic characteristics associated with low and stable HI premiums. Empirical evidence suggests that the workforce composition in small firms might have shifted as a result of HI regulations and costs (Kapur, 2004). Similarly, workforce composition might be affected by the possibility of health and safety violations in small firms.

A business might also respond to the regulatory environment by attempting to reduce its compensation costs by encouraging employees with working spouses to take family coverage from the other employer. The use of practices of this sort might vary by firm size. For example, earlier research found that about 10 percent of employees and dependents with coverage from a large firm have a working family member in a small firm, suggesting that large employers may "subsidize" small employers (Monheit and Vistnes, 1994). Some empirical support has been presented for the idea that employers adopt strategies, such as raising contribution rates, to encourage employees to use HI coverage provided by the employer of a spouse or another family member. However, there is further scope for research that examines whether small firms systematically shift their workforce composition to reduce HI costs.

Even though the primary goal of HI regulation has been to improve HI access and affordability, the policy community has also claimed that such regulations have reduced labor-market distortions by, for example, providing HI protections to certain groups of people. While there is evidence that small-group policy reform may have reduced distortions for some groups (such as workers with certain preexisting medical conditions), others who are not explicitly protected by the reforms might now face higher costs. In addition, with rising HI costs, we are likely to see a growing trend toward hiring part-time and other types of employees who do not have to be offered HI.

Effect on Worker Turnover. HI regulations might also potentially affect worker turnover. For instance, small-group HI legislation and HIPAA include portability and preexisting-condition exclusion provisions that might make it easier for individuals to accept jobs at small firms. However, two existing studies that examine the labor-market effects of small-group HI reform, including job mobility, find little or no effect on mobility; however, no research has examined the labor-market implications of HIPAA (Kaestner and Simon, 2002; Kapur, 2003). Other research has examined the effect of continuation-coverage mandates and has found that these mandates increase mobility and therefore reduce labor-market inefficiency (Gruber and Madrian, 1994). Further research on worker turnover may benefit from focusing more closely on the variation in state continuation-coverage laws and their effect on small businesses.

The lack of controls on premiums is likely to be the most important factor preventing HIPAA from increasing transitions and HI coverage. Policymakers will need to balance pricing policies with the potential distortions that might arise from instituting price regulations.

Effect on Business Size. Virtually no prior research has examined the effect of HI regulations on business size. The explicit size thresholds in many HI regulations suggest that firms considering changing their workforce size might be influenced by HI regulations. For instance, in the case of small-group HI regulations, small firms that can obtain HI that is protected by small-group regulations might choose not to expand beyond the upper size threshold. On the other hand, if the regulations result in higher premiums and lower availability, small firms might prefer to expand to a size that is beyond the reach of small-firm regulations. Other regulations such as state-mandated benefits may also affect business size, since larger firms can self-insure and avoid state regulation. Chapter Three provides evidence that state HI mandates have led small firms to adjust their size to escape the more highly regulated market for HI.

Section Conclusion

Businesses face a vast array of HI regulations either directly or indirectly via their contracts with health insurers. These regulations might be expected to affect HI choices, workforce composition, turnover, and size. Even though there is some research that examines the differential effect of these regulations on small and large firms, there is substantial scope to expand this research agenda. An important policy issue is whether policymakers should consider pricing regulation to accompany HI access regulations. Premium regulations are likely to lead to an increase in the number of small firms offering HI. However, the magnitude of the increase depends on small firms' price sensitivity. In general, small firms have not been very responsive to price incentives. Excessively stringent premium regulations may also drive insurers away from unprofitable markets, resulting in worse HI availability. Furthermore, premium regulations may change the landscape of labor-market distortions. Policymakers will need to carefully balance these considerations in revising existing HI regulation.

Chapter Conclusion

In this chapter, we have considered the impact of regulation and litigation on small businesses and entrepreneurship in the context of four key regulatory areas: corporate securities, environmental protection, employment, and HI.

Across these four areas, we find that regulation tends to originate from concerns about the behavior of large businesses and that the strategies for addressing these concerns tend to focus on actions that would most effectively influence the behavior of larger businesses. This is true even for HI regulations, which, although intended to benefit small businesses and to improve their ability to offer affordable HI to their employees, are directed at the HI companies—which are large businesses. However, the attention given to large businesses does not mean only that regulators are unconcerned about the potential impact of small firms' behavior on employees, customers, or society as a whole, but perhaps more that the policy debate is dominated by the magnitude of large-business interests.

There is broad recognition that regulation impacts small businesses differently from the way in which it affects large businesses. For example, compliance with environmental regulations can be costlier for small firms than for large ones because of the financial and other costs of compliance. To cite another example from this chapter, there are also reasons to believe that small-business owners will face higher WC costs than will large-business owners. To mitigate the potential negative impacts of regulation, small businesses often receive special consideration in the policymaking process. Such special consideration takes many forms, including opportunities to voice specific concerns or raise issues about proposed regulations before they go into effect or alterations in the regulatory environment that small firms face (e.g., exemptions from regulation, modified compliance procedures, reduced penalties for violation of regulation, special programs to assist small firms in complying with regulation).

The existence of a different regulatory environment for small firms is referred to as *regulatory tiering* and is a common approach to addressing the concerns of small businesses. As we have described in this chapter and further detail in Appendix A, the size thresholds that are used to determine whether a firm is eligible for a different regulatory environment vary dramatically across regulatory contexts. Although these thresholds create clear incentives for firms to limit growth to avoid them, in our review of the literature, we uncovered no research on whether regulatory thresholds affect firm growth in the United States or on the magnitude of that effect.

Across the board, there is little empirical evidence to demonstrate that the special consideration offered to small businesses in the regulatory context makes sense from a cost-benefit perspective. Further, it is not always clear that regulations designed to benefit small businesses always achieve their intended aims, that programs designed to assist small businesses in complying with regulations are well targeted or well utilized, or that thresholds that define exemptions from regulations are based on a careful consideration of the relative costs and benefits of regulation. For example, although much of the regulatory regime surrounding HI was designed explicitly to increase access to HI among small businesses, it appears that these regulations have had little effect on premiums or HI coverage. In the environmental realm, consensus is lacking over whether environmental regulation put small firms at a disadvantage relative to larger ones, and it has been difficult to judge the success of recent efforts to make it easier for small firms to comply. In the area of securities and exchange law, data have been lacking to address key questions, such as whether new regulatory requirements such as SOX have affected the willingness of small firms to enter public capital markets. Finally, the discussion of employment law shows that, despite the existence of size thresholds, many policy instruments designed to regulate aspects of the employer-employee relationship might have had unintended consequences that impose higher costs on small businesses than on larger ones.

The remainder of this book attempts to expand our understanding of the influence of public policy on small businesses. Although each of the studies is focused on a specific policy area, many of the lessons learned are potentially generalizable.

Regulations or programs designed to benefit small businesses are rarely criticized or questioned. However, as has been described in this chapter, even programs that are well targeted may fail to achieve their intended aims and also have unintended consequences. Chapter Three examines the issue of the unintended effects of policies in the context of regulation of HI. This chapter also explores effect of regulatory thresholds on business growth.

Research on small businesses rarely makes a distinction between small establishments (workplaces) and small firms (business operations). Indeed, data on establishment size is often used to draw conclusions about differences by firm size. The importance of this distinction and its implications for understanding the effects of policy are illustrated in the study on workplace fatalities and firm size described in Chapter Four. This study illustrates how important it is for the research unit of analysis to be congruent with the policymaking unit of analysis.

A major challenge facing research on the effect of regulation on small businesses is isolating the effect of the regulation's introduction or reform from other factors. This issue is a key element of the assessment, provided in Chapter Five, of the impact of SOX on small businesses.

The choices that entrepreneurs make regarding incorporation, organizational status, and publicly held status can have important implications for firm behavior, growth, and success. Chapter Six considers whether organizational forms that were designed, at least in part, with small businesses in mind have actually benefited small law firms.

CHAPTER THREE

State Health-Insurance Mandates, Consumer-Directed Health Plans, and Health Savings Accounts: Are They a Panacea for Small Businesses?

Susan M. Gates, Kanika Kapur, and Pinar Karaca-Mandic

Small firms in the United States that seek to offer HI to their employees have historically reported problems with the availability and affordability of their options. The cost of HI has been the primary concern of small-business owners for several decades. In 2004, two-thirds of small-business owners listed health-care costs as a critical problem—a proportion that increased by 18 percentage points between 2000 and 2004 (NFIB, 2004). Small businesses are likelier to report problems with their health-care availability and costs than larger businesses (Charles Brown, Hamilton, and Medoff, 1990; McLaughlin, 1993; Fronstin and Helman, 2000). Extending HI to workers and the families of workers in small firms continues to be a pressing issue.

HI plans offered to small businesses tend to suffer from limitations that are widely acknowledged. First, small-group HI premiums have varied dramatically depending on the expected cost of the group (Cutler, 1994). In addition, the HI policies offered to small firms often contain preexisting-condition clauses that exclude expensive conditions from coverage (U.S. Congress, 1988). Some insurers simply do not offer policies to small firms, resulting in limited choices for small firms. These limitations, along with double-digit increases in HI costs and consumer dissatisfaction with managed care, have led to both employers and government policymakers seeking new ways to contain health-care costs.

Policymakers have pursued various avenues to address the problems that small businesses face in the market for HI. In this book, we provide a summary of the success of two different approaches: one that is regulatory in nature and the other that is market based. The first is state HI mandates. To try to address problems with the small-group market, most states passed small-group HI reforms in the 1990s. These reforms have three key characteristics. First, they restrict insurers' ability to deny coverage to small firms. Second, they restrict premium variability, and, finally, they encourage portability when employees move from job to job. In this chapter, we summarize the evidence of the influence these mandates had not only on HI premiums and HI availability, but also on business size.

An alternative solution to the HI crisis that has been advocated by the Bush administration and by some policy analysts is the development of consumer-directed health plans (CDHPs). These plans aim to control costs by increasing consumers' financial responsibility and involvement in their health-care choices. Since CDHPs are potentially less costly than traditional health plans and may appeal to younger workers with low health-care demands, these plans may be well suited to workers in small businesses (Laing, undated).

In this chapter, we examine the effect to date of two types of policy initiatives that could have substantial benefits for small businesses: state HI mandates and key components of CDHPs—HSAs, health reimbursement arrangements (HRAs), and HDHPs. We summarize the key policy issues, review existing research evidence, including our own research, on the effect of these initiatives on small businesses, and offer some conclusions for policymakers.

Small Businesses Typically Face Restricted Health-Insurance Options

The difficulties that small firms face in obtaining and maintaining HI for their employees have been widely documented (Charles Brown, Hamilton, and Medoff, 1990; McLaughlin, 1993; Fronstin and Helman, 2000). Only 43 percent of firms with fewer than 50 employees offer HI, compared to 95 percent of firms with 50 or more employees (AHRQ, 2003). This low proportion has been attributed, in part, to the high administrative cost of HI for small firms, the low demand for HI among workers in these firms, and the unwillingness of insurers to take on small-firm risks (McLaughlin, 1993; Fronstin and Helman, 2000; Monheit and Vistnes, 1999).

According to surveys conducted by the National Federation of Independent Business (NFIB, 2004), the cost of providing HI has been the number-one concern of small-business owners since 1986. In 2004, nearly two-thirds of small-business owners cited it as a critical issue. While the cost of HI is a concern for all employers irrespective of size, it is well documented that the administrative cost of HI is substantially higher for small employers—20 to 25 percent of employee premiums in small firms compared to 10 percent of premiums in large firms—and is one possible reason that so few small businesses offer HI to their employees (U.S. General Accounting Office, 2001).[1] Several studies have shown that small-firm employees who do not have HI are relatively young and healthy and are likelier to have higher job turnover and therefore have a lower demand for employment-based HI (Monheit and Vistnes, 1994, 1999, 2006). Even though the demographic characteristics of small-firm employees as a whole (insured and uninsured combined) appear to be quite similar to those of other employees, small firms employ a slightly larger share of workers under age 25 and a much larger share of workers over age 65 (Headd, 2000). This suggests that small firms are likelier to employ individuals with a relatively low demand for employer-sponsored HI: the youngest and healthiest workers but also the oldest workers who are eligible for HI coverage under Medicare.

---

[1] The lower administrative costs in large firms may be due to the fact that large firms tend to have a benefits manager to coordinate health claims and complete paperwork. The benefits office in large firms acts as an intermediary between employees and insurers, reducing administrative burden for large-firm insurers. Large firms are also less likely to drop insurance, resulting in lower transition costs for insurance companies.

State Health-Insurance Mandates Seek to Expand Small-Business Options

To address the aforementioned problems with the small-group market for HI, virtually all states passed some form of small-group HI reform in the 1990s. Although the extent of and approach to the reforms vary from state to state, they contain broadly similar elements.

Rating Reforms

State reforms have placed restrictions on the factors that can be used to set HI premiums or limited the rate variations to specified ranges. Most states' premium rating reforms follow the rate-banding approach, which limits insurers to a set number of classes for which they can charge separate rates. Age, geographic location, family size, and group size are often allowable factors that can be used to set classes. The reform restricts the variation in premiums that the insurer can charge to firms within each of these classes and restricts the variation allowed between business classes. Most states allow nine business classes and about 15 to 30 percent premium variation within and between classes, although these numbers vary somewhat from state to state. Rating reforms do not regulate the dollar value of the premium; however, they do often restrict the percentage increase in premiums from year to year. About 10 states have implemented modified community rating, in which the use of claims experience and employee health status in setting premiums has been restricted, and premiums can be set only on the basis of demographic factors such as family size and age. Community rating, the strongest form of rating reforms, has been implemented only by a few states and disallows variation in premiums due to demographic and health factors.

It is plausible that these restrictions on premiums may have limited premium variability for a small firm. In addition, these reforms may have succeeded in reducing premiums for small firms that employ individuals with high health costs. The rate-banding approach is the most common premium rating reform, and this form of reform often allows claims experience to be used to set premiums. Therefore, in practice, in most states, premiums still do vary substantially due to claims experience and the health characteristics of the insured (U.S. General Accounting Office, 1995; Hall, 2000).

Guaranteed-Issue and Guaranteed-Renewal Reforms

Every state (except Georgia) that has passed small-group HI reform has included guaranteed-renewal reform in its package. This reform requires insurers to renew coverage for all groups, except in cases of nonpayment of premium or fraud. Guaranteed-issue legislation, on the other hand, is excluded from the reform packages of eight states that have passed guaranteed-renewal laws. Guaranteed-issue legislation requires HI companies to offer HI coverage to any small employer in the state. Some guaranteed-issue legislation requires HI companies to offer only one or two specific benefit plans, while some requires insurers to offer every small-group health plan they sell to each small employer. Guaranteed-issue legislation limits the ability of insurers to circumvent rating reform by insuring only low-cost, small firms.

Preexisting-Condition Limitation and Portability Reforms

Health plans often impose waiting periods for coverage. These waiting periods may pertain to all coverage or only to coverage for preexisting health conditions. In some instances, health plans permanently exclude coverage for specific health conditions. State preexisting-condition reforms limit the length of time for which preexisting health conditions can be excluded from coverage. Most states limit the waiting period for coverage for preexisting conditions to a maximum of 12 months and allow only conditions present in the past six months to be defined as *preexisting*.

Portability reforms ensure that an individual who is covered by HI on a previous job does not face any new preexisting-condition exclusions or waiting periods as a result of changing jobs. Note that portability reforms do not place any restrictions on either premiums that HI companies charge small firms or premium contributions that firms charge workers. Portability and preexisting-condition limitation laws have been enacted at the same time in most states.

HIPAA reinforces preexisting-condition exclusion limitations. In essence, these laws virtually remove small-group insurers' ability to exclude coverage for certain conditions or to deny individuals coverage in small-firm policies. Therefore, after the passage of these laws, charging higher premiums, subject to the state's premium rating reforms, may be small-group insurers' only available underwriting option.

Small-group HI reforms regulate the type of HI that HI companies can sell to small firms. They have no direct effect on the HI offered to other firms, although they may have an indirect effect if insurers adjust policies in the large-group market to make it easier to comply with the regulations in the small-group market.

State Mandates Have Not Improved Small-Business Access to Health Insurance

Research examining the effect of state HI mandates on HI coverage, firms' propensity to offer coverage, and HI premiums generally has shown a small effect or no effect on small firms' propensity to offer HI or on employees' HI coverage (Sloan and Conover, 1998; Gail Jensen and Morrisey, 1999; Zuckerman and Rajan, 1999; Monheit and Schone, 2004; Buchmueller and DiNardo, 2002; Marquis and Long, 2001). A few studies do find modest effects of the reforms on HI offer rates and HI coverage; however, the direction of the effects found varies among the studies (Uccello, 1996; Hing and Jensen, 1999; Simon, 2005; Buchmueller and Jensen, 1997). In addition, some work has demonstrated that stronger reforms increased HI coverage for high-risk workers relative to low-risk workers (Monheit and Schone, 2004; Davidoff, Blumberg, and Nichols, 2005). Most of these studies exploit cross-sectional and time-series variations in the implementation of state reforms to identify the reforms' effects on HI coverage and do not focus on analyzing employment and employment flows in small and large firms as a result of the reforms.

The overall effect of reforms is likely to depend on the characteristics of those reforms. The Health Insurance Association of America estimates that guaranteed-issue provisions have only a small impact on premiums—2 to 4 percent (Roger Thompson, 1992). Gail Jensen, Michael Morrisey, and R. J. Morlock (1995) found no evidence that guaranteed-issue laws, preexisting-condition limits, or laws limiting exclusions on the basis of condition or occupation resulted in premium increases. Premiums in New York, which enacted very stringent rating reforms in the small-group market, rose about 5 percent during the first year that community rating was in effect (Chollet, 1994). Minnesota, which adopted restrictions on premium rate variations, also experienced premium rate increases of less than 5 percent in the year after it enacted these rating reforms in combination with a number of other small group reforms (Blumberg and Nichols, 1996). Two studies examined the labor-market effects of small-group HI reform and find small or no effect on mobility among workers with high expected health costs and no effect on wages or hours worked (Kapur, 2003; Kapur et al., 2005; Kaestner and Simon, 2002).

Because of the way in which these HI mandates were implemented—applying only the HI products offered to firms below a certain size threshold—we were also curious as to whether the mandates had any unintended effect on the size of firms. While there is no prior research on the effect of small-group HI reforms on the size of small firms, a few studies have examined the effect of other regulations on business size. Schivardi and Torrini (2004) examine the effect of employment-protection legislation on business size in Italy. Employment-protection legislation, which imposes higher unfair-dismissal costs on firms that employ more than 15 employees, was found to reduce business size and growth for firms that were just below the size threshold. Using the same data source, Garibaldi, Pacelli, and Borgarello (2004) find results that are consistent with Schivardi and Torrini's. Germany's Protection Against Dismissal Act allows firms above a certain size threshold to sue for wrongful termination. The threshold size has varied over time. Verick (2004) examined the effect of this size threshold on firm size and found mixed effects.

We undertook a study to examine whether there was a size effect (Kapur et al., 2006). We summarize our findings in the next section of this chapter.

State Health-Insurance Mandates Have Had Unintended Effects

In our study, we used data from a nationally representative, employer-based survey conducted by KMPG Consulting (now BearingPoint). This data source contains information on HI offering, number of workers employed in the firm, and the industry to which the firm belongs.[2] Because most states adopted small-business HI reforms during the early 1990s, we used the surveys from 1993, 1996, and 1998. These were the only years during the 1990s in which the survey included smaller firms with fewer than 200 employees.

We also used a data set that characterizes the presence of a small-business HI reform for any given state and year, as well as the detailed characteristics of the reform, if one exists. These data come from the state small-group reform survey conducted by Simon (2005) and Marquis and Long (2001). Our analysis used the upper and lower limits of the firm-size thresholds for the reform to be applicable. The HI reform data and the firm-level survey data were merged using the survey year and the state of the firm. Small-group HI reform was coded using a binary indicator of having a reform or not.

Table 3.1 provides a data summary of the state health reforms. As the table indicates, in 1993, 14 states had no reform; by 1997, all states except for one (Michigan) had adopted some type of small-business health-care reform. Most states have a moderate reform that includes restrictions on premiums using a rate-band approach rather than by imposing community rating or modified community rating.

Table 3.2 presents the upper size limit for small-group HI reforms. During these years, most states with reforms had either 25 or 50 employees as the upper size threshold. In our data, 81 percent of state-year observations had thresholds at either 25 or 50 employees. Over time, states tended to raise their thresholds, and the number of states with

---

[2]   We used data on the number of workers employed in the entire firm rather than in a single location because HI decisions tend to be made at the firm level rather than the plant level. However, as a sensitivity check, we reestimated our models for the sample of single-location firms. We found results that were qualitatively similar but far less precise, primarily because we lost about half the sample while conducting this check.

Table 3.1
State Counts by Reform Level and Year

Reform Level	1992	1993	1995	1996	1997	1998
No reform	27	14	5	4	1	1
Reform	23	36	45	46	49	49

NOTE: Does not include Hawaii but does include Washington, D.C.

Table 3.2
State Counts by Firm-Size Upper Limit for State Small-Group Health-Insurance Reform, by Year

Firm-Size Upper Limit	1992	1993	1995	1996	1997	1998
25	18	24	12	11	0	0
26–50	5	11	30	32	48	48
51–100	0	1	3	3	1	1
No reform	27	14	5	4	1	1

NOTE: Does not include Hawaii but does include Washington, D.C.

upper size thresholds of 25 employees decreases. By 1997, no state had 25 employees as the upper size threshold.[3]

As mentioned, the definition of *small firm* varies among states and, in some cases, over time within the same state. The upper size threshold for a small firm varies between 25 and 100 employees, depending on the state and year. The lower threshold varies between one and five employees.

Small-group HI reform may affect the scope, price, and availability of HI for small firms. For the sake of exposition, let us assume that there are two types of small firms: low-cost firms, which employ

---

[3] The lower size limit for the reforms was one, two, or three employees, depending on the state and year. However, California, in 1993, had a lower threshold of five employees. Our data set includes only firms that had three or more employees. We have reestimated our models, excluding Californian firms with fewer than five employees in 1993 (N = 8), and find virtually identical results.

a high proportion of young and healthy workers, and high-cost firms, which employ workers with high expected health-care costs (either older workers or workers at risk for injury or illness). Small-group HI reforms prevent insurers from excluding preexisting conditions from HI coverage, implying more complete HI for all small firms. However, in states that impose tight premium rating restrictions and guaranteed issue, the combination of the two types of reforms may drive insurers to set premiums in a way that increases premiums for low-cost firms and reduces premiums for high-cost firms. Alternatively, the regulations might affect the completeness of the plans offered if insurers find it impossible to offer comprehensive plans to all small firms at a reasonable price. In states with weak premium rating restrictions, premiums may be affected relatively little.

Guaranteed-issue and -renewal laws directly affect the availability of HI. In particular, in states with guaranteed issue, high-cost firms that may have had problems obtaining access to HI should find obtaining a policy much easier. However, the overall burden of complying with the state small-group HI regulations may be a disincentive for offering HI in the small-group market for some insurers, and insurers may consider exiting the market in highly regulated states or consider reducing their marketing efforts in those states. As a result, the reforms may have an adverse effect on availability for low-cost firms. Therefore, the reforms may have heterogeneous effects on price and availability, depending on the strength of their component provisions and the market composition of low-cost versus high-cost small firms.

In our empirical estimation (see Kapur et al., 2006), we focus on firms that offer HI right around the legislative threshold—since the reform is likeliest to affect their decisions. We estimate whether reform states are likelier than nonreform states are to have a higher or lower proportion of firms offering HI below the threshold. If firms value the reforms, the proportion of firms below the threshold to those above it should be higher in reform states as firms attempt to manipulate their size to remain below the reform threshold. If firms do not value the reforms, they will do just the opposite: They will expand so that they are no longer subject to the reforms, and then the proportion of firms under the threshold relative to firms over the threshold will be lower in reform states.[4]

Our analysis provides evidence that, in states that implemented these reforms, firms offering HI are significantly likelier to be just above the threshold than just below the threshold. In states that implement a 25-employee threshold, we estimate that 31 percent of firms with 20 to 30 employees would fall below the 25-employee threshold, compared with 75 percent in states that did not have a reform. In states that implement a 50-employee threshold, we estimate that 65 percent of firms with 45 to 55 employees would fall below the threshold, compared with 82 percent of firms with 45 to 55 employees in states that did not have a reform. The magnitudes of these predicted changes in firm-size distribution are large; however, they apply to a relatively small segment of the firm distribution that is clustered around the regulatory threshold.

These findings suggest that small employers near the threshold that offered HI found the state HI mandates to be onerous and increased their size to avoid the regulated market. As expected, our analyses suggest that firms' ability to make such an adjustment was greater for firms that were closest to the regulatory threshold. The magnitude and statistical significance of the effect declined as we expanded the size of the band around the threshold under consideration.

Our study shows that the small-group HI reform implemented by states in the mid-1990s likely had unintended consequences. The reforms appear to have led firms to distort their firm-size decisions to avoid the more regulated market. What happened to the HI market in reform states to lead to these outcomes? There is evidence from previous research to suggest that the implementation of reforms increased

---

[4]   To capture proximity of firm size to the reform threshold, we restrict our analysis to states that implemented a reform with an upper size threshold of either 25 or 50 and use separate models to examine the effect of each threshold. Since the inherent distribution of firms around the 25-employee size threshold differs from the distribution of firms around the 50-employee size threshold, we cannot estimate a model that compares distributional changes across different thresholds. Our empirical strategy is to focus on a narrow set of firms around the threshold and study whether the proportion of firms under the threshold differs across reform and nonreform states.

the breadth of HI policies but also led to an increase in premiums as insurers that found the small-group regulations burdensome exited the market. For example, in New York, premiums were estimated to have risen for about 30 percent of the insured, and 500,000 New Yorkers were estimated to have cancelled their individual or small-group policies after the implementation of reforms (NCPA, 1994). In Oregon, insurers were reported to have exited the small-group market in response to the reforms (Brock, 1998). However, Buchmueller and DiNardo (2002) compared the New York market that had community rating (strong reform) to the markets in Pennsylvania and Connecticut (states that did not have strong reform) and found no evidence that HI offering levels had fallen in New York.

These reports suggest that the reforms may have resulted in changes in the small-group market that some, but not other, small firms valued. High-cost firms (that is, firms that employ workers with high expected health-care costs, as defined in the conceptual framework section) that previously could not obtain HI are able to access coverage after the reform. Some of these firms may value the access to HI and the broad coverage offered under reform, even if it means higher premiums. Low-cost firms (that is, firms that employ workers with low expected health-care costs), on the other hand, may place little value on the breadth of coverage offered under reform. For example, many small firms hire a younger, healthier workforce and have higher worker turnover than larger firms have (Kapur, 2004), and these workers may not value the more complete policies and higher premiums associated with small-group HI reforms. If it is at all feasible, these firms may increase their firm size to avoid the reform and purchase HI in the unregulated market.

Consumer-Directed Health Plans Could Expand Options for Small Businesses

Our review of the effects of state HI mandates suggests that this regulatory approach was not terribly successful in terms of expanding access to HI for small businesses. Recently, policymakers have advocated an alternative approach to achieving this aim. Since high and increasing costs of health services and HI are perceived as the primary barrier to access, new innovations in the HI market, CHDPs, are designed to encourage individual responsibility in health-care choices in the hope of increasing price sensitivity, controlling cost escalation, and ultimately improving access. This approach would yield benefits for all businesses, but particularly for small businesses that are often shut out of the traditional HI market because of high costs of coverage.

The basic logic behind this argument is that CDHPs change individual incentives by making consumers financially responsible when they choose costly health-care options (Robinson, 2003). Ultimately, this change in individual incentives should reduce the cost of HI and possibly the cost of health care as well. Increases in consumer cost-sharing, especially deductibles, are part of this new strategy (Gabel et al., 2002). Despite the popular notion that encouraging the provision of CDHPs could improve the health-care market, economic theory can also support the opposite conclusion. In a market in which there is a trade-off between making consumers financially responsible for their health care and providing consumers with complete HI, reducing HI to increase financial responsibility can lead to a suboptimal outcome (Zeckhauser, 1970). This possible consequence of CDHPs has received little attention in a policy debate that is focused primarily on the potential role of CDHPs in reducing overall medical expenditures.

HDHPs are an important feature of CDHPs. Often, these HDHPs are combined with a personal health-care spending account that provides individuals with favored tax treatment for money spent to pay for deductibles and copayments. Federal legislation has facilitated the formation of HRAs and HSAs.

HRAs and HSAs potentially make HDHPs more palatable to individuals by providing them with a means to avoid taxes on money used to pay health expenses not covered by HDHPs. The accounts can compensate individuals somewhat for the risk associated with HDHPs. The employee can use money in these accounts to pay for unreimbursed, qualified medical expenditures. Unused funds in the account may be carried over from year to year.[5] This carryover provision of HRAs and HSAs is intended to benefit employees who use fewer and less costly services and encourage them to do so.

The legal foundation for HSAs was established in 2003 under the Medicare Prescription Drug, Improvement, and Modernization Act (P.L. 108-173), creating the newest form of personal savings accounts. HSAs are available to all individuals and employer groups. To operate an HSA, employers or enrollees make deposits into a specially designated account that is then used to purchase health services. If an enrollee spends all of the funds allocated to his or her account in a given year and if this amount is less than the plan deductible, the enrollee must then pay for additional health services out of pocket until the plan deductible is met. (The expenditure amount between the annual account contribution and the deductible is often referred to as a *doughnut hole*). Above the deductible, enrollees' health plans cover most costs. The earlier generation of personal health accounts, flexible spending accounts (FSAs), did not permit enrollees to roll funds over from year to year.

An HSA must be combined with an HI plan with a deductible of at least $1,100 for an individual and $2,200 for a family. The maximum account contribution is the lesser of 100 percent of the deductible or $2,850 for an individual or $5,650 for a family.[6] While contributions can be made by the employee, the employer, or by both parties, the employee owns the account, and, thus, the account is fully portable across jobs. Unused funds are rolled over from year to year. Moreover, accounts can earn investment income that is not taxed as earned. In addition, funds in HSAs can be withdrawn to pay for nonmedical expenses, though they are then subject to taxes and to a penalty if the accountholder is under age 65.

HRAs, available since 2002, differ from HSAs in several important respects: They need not be paired with HDHPs with federally mandated characteristics; only the employer contributions to the

---

[5] In the case of HRAs, the employer chooses whether the accounts have this carry-over provision.

[6] The amounts reflect the requirements for 2007 and are indexed to inflation.

account receive favorable tax treatment; portability across employers and annual carry-over is permitted but not required; accounts are funded by employers only; and third-party administration of the accounts is required.

Some observers have argued that HSAs are particularly well situated to help small firms without medical plans to offer some form of HI to their employees (Laing, undated). HDHPs typically have lower premiums and are more accessible than other types of health-care offerings are to small businesses. The Small Business and Entrepreneurship Council supported the implementation of HDHPs, and HSAs in particular, as a way to provide small-business owners and their employees greater access to affordable choices in HI.

Early evidence suggests that CDHPs are associated with both lower costs and lower cost increases (Buntin et al., 2006). However, CDHPs continue to be controversial as a mechanism for controlling costs and shifting responsibility to consumers (Ginsburg, 2006; Lee and Hoo, 2006). Among other things, there is some evidence that healthier individuals are likelier than less healthy people to opt for these plans (Buntin et al., 2006). Early evidence also raises questions as to whether CDHPs really are a panacea for small businesses.

Small Firms Have Not Been Especially Quick to Adopt Consumer-Directed Health Plans

Insurers' interest in HRAs and HSAs is widespread and growing rapidly. According to a recent survey by America's Health Insurance Plans (AHIP), the number of individuals covered by an HSA or other HDHP reached 3.2 million in January 2006—having tripled in less than one year (AHIP, 2006). Approximately 30 percent of HSA purchasers did not previously have HI, according to the AHIP survey, with 16 percent of new small-business HI-plan purchasers previously not offering HI (AHIP, 2006).

This growth in coverage was due to increases in both the group and the individual market. Today, at least 75 insurers offer account-compatible plans nationwide (KFF, 2004; AHIP, 2005). Fifty-eight offer high-deductible, account-compatible plans to large employers, 56 to small employers, and 47 to individuals. Most large insurers will also have full integration of HSAs and high-deductible plans by 2006, meaning that the carrier has an established relationship with a bank and can provide information about the account along with information about total claims (CDMR, 2005).

There is some evidence that, while HSA products were more popular among small businesses and individuals than among larger groups initially, their use is growing most rapidly among large employers. Large employers are generally introducing these products in a gradual way. Few large employers have chosen the full-replacement route of abandoning traditional plans in favor of CDHPs (Schieber, 2004). HI-industry officials report that employee take-up is low when CDHPs are offered alongside traditional plans. Insurers and employers also report that employers' success in enrolling employees in these new plans to date depends on comprehensive education and communication efforts rather than waiting for employees to respond to premium differences.

An AHIP survey of member companies found that only 3 percent of HSA enrollees in 2004 were in large-group plans (see AHIP, 2005). However, by January 2006, that figure had grown to 33 percent. Small-group plans represented 18 percent of enrollees in 2004 and 25 percent in January 2006 (AHIP, 2006).

Some smaller businesses that might not otherwise offer HI see HSAs as a way to provide low-cost coverage. According to the 2006 survey of AHIP member companies, 33 percent of small-group HSA policies were sold to businesses that previously did not offer HI. This suggests that HSAs have the potential at least to serve as a meaningful tool for expanding health-care coverage to small-business employees, a finding that a simulation study conducted by Goldman, Buchanan, and Keeler (2000) supports. Goldman, Buchanan, and Keeler found that similar plans could increase the proportion of small businesses offering HI.

The 2006 AHIP survey of insurance companies provides information on the characteristics of the HSAs and other HDHPs provided to individuals, small groups, and large groups. This information suggests that small businesses are on a more level playing field with large businesses in this market. A comparison of the HSA and HDHP policies offered in the small- versus large-group markets[7] reveals that average annual deductibles are somewhat higher in the small-group market but that other characteristics are remarkably similar (AHIP, 2006). In the small-group market, the average annual deductible is $2,143 for individual coverage and $4,311 for family coverage, compared with $1,754 and $3,494, respectively, in the large-group market. The average annual premium is $2,772 for individual coverage and $6,955 for family coverage in the small-group market, compared with $2,745 and $6,715, respectively, in the large-group market.

A survey of employers by the Henry J. Kaiser Family Foundation (KFF) and the Health Research and Educational Trust (HRET) (2006) provides information on the availability, enrollment, and characteristics of HDHPs that are either offered with HRAs or are HSA-compatible (Claxton et al., 2005). This type of plan is referred to as an *HDHP with a savings option* (HDHP/SO). The data reflect the situation as of 2006. The survey finds that 7 percent of employers offer one of these arrangements, with 1 percent offering HRA HDHPs and 6 percent offering HSA HDHPs. The fraction of employers offering HSAs was up significantly from the previous year.

Large firms are likelier than small firms to offer an HSA-qualified HDHP. Twelve percent of firms with more than 1,000 employees offered such a plan in 2006, up from 4 percent in 2005. Firms with 3 to 999 employees were half as likely to offer an HSA-qualified HDHP—6 percent of such employers offered one.

Confirming the findings of other studies that suggest that individuals who have a choice among several plans are not likely to choose an HDHP/SO, the KFF survey reveals that 40 percent of workers covered by an HDHP/SO are in firms in which 100 percent of covered workers are enrolled in an HDHP/SO. In firms that provide other options in addition to HDHP/SOs, on average, 19 percent of those employees enroll in an HDHP/SO (KFF/HRET, 2006).

---

[7] The AHIP survey defines the small-group market as one covering groups of 50 or fewer employees.

Employer contributions to the savings accounts also vary tremendously. Thirty-seven percent of employers offering HSA-qualified HDHP/SOs do not contribute to an HSA. Twenty-seven percent contribute $1,200 or more (KFF/HRET, 2006). This information is not broken down by firm size in the report.

Additional Evidence on the Use of Health Reimbursement Arrangements, Health Savings Accounts, and High-Deductible Health Plans by Small Businesses

In this section of the chapter, we expand on existing descriptive analyses of HSA and HDHP offerings, focusing in particular on small firms. We compare the profile of small-firm offerings to that of larger-firm offerings. We also perform a multivariate analysis of HSA and HDHP offerings. Our goal in this analysis is primarily to describe the CDHP offerings in small businesses and to assess whether the popularity of these plans varies by firm size. Our analysis does not test whether the advent of CDHPs has increased the propensity of small businesses to offer HI.[8] However, the descriptive profile in this report provides a useful backdrop for understanding the role of CDHPs in small-business HI.

Following most of the literature, we use the term *CDHP* to refer to any HDHP; typically, *high-deductible* refers to a plan with a deductible of $1,000 or more. HDHPs may be coupled with HSAs or HRAs (Buntin et al., 2006).

Our work on HSAs, HRAs, and CDHPs uses data from the 2003, 2004, and 2005 KFF/HRET annual employer health-benefits surveys (KFF/HRET 2003, 2004, 2005). This is an annual, national telephone survey of about 5,000 randomly selected public and private employers. Firms range in size from small enterprises with a minimum

---

[8]   Identification of the effect of CDHP availability on HI offering would require exogenous cross-sectional or time-series variation in the availability of CDHPs. Given that our data have only a limited time-series variation, we do not undertake to test the effect of CDHP availability on HI offering.

of three workers to corporations with more than 300,000 employees (see Claxton et al., 2005, for a detailed description of the survey).

The data contain detailed information about the health benefits offered by the firm and about other firm characteristics. In particular, the survey asks about the types of health plans offered (PPO, HMO, fee for service), enrollment in each type of plan, and whether the firm offers an HSA or HDHP or both in conjunction. Moreover, the survey asks firms that do not offer these plans about the likelihood of offering HSA plans combined with an HDHP. The survey also asks additional details about the features of these plans such as the deductible, premiums, and plan enrollment. Additional information about whether the firm is considering CDHPs in the future and whether the firm is aware of these products is also available. The survey does not ask this full set of questions every year—for example, it requested information on offering and characteristics of HRA plans in 2005 only.

Other firm data include the composition of the workforce (such as percentage that is low wage), the unionization of workers, and the number of workers in the firm, industry, rural versus urban, employee turnover, whether the firm laid off any workers in the previous year, and percent of the workforce that is part time. There are also measures of the cost and quality of health-benefit offerings such as whether the firm offers retiree benefits, wait periods, and employer contribution to each plan offered. A subsample of firms is interviewed for two consecutive years, allowing us to construct a two-year longitudinal sample as well as a cross-sectional sample. Our analyses using these data are weighted using firm-level weights.

Consumer-Directed Health Plan Utilization and Growth Do Not Vary by Firm Size

As is well known, the smallest firms (3 to 49 employees) are less likely than larger firms to offer HI, as shown in Table 3.3. About 58 percent of small firms offer HI, compared to 60 percent of firms with 50 to 199

Table 3.3
Descriptive Profile of Health Insurance Offerors, by Firm Size and Year

Characteristic	All Firms	Firms with 3–49 Employees	Firms with 3–199 Employees
2003–2005			
Offering HI (%)	61	58	60
Sample size	5,794	1,611	2,415
HI offerors offering HDHPs (%)	12	12	12
Sample size	5,288	1,157	1,925
HDHP offerors offering HSAs (%)	9	8	9
Sample size	719	137	235
2003			
Offering HI (%)	62	59	61
HI offerors offering HDHPs (%)	5	5	5
HDHP offerors offering HSAs (%)	13	11	13
2004			
Offering HI (%)	62	60	61
HI offerors offering HDHPs (%)	10	10	10
HDHP offerors offering HSAs (%)	4	3	3
2005			
Offering HI (%)	60	57	59
HI offerors offering HDHPs (%)	20	20	20
HDHP offerors offering HSAs (%)	12	11	11
HDHP offerors offering HRAs or HSAs (%)[a]	20	18	19

[a] Information on HRAs is available only in the 2005 data.

employees and 61 percent of all firms regardless of size.[9] Despite the notion that CDHPs may be especially attractive to small firms, there is no evidence that offering HDHPs, conditional on offering HI, or offering HSA plans conditional on offering HDHPs is higher in small firms. Twelve percent of small and large firms that offer HI also offer HDHPs. Conditional on offering HDHPs, 8 percent of small firms and 9 percent of all firms offer HSAs; however, this difference is not statistically significant.

CDHPs have grown in popularity between 2003 and 2005. In 2003, only 5 percent of firms that offered HI also offered HDHPs, and 13 percent of firms that offered HDHPs also offered HSAs. By 2005, these percentages had grown to 20 percent offering HDHPs and 20 percent offering HRAs or HSAs, conditional on offering HDHPs. However, there was no difference in the growth rate between small and large firms.

Even though we observe little difference between small and large firms in HRA and HSA offerings, simply examining the propensity to offer these plans provides a partial picture. Firms may differ in the generosity of their HSA and HRA plans—some may provide generous contributions and use these plans as a mechanism for subsidizing health-care expenditures, and others may have very high deductibles and large doughnut holes to shift costs to employees. In a later section, we examine benefit-generosity variations in plans to develop a full picture of the differences in CDHP offerings between small and large businesses.

Persistence in Consumer-Directed Health Plan Offerings

Given that CDHPs are new products, we may expect a moderate degree of churning in the offering of these plans. Firms may choose to offer CDHPs in one year and drop them the following year if take-up

---

[9] While these differences may not seem large, HI offer rates do drop precipitously as firm size falls—only 48 percent of the smallest firms (three to nine employees) offer HI, compared to 98 percent of the largest firms (200 or more employees) (KFF/HRET, 2005).

was poor or if they proved to be onerous to administer. To examine this issue, we analyze firms that are surveyed both in 2004 and 2005 to develop a longitudinal descriptive profile of CDHP offering. We find that 75 percent of firms that offered HDHPs in 2004 continued to offer them in 2005. Small firms (3 to 49 employees) appear to be slightly less likely to offer HDHPs in 2005, conditional on having offered them in 2004. Sixty-six percent of firms with 3 to 49 employees offer HDHPs in 2005, conditional on having offered them in 2004; however, this statistic is based on a very small sample. In addition, 99 percent of firms that offered HSAs in 2004 offered either HRA or HSA plans in 2005; however, again, this statistic is based on a very small sample (N = 21). Conversely, 25 percent of firms offering HDHPs in 2005 also offered them in 2004. Twenty-six percent of firms offering HRAs or HSAs in 2005 also offered HDHPs in 2004. Among firms that offered HRAs or HSAs in 2005, 16 percent offered HSAs in 2004; however, this number is based on a very small sample size. Smaller firms appear to be slightly likelier than larger firms to be new adopters of CDHPs—22 percent of small firms offered HDHPs in 2004, conditional on offering HDHPs in 2005, compared to 25 percent for firms of all sizes. In summary, it appears that there is some evidence of higher churning in small-firm CDHP offerings—small firms are likelier to be new adopters and less likely to retain their CDHP offerings from year to year.

Which Firms Are Likelier to Offer Consumer-Directed Health Plans?

We estimate logit models of CDHP-offering behavior to parse out the firm and worker characteristics that are associated with a firm's propensity to offer CDHPs. We estimate a three-equation model to develop a complete picture of the CDHP-offering decision. First, we estimate a model of the propensity to offer HI. Second, we estimate a model of the propensity to offer HDHPs, conditional on offering HI. Lastly, we estimate a model of HSA offering, conditional on offering HDHPs.

The explanatory variables used in the models are firm-composition variables, industry indicators, firm location, and survey year. Firm-composition variables include firm size (3 to 49 workers, 50 to 199 workers, 200-plus workers), and variables to capture workforce composition and worker demand for HI such as the percentage of the workforce earning $20,000 or less, percentage of the workforce working part time, percentage of covered employees, and union coverage. We also include a full set of industry-indicator variables to measure variations in insurance practices, insurance availability, and industry-level worker demand. The firm's geographical location is measured by indicators for region and an indicator for location in an urban area. HI premiums and safety-net availability vary by region and population density, therefore, location variables are useful proxies to capture this variation. Year indicators are included in the model to capture annual trends in CDHP availability and demand as well as annual variations in survey administration. We use firm-level data from 2003 to 2005 and apply firm-level sample weights to the models.

The estimates from the three logit models are reported in Table 3.4. The first and second columns show that small firms are no different from larger firms in their propensity to offer HSAs and HDHPs. This result is in keeping with the descriptive data reported earlier. The third column shows that small firms are substantially less likely to offer HI, consistent with the rest of the literature on small firms and HI.

The results also show that firms with a higher proportion of low-income workers are both less likely to offer HSA plans and less likely to offer HI. The model predicts that the percentage of firms offering HSA plans increases from 0.3 percent to 9 percent as the fraction of the workforce that is low income falls from 1 to 0.2 (75th to 25th percentile of the income distribution). This result is consistent with media reports that HSA plans may have more appeal for educated, higher-income workers. Firms that have union workers are significantly likelier to offer HDHPs as well (20 percent for union firms compared to 11 percent for nonunion firms), suggesting that unions have been lobbying for the introduction of more choice in HI offerings.

CDHP offering also varies by industry and location. Construction and health-care industries are likelier than manufacturing

Table 3.4
Determinants of Consumer-Directed Health Plan Offerings: Estimates from Logit Model (2003–2005)

Determinant	HDHP Offerors Offering HSA		HI Offerors Offering HDHP		Offering HI	
	Estimate	Standard Error	Estimate	Standard Error	Estimate	Standard Error
Firm composition						
Size: 3–49 workers	−0.43	0.52	0.09	0.23	−2.14[a]	0.52
Size: 50–199 workers	−0.25	0.55	0.21	0.20	−1.95[a]	0.62
Workforce earning $20,000 or less (%)	−4.73[a]	1.44	0.60	0.59	−1.89[b]	0.88
Workforce working part time (%)	−1.12	1.50	−1.03	0.81	−3.67[a]	1.03
Covered employees (%)	0.13	1.15	−0.58	0.69		
Union	−0.41	0.74	0.77[b]	0.37	1.84[b]	0.85
Industry						
Mining	−1.17	1.31	0.30	0.78	0.60	0.78
Construction	1.75[c]	0.98	−0.33	0.48	−0.48	0.73
Transportation, utilities, communication	1.65	1.09	−0.45	0.48	−0.55	0.85
Wholesale	1.68	1.06	0.48	0.56	0.63	0.70
Retail	0.76	0.93	1.16[b]	0.51	−1.05	0.73
Financial	−0.98	0.98	0.25	0.47	0.38	0.74
Service	−0.48	0.82	1.16[a]	0.40	0.07	0.62
Government	0.56	0.91	−0.69	0.44	2.51[a]	0.69
Health care	1.65[b]	0.80	0.18	0.47	−0.27	0.78

Table 3.4—Continued

Determinant	HDHP Offerors Offering HSA		HI Offerors Offering HDHP		Offering HI	
	Estimate	Standard Error	Estimate	Standard Error	Estimate	Standard Error
Location						
Midwest	2.22[b]	0.93	0.96[b]	0.44	−0.10	0.50
South	1.99[b]	0.97	0.61	0.47	0.21	0.45
West	0.94	1.02	0.23	0.56	0.01	0.62
Urban	−1.18[c]	0.64	0.13	0.31	0.20	0.42
Year						
2003	0.19	0.73	−1.64[a]	0.39	0.26	0.40
2004	−1.46[c]	0.82	−0.76[b]	0.36	0.55	0.40
Observations	719		5,288		5,794	

[a] Significant at 1 percent.
[b] Significant at 5 percent.
[c] Significant at 10 percent.

(the omitted category) to offer HSAs, and retail and service industries are likelier to offer HDHPs than manufacturing industries. Furthermore, CDHPs (particularly HSAs) appear to be most popular in the Midwest, followed by the South, and less popular in urban areas than in rural areas. There also appears to be an increase in CDHP offerings in 2005 from earlier years, suggesting that these plans are growing in popularity.

The models presented in Table 3.4 focus on HDHP and HSA offerings. Recently, HRAs have become an important part of the CDHP landscape. Given that HRAs are a recent development, our data set contains information on these plans for 2005 only. We have reestimated the logit models on 2005 data including a separate logit model that includes firms that offer either an HSA or HRA, conditional on offering HDHPs. Consistent with the results reported for HSA plans, we found no differences in offering by firm size. We have not reported these results in Table 3.4; however, they are available on request.

Longitudinal Analysis of Consumer-Directed Health Plan Offerings

Our data allow us to follow firms for a two-year period. We use our two-year analytic database for 2004–2005 to analyze the effect of HI status in 2004 on CDHP offering in 2005. This analysis provides us with a picture of the dynamics of plan determination and the importance of persistence in health-plan offerings.

We estimate two logit models for 2005. First, we model a firm's propensity to offer HDHPs, conditional on offering HI. Next, we model a firm's propensity to offer an HRA or HSA, conditional on offering an HDHP. The explanatory variables in these models are, for the most part, the same as those in the logit models presented earlier. We include a set of firm-composition variables (firm size and workforce characteristics), industry indicators, and location indicators. We also include a set of current HI offering variables—these are whether the firm offers only one plan, two to four plans, or five or more plans. We expect that firms that offer many plans may be likelier to choose a CDHP as one of the options. We also include a set of lagged (2004) HI variables. These are whether the firm offered an HDHP in 2004 and whether the firm offers only one plan, two to four plans, or five or more plans in 2004.

Our results in Table 3.5 show that, while there continues to be no difference among small and large firms in HDHP offering, we do find that HRA and HSA plan offering is 26 percent lower in the smallest firms (3 to 49 employees) than in firms that employ 200 or more workers and that this result is statistically significant. This result controls for all other variables that may be associated with HRA and HSA offering, including lagged and current HI offerings. We also find that firms that offered only one plan or two to four plans were significantly less likely to offer HRAs or HSAs than were firms that offered five or more plans. In addition, firms that offered two to four plans in 2004 were significantly less likely to offer HDHPs in 2005 than were firms that offered

Table 3.5
Determinants of Consumer-Directed Health Plan Offerings in 2005:
Estimates from a Logit Model

Determinant	HI Offerors Offering HDHP		HDHP Offerors Offering HRA or HSA	
	Estimate	Standard Error	Estimate	Standard Error
Firm composition				
Size: 3–49 workers	0.12	0.41	−2.12[a]	0.78
Size: 50–199 workers	0.54	0.36	−0.89	0.76
Workforce earning $20,000 or less (%)	−0.43	0.71	−7.53[a]	1.72
Union	0.33	0.52	0.50	0.96
HI				
Offer only one plan	0.10	0.85	−1.98[b]	1.05
Offer 2–4 plans	0.38	0.86	−4.90[a]	1.18
Lagged HI (2004)				
Offered HDHP	3.20[a]	0.54	0.46	0.82
Offered only one plan	−0.93	0.93	−1.42	1.14
Offered 2–4 plans	−1.70[b]	0.92	−1.09	1.13
Industry				
Mining	0.41	1.24	1.42	1.38
Construction	−0.1	0.84		
Transportation, utilities, communication	−0.96	0.72		
Wholesale	2.28[a]	0.87		
Retail	0.84	0.78	1.34	1.08

Table 3.5—Continued

Determinant	HI Offerors Offering HDHP		HDHP Offerors Offering HRA or HSA	
	Estimate	Standard Error	Estimate	Standard Error
Financial	0.71	0.77	−1.29	1.74
Service	0.07	0.67	2.52[b]	1.00
Government	−0.49	0.74	2.93	1.83
Health care	1.69[b]	0.87	4.38[a]	1.29
Location				
Midwest	1.80[a]	0.51	1.22	1.00
South	0.94[b]	0.51	1.95[c]	0.94
West	1.32[c]	0.58	−1.27	1.05
Observations	1,169		268	

NOTE: Sample consisted of all firms surveyed both in 2004 and 2005.
[a] Significant at 1 percent.
[b] Significant at 10 percent.
[c] Significant at 5 percent.

five or more plans. These results are consistent with the notion that firms that offer more choice are likely to also offer CDHP options.

Benefit Design of Health Reimbursement Arrangements and Health Savings Accounts

The 2005 survey data provide detailed information on the benefit design of HRA and HSA plans. We analyze the existence and magnitude of differences in the benefit design of HRA and HSA plans by firm size. In general, small firms are thought to provide HI policies that are less generous than larger firms, though recent evidence suggests that small-firm and larger-firm policies are similar along many dimensions (KFF/HRET, 2005).[10] We revisit this issue, focusing on benefit generosity in HRA and HSA plans.

We estimate ordinary least squares (OLS) models for the monthly premium for a single individual, monthly worker contribution to the single premium, annual deductible for a single worker, annual firm contribution to a single worker, and the maximum out-of-pocket liability for a single worker. We estimate one set of models for HRA plans and another set of models for HSA plans. An important caveat with these models is that they have a relatively small number of observations—50 to 60 depending on the model. However, the key findings from the models remain the same after reestimating a parsimonious specification that excludes detailed firm and industry characteristics.

Table 3.6 reports the OLS regression estimates for HRA plans in 2005. We find that small firms with 3 to 49 employees have significantly lower premiums ($86.46) and significantly higher deductibles ($912.35) than large firms, suggesting that they have somewhat lower-quality policies. However, firms with 50 to 199 workers have significantly lower worker contributions ($52.15) and higher firm contributions ($730.94) and lower maximum out-of-pocket liabilities ($1,490) than large firms, suggesting that these firms are more generous than large firms.

Firms with a higher proportion of low-income employees appear to offer HRAs that have higher deductibles, however, we do not observe that these firms have significantly lower premiums to account for the higher deductibles. Firms with a high proportion of part-time workers also have a lower firm contribution to HRAs, suggesting that worker demand for HI influences the firm's contribution decision. We also observe differences in plan benefits by industry and region.

---

[10] The KFF/HRET employer surveys on HI benefits have showed that there are no statistically significant differences among small-firm plans and large-firm plans in their offerings of prescription drugs, adult physicals, outpatient mental, inpatient mental, annual OB-GYN visit, oral contraceptives, and well-baby care. Only the propensity to offer prenatal and chiropractic care differed significantly. Small-firm policies were likelier to have no policy limit (60 percent in small firms and 45 percent in large firms) and likelier than large-firm policies to have a limit on out-of-pocket spending (87 percent in small firms and 77 percent in large firms), and likelier to have higher deductibles ($559 in large firms and $280 in small firms for individual coverage) (KFF/HRET, 2004).

Table 3.6
Benefit Design of Health Reimbursement Arrangement Plans (OLS Regressions, 2005)

Determinant	Monthly Total Premium (individual)		Monthly Worker Contribution to Premium (individual)		Annual Deductible (individual)		Annual Firm Contribution (individual)		Maximum Out-of-Pocket Liability (individual)	
	Estimate	Standard Error	Estimate	Standard Error	Estimate	Standard Error	Estimate	Standard Error	Estimate	Standard Error
Firm composition										
Size: 3–49 workers	-86.46[a]	47.93	-4.51	22.22	912.35[b]	391.74	209.48	209.01	738.26	719.72
Size: 50–199 workers	44.54	41.74	-52.15[b]	19.35	181.36	323.58	730.94[c]	172.64	-1,490.23[b]	626.85
Workforce earning $20,000 or less (%)	-24.83	67.96	20.02	31.51	1,171.64[b]	481.99	-362.04	257.16	161.47	1,020.61
Workforce working part time (%)	-9.94	85.08	-52.37	39.44	-501.39	734.24	-783.82[a]	391.74	523.07	1,277.63
Covered employees (%)	137.12[a]	74.97	-11.18	34.76	-255.82	673.78	-686.43[a]	359.48	1,241.56	1,125.88
Union	37.49	32.14	-5.68	14.90	-274.56	271.12	-48.14	144.65	-605.66	482.61

Table 3.6—Continued

Determinant	Monthly Total Premium (individual)		Monthly Worker Contribution to Premium (individual)		Annual Deductible (individual)		Annual Firm Contribution (individual)		Maximum Out-of-Pocket Liability (individual)	
	Estimate	Standard Error	Estimate	Standard Error	Estimate	Standard Error	Estimate	Standard Error	Estimate	Standard Error
Industry										
Mining	46.52	64.27	20.1	29.80	572.46	578.38	-83.24	308.58	-150.35	865.10
Construction	32.65	53.64	37.99	24.87	722.41	480.98	-58.88	256.62	670.87	805.46
Transportation, utilities, communication	-17.64	84.55	-7.01	39.20	241.47	765.44	50.4	408.39	-1,523.54	1,269.77
Wholesale	12.99	94.36	10.17	43.75	-315.18	454.19	-647.98[b]	242.33	-93.25	1,417.04
Retail	129.09[b]	54.91	31.14	25.46	668.17	475.13	4.92	253.50	-102.84	824.56
Financial	89.93[b]	42.29	17.71	19.61	85.4	357.83	-389.10[b]	190.91	76.7	635.04
Service	51.33	40.10	-3.78	18.59	123	328.67	-131.39	175.35	-490.03	602.16
Government	79.9	70.17	-32.95	32.53	-431.77	614.93	-226.92	328.08	-2,120.78[a]	1,053.81
Health care	52.05	48.33	-7.24	22.41	-321.71	388.04	-412.73[a]	207.03	-399.78	725.85

Table 3.6—Continued

Determinant	Monthly Total Premium (individual)		Monthly Worker Contribution to Premium (individual)		Annual Deductible (individual)		Annual Firm Contribution (individual)		Maximum Out-of-Pocket Liability (individual)	
	Estimate	Standard Error	Estimate	Standard Error	Estimate	Standard Error	Estimate	Standard Error	Estimate	Standard Error
Location										
Midwest	-1.92	36.03	-5.49	16.70	226.91	313.47	84.19	167.25	149.1	541.04
South	10.43	33.46	9.83	15.51	141.4	288.86	10.55	154.12	1,124.76[b]	502.54
West	51.01	49.13	15.38	22.78	273.21	398.62	245.36	212.68	1,660.42[b]	737.77
Urban	25.39	42.16	-30.09	19.55	-355.69	325.46	97.66	173.64	-130.11	633.14
Observations	54		54		66		66		54	
R-squared	0.41		0.38		0.45		0.53		0.41	

[a] Significant at 10 percent.
[b] Significant at 5 percent.
[c] Significant at 1 percent.

Table 3.7 reports OLS regression estimates for HSA plans. Unlike the models for HRA plans, we observe almost no difference in benefit design by firm size. The only exception is that it does appear that firms with 3 to 49 workers have significantly higher individual premiums ($128.49 per month); however, we do not observe a statistically significant difference in any other feature of the plan benefit. Firms with a higher proportion of low-income workers have plans with a higher worker contribution to the premium, but we do not observe a statistically significant difference on any other measure of plan benefit. In summary, it appears that the evidence on plan generosity for small firms is mixed—HSA plans in small firms appear to have lower premiums and lower quality, but HRA plans appear to have somewhat higher premiums and do not appear to differ in other dimensions. In general, it does not appear that small businesses are offering plans that are systematically different from larger businesses in generosity, along the full spectrum of benefit features.

Consumer-Directed Health Plans Are Growing in Popularity but Do Not Appear to Be a Panacea for Small Businesses

Our analysis of the KFF/HRET survey shows that, in general, small firms are no likelier than larger ones to offer CDHPs and that their uptake of CDHPs has not grown any more rapidly than has that of larger firms. Small firms appear to have slightly higher rates of churning in their CDHP offerings and seem to be somewhat likelier to adopt and drop CDHP policies. However, we find no consistent evidence that CDHP offerings vary systematically in premiums or generosity between small and large firms.

Table 3.7
Benefit Design of Health Savings Account Plans (OLS Regressions, 2005)

Characteristic	Monthly Total Premium (single)		Monthly Worker Contribution to Premium (single)		Annual Deductible (single)		Annual Firm Contribution (single)		Maximum Out-of-Pocket Liability (single)	
	Estimate	Standard Error	Estimate	Standard Error	Estimate	Standard Error	Estimate	Standard Error	Estimate	Standard Error
Firm composition										
Size: 3–49 workers	128.49[a]	62.44	26.57	33.90	–311.52	442.60	–16.29	278.44	–418.41	752.52
Size: 50–199 workers	12.59	65.23	30.2	35.42	–219.53	429.96	9.24	270.49	–367.71	786.20
Workforce earning $20,000 or less (%)	107.53	105.74	117.19[b]	57.42	–865.69	706.08	–332.01	444.19	805.45	1,274.43
Workforce working part time (%)	237.63[b]	137.28	57.89	74.54	–1,581.18	999.19	133.51	628.59	–2,789.86	1,654.56
Covered employees (%)	256.44[b]	126.18	121.49[b]	68.52	–1,355.90	869.10	432.36	546.75	–989.43	1,520.78
Union	85.30[b]	44.06	66.14[c]	23.92	81.83	324.33	121.05	204.03	–86.37	530.96

Table 3.7—Continued

Characteristic	Monthly Total Premium (single)		Monthly Worker Contribution to Premium (single)		Annual Deductible (single)		Annual Firm Contribution (single)		Maximum Out-of-Pocket Liability (single)	
	Estimate	Standard Error	Estimate	Standard Error	Estimate	Standard Error	Estimate	Standard Error	Estimate	Standard Error
Industry										
Mining	-357.72[a]	160.16	-36.18	86.97	817.11	1,165.77	339.5	733.39	987.01	1,930.29
Construction	-176.81[b]	102.23	37.44	55.51	596.17	738.76	257.73	464.75	-1,265.21	1,232.10
Transportation, utilities, communication	-4.83	86.17	-9.2	46.79	-125.43	530.33	119.64	333.63	-1,010.49	1,038.50
Wholesale	-230.27[b]	134.86	-26.73	73.23	1,311.86	929.79	655.8	584.93	-199.55	1,625.31
Retail	62.19	101.48	94.49[b]	55.10	-17.28	624.60	880.02[a]	392.93	1,161.10	1,223.08
Financial	50.14	86.80	7.04	47.13	4.69	567.55	64.24	357.05	-899.46	1,046.14
Service	-27.32	64.77	21.29	35.17	797.04[b]	441.05	264.97	277.46	-128.06	780.61
Government	37.33	89.10	3.47	48.38	868.98	611.92	-53.69	384.96	-638.74	1,073.85
Health care	16.69	74.30	57.54	40.34	330.16	517.07	190.13	325.29	33.26	895.46

Table 3.7—Continued

Characteristic	Monthly Total Premium (single)		Monthly Worker Contribution to Premium (single)		Annual Deductible (single)		Annual Firm Contribution (single)		Maximum Out-of-Pocket Liability (single)	
	Estimate	Standard Error	Estimate	Standard Error	Estimate	Standard Error	Estimate	Standard Error	Estimate	Standard Error
Location										
Midwest	−61.13	61.34	5.17	33.31	146.94	434.17	−92.04	273.13	−188.73	739.33
South	−38.12	58.13	−10.45	31.56	419.86	432.06	−49.34	271.81	−545.28	700.59
West	137.29[b]	78.32	25.09	42.53	289.32	543.06	−240.93	341.64	311.87	943.91
Urban	−70.23	51.46	−6.35	27.94	−482.92	352.28	−170.48	221.62	−373.93	620.24
Observations	50		50		59		59		50	
R-squared	0.52		0.42		0.3		0.23		0.31	

[a] Significant at 5 percent.
[b] Significant at 10 percent.
[c] Significant at 1 percent.

Conclusion

Small-business HI reform is a policy issue that is continually in the limelight. Since the majority of uninsured working Americans are employed in small businesses, extending HI coverage to small businesses is an important mechanism for reducing the number of uninsured. States have continued to adjust their small-group HI-reform packages to make them more effective. However, these incremental pricing and access reforms cannot be expected to solve the fundamental problems of high administrative costs, adverse selection, and a shallow risk pool that afflict the small-group HI market. Regulations that restrict premium variation may lower prices for some but increase prices for others; they may drive some insurers out of the market. Evidence reveals that policy approaches focused on regulating the insurance market have not improved access to or affordability of HI to small businesses across the board and have led to distortions in the size of businesses right around the regulatory threshold. In other words, the regulations have not only failed to achieve their core aims, but they also have had unintended consequences related to business operations. Research suggests that policymakers need to be aware that legislative size thresholds may have unintended consequences on business size. Furthermore, incremental legislation that makes only small changes in the small-group HI market is unlikely to have large-scale effects on HI offering among small firms.

Solutions to the problem of HI access and affordability will likely need to address fundamental issues driving the escalation in HI costs. Indeed, the policy debate has shifted in this direction. For example, the Small Business Health Plan legislation in the House and Senate proposes to improve access and availability to HI by allowing small businesses to band together to purchase HI through their industry associations (U.S. Chamber of Commerce, undated). Another solution that has been advocated by the Bush administration and by policy analysts is the development of CDHPs. These plans aim to control costs by increasing consumers' financial responsibility and involvement in their health-care choices. Since CDHPs are potentially less costly than traditional health plans and may appeal to younger workers with low health-care demand, these plans may be well suited to workers in small businesses (Laing, undated). However, despite the enthusiasm for such plans among small-business advocates, evidence to date suggests that small businesses have been no likelier than larger businesses to offer such plans. We examine evidence from the KFF/HRET survey and show that, in general, small firms are no likelier to offer CDHPs and that their uptake of CDHPs has not grown any more rapidly than larger firms. We do find some evidence that small firms are likelier to add and drop CDHPs. More information on the implementation of CHDPs, particularly within smaller firms, would be valuable in assessing the causes of such churning and, ultimately, whether CDHPs are indeed a panacea for small businesses. Because the marketplace for such options is changing rapidly, it will be important to monitor changes over the next few years. For example, as more firms enter the marketplace offering services to manage HSAs, a small business with a small benefits office might find it plausible to offer HSAs by contracting with such a firm. It may simply take time for these providers to emerge and for small businesses to learn about them.

CHAPTER FOUR

Small Businesses and Workplace Fatality Risk: An Exploratory Analysis

John Mendeloff, Christopher Nelson, Kilkon Ko, and Amelia Haviland

In 2002, some 56 percent of Americans were employed in businesses with fewer than 100 workers. It has long been argued that the burdens of safety and health regulation fall more heavily on these firms. Adopting prevention technologies and processes often involves considerable fixed costs, which are more difficult for smaller operations to absorb. Similarly, small businesses are less likely than their larger counterparts to be able to hire in-house safety experts and often lack the resources to remain aware of voluminous and changing safety regulations.

Concern about regulatory burdens on small businesses has not escaped the attention of policymakers. SBREFA (P.L. 104-121) and its predecessor, RFA (P.L. 96-354), seek to increase the weight given to small-business concerns in the regulatory rulemaking and enforcement processes. Similarly, OSHA exempts workplaces with fewer than 11 workers from regular, programmed inspections and considers firm size when assessing penalties for violations of its safety and health standards. For firms with fewer than 500 workers, OSHA developed a consultation program that provides services largely independently of the enforcement program.

Yet, regulations and other policies toward small businesses should be guided both by concern for potential costs to small businesses *and* by an understanding of the magnitude of the risks they face and the potential benefits of prevention activities. Therefore, it is important to understand whether working for a small business is any more or less risky than working for a large business. If working for a small business is riskier, then we also need to understand whether the risk is due to the size of the *establishment* (i.e., the individual worksite) or to the size of the *firm* (i.e., the business organization, which consists of one or more establishments). Should policy efforts be directed toward small firms, toward small establishments, or both? A better understanding of the distribution of risks can help policymakers design and target appropriate policies.

Unfortunately, empirical research on the topic has been surprisingly scant, especially given the significant number of policy initiatives targeting small businesses. While a small group of studies focuses on how risk changes with establishment size and a few look at the role of firm size, there has been no systematic attempt to disentangle the effects of establishment and firm size.

To shed light on these issues, we examined the relationship between the fatality rate, i.e., the number of deaths per 100,000 workers, and business size, both in terms of establishment size and firm size. Most of the analyses use fatalities investigated by OSHA between 1992 and 2001. We excluded the construction sector from most analyses due to concerns about the accuracy of the distinction between establishment and firm in these nonfixed work settings.

As indicated in the chapter title, this work should be regarded as exploratory, not definitive. Data limitations and the scope of the problem limit our ability to understand fully the drivers of the size-fatality risk—and even, in some cases, to provide a full picture of the nature of the relationship. Rather than trying to provide the last word on the subject, our goal is to enrich the debate over safety in small businesses by providing a factual baseline and considering possible causal mechanisms and policy approaches.

The remainder of the chapter proceeds as follows. First, we review some reasons we might expect the risk of injury or fatality to be higher at small firms than at large firms and discuss the results of previous research on the topic. We then briefly describe the data and methods used in our analysis. We next present our findings, first examining the simple relationships of risk to establishment and firm size, then considering the relationship between fatality risk and establishment and firm size, holding the other constant. We also discuss other issues, such as variables that might affect the results, trends over time, the issue of underreporting, and the relationship between fatalities and violations of OSHA standards. Finally, we discuss the implications of our study for public policy and suggest directions for further research.

The Relationship Between Firm Size and Risk

Previous research and theory lead us to expect that fatality risks will be higher in smaller firms and establishments. Understanding the reasons behind this expectation will help with data interpretation and policy implications.

- Smaller firms might be expected to save less than larger firms do by preventing injuries. The limited actuarial experience at small firms means that they are subject to little or no experience rating by WC insurers. Thus, small firms will not see reductions in their WC premiums even if their injury losses decline. Small firms are also less likely to be unionized, and some evidence indicates that the presence of unions increases the probability that workers will receive higher wages to compensate for higher risks (Viscusi, 1983). Small firms also get reductions in OSHA fines, which also decreases the incentive to correct hazards.

- Smaller firms are also likelier than larger firms to employ higher-risk workers (i.e., workers who are younger and unmarried and those have lower levels of education and experience) (Belman and Levine, 2004). They may not pressure management on safety issues as much as older or married workers would. These worker characteristics also may make it costlier for firms to achieve a given level of safety.

- Both smaller firms and smaller establishments will be less able to realize economies of scale in the production of safety. Lacking in-house expertise, they may face higher marginal costs to obtain information about risks and how to reduce them.

- Smaller establishments are less likely than large ones to be inspected, reducing the marginal benefit of compliance.

In sum, there appear to be good reasons to expect that both smaller firms and smaller establishments will exhibit higher levels of risk than larger ones. The reasons are more numerous and perhaps more powerful at the firm level. Tables 4.1 and 4.2 present a full list of potential factors considered.

Previous Research on Size and Risk

A few studies have examined the relationship between establishment or firm size and risk. We briefly review the findings from these studies here.

Table 4.1
Factors Influencing the Predicted Effects of Establishment and Firm Size on Safety: Marginal Benefits

Affected Entity	Factor
Firms	Smaller firms have less experience rating in WC than larger firms have, reducing financial incentive for investments in prevention.
	Smaller firms pay lower wages than larger firms do, reducing wage-replacement costs.
	Smaller firms are less likely than larger firms are to have unions and to pay high wage-risk premiums, reducing wage-replacement costs.
	Smaller firms face lower penalties than larger firms face from OSHA inspections and are less subject than larger firms to repeat violations if similar violations have been recently cited at other workplaces.
Establishments	Smaller establishments are less likely than larger establishments to have unions and to pay high wage-risk premiums; therefore, a reduction in risk may not save them as much in compensation costs as larger establishments might save.
	Smaller establishments are less likely than larger establishments to be inspected; therefore, compliance will have lower expected benefits for them than for larger establishments.

Table 4.2
Factors Influencing the Predicted Effects of Establishment and Firm Size on Safety: Marginal Costs

Affected Entity	Factor
Firms	Smaller firms have higher costs of capital than larger firms have, making investments in prevention costlier.
	Smaller firms are likelier than larger firms to have higher-risk workers.
Establishments	Smaller establishments are less likely than larger ones to have easy access to safety expertise, increasing costs of prevention.
	Smaller establishments are less likely than larger ones to engage in safety training.

Fatalities and Other Serious Injuries

Previous studies have found an association between establishment size and occupational injury and illness risk.[1] A 1990 study of more than 14,000 OSHA fatality investigations from 1977 to 1986 showed that reported fatality rates were usually highest at smaller workplaces across all major industry sectors (Mendeloff and Kagey, 1990). The fatality rates for the smallest establishments (1 to 19 employees) were about four times the rates for the largest (more than 1,000 employees). To investigate whether the result was due to a compositional effect (i.e., industries with a high fatality rate just happen to be those that are dominated by small establishments), the study examined rates within detailed industry categories—four-digit standard industrial classifications (SICs)—in manufacturing.[2] Similarly sharp drops for establishment with more than 20 workers were observed in most industries in the analysis.

---

[1] In this chapter, *injury*, unless noted, will refer to both injuries and illnesses. However, none of the data sources examined can be expected to do a good job of capturing illnesses with long latency periods.

[2] For example, *food and kindred products* is a two-digit category within manufacturing, *meat products* is a three-digit category within food, and *sausages and other prepared meats* is a four-digit category within meat products.

Other studies have found an association between smaller establishments and serious injury. An examination of the 1990 Workplace Industrial Relations Survey (WIRS) of British manufacturing establishments with 25 or more employees (Nichols, Dennis, and Guy, 1995) cites earlier work by Thomas (1991), which found that the health and safety executive (HSE) major rate (which includes relatively serious categories of injuries, e.g., amputations) decreased with establishment size.[3] Fenn and Ashby (2001), reporting on the findings from the 1998 WIRS of about 2,000 British establishments with more than 10 employees, found that doubling the number of employees at an establishment was associated with a 33-percent reduction in reported injuries and a 25-percent reduction in reported illnesses. Finally, Bennett and Passamore (1985) found that fatality rates in coal mining decreased as establishment size increased.[4]

Less Serious Injuries

Some research on less serious injuries has shown that small establishments (i.e., with 1 to 19 employees) have *lower* rates of such injuries than large establishments have. For example, the U.S. Bureau of Labor Statistics has regularly reported that small establishments have a relatively low lost-workday frequency rate.[5] The rates increase from the smallest size category to the category with 100 to 250 employees and then decline with increasing size for establishments with more than 250 employees. In all sectors except construction and mining, the

---

[3] Nichols, Dennis, and Guy (1995) also present data that indicate that establishments that are part of larger firms have higher HSE major rates than those that are independent, but the conclusion is based on small numbers and fails to control for industry composition.

[4] Using the U.S. Bureau of Labor Statistics (BLS) National Census of Fatal Occupational Injuries (CFOI), Peek-Asa et al. (1999) analyzed fatalities in the retail trade sector, in which 89 percent of the deaths were due either to transportation accidents or to assaults. They found that establishments with fewer than 20 workers had higher-than-average fatality rates. It is plausible that workers in, for example, minimarts are more vulnerable to assaults than are workers in department stores. The possible patterns for car-crash deaths are less clear-cut and deserve further attention. In our analyses, we exclude fatalities from these two causes.

[5] *Lost-workday injuries* includes both injuries resulting in one or more days away from work and injuries resulting only in restricted work activity.

smallest establishment-size category has the lowest rate. For those two exceptions, the smallest size has the second lowest rate, second only to establishments with more than 1,000 workers.

In contrast to his findings for the HSE major injury category, Thomas (1991) found, in the same study, that the rates for a somewhat less serious injury category (more than three days off work but not in the HSE major category) increased with establishment size. One study of less serious injuries that did find decreases in rates with larger sizes was by Haberstroh (1961). His study of 53 integrated steel mills found that, from 1948 to 1957, a 10-percent increase in employment, for both establishment and firm size, led to about a 3-percent decrease in the frequency of disabling injury rates.

What could explain the disparity we usually find between the size patterns for more and less severe injuries? The fairly consistent pattern we find is that, as injuries become severer, the relative performance of smaller establishments worsens. Rates for fatalities and HSE major injuries show higher rates for the smallest establishments; rates for the less serious injuries in Britain and for the U.S. lost-workday rate show better performance there.[6] One explanation could be that establishments in different size categories truly differ in their rates for more and less severe injuries. Another explanation could be that smaller establishments have a higher rate of underreporting but that the underreporting is less for more serious injuries. We discuss each explanation in turn.

Accident Types and Size
It is plausible that different types of injury-causing events might display different frequencies across size groups. This result would require two elements: first, that different accident types vary in the probability that death will result; and second, that workplaces of different sizes vary in the composition of these accident types.

---

[6] One exception is a comparison we made between the rates from the BLS survey for lost-workday injuries and the rates from the survey for *medical only* cases, which do not involve time lost from work or restricted work activity. The patterns by establishment-size category were almost identical for the two groups of injuries; the relative rates for the smallest workplaces were only slightly higher for the severer category.

The first element is certainly present. The causes of fatalities do differ considerably from the causes of nonfatal injuries and illnesses. Even ignoring highway motor-vehicle crashes and assaults (which are largely excluded from the database we examine here), we find that other causal event types such as fires and explosions also account for a much larger share of fatalities than they do of nonfatal injuries. Similarly, injuries caused by overexertion (e.g., sprains and strains) comprise about 40 percent of all lost-workday injuries but only a tiny share of deaths.

Whether the rate of different accident types varies for workplaces of different sizes and whether these differences could account for major differences in fatality rates will be explored in our analysis of the relationship between establishment size and the causes of fatalities.

Underreporting and Size

It seems plausible that more serious injuries might be less subject to underreporting. For example, Leigh, Marcin, and Miller (2004) reviewed many studies that indicate that the BLS survey substantially undercounts nonfatal injuries, perhaps by 40 percent for the sectors covered. They note that "evidence suggests that small firms are especially prone to underreport" (Leigh, Marcin, and Miller, 2004). Similarly, Seligman et al. (1988) reported that compliance with OSHA recordkeeping requirements was poorest at small firms and best at the largest ones. However, Glanzer et al.'s (1998) study of a large construction project found fewer instances of underreporting for injuries that involved lost workdays than for injuries without lost workdays.

Oleinick, Gluck, and Guire (1995) suggest that lower reported rates for less severe injuries at smaller establishments in Michigan were probably due underreporting. They found that smaller establishments tended to have more risk factors for injury than did larger workplaces. For example, they found that smaller establishments had such risk factors as younger workers, a higher percentage of males, and more construction work.[7] Because they found evidence that there were more risk

---

[7]   A higher turnover rate of workers has also often been linked to higher injury rates. Oleinick, Gluck, and Guire (1995) cite a study by Berkeley Planning Associates and SBA (1988)

factors at smaller establishments, Oleinick, Gluck, and Guire (1995) concluded that the lower reported rates for less severe injuries at these workplaces were probably a result of underreporting.

Morse et al. (2004) also concluded that both large and small businesses have underreported cases of occupationally related musculo-skeletal disorders (MSDs) but that there appeared to be more under-reporting in smaller businesses. (It was unclear in this study whether the survey responses pertained to establishment or firm size.) The researchers conducted a population-based survey in Connecticut that found that, controlling for age, gender, physical risks, and occupation, employees of smaller businesses had a marginally significantly higher risk of occupationally related MSDs than did employees of larger businesses. The authors thus concluded that there was general underreport-ing of MSDs but that there appeared to be more underreporting in smaller firms.

Summary

This review of studies done to date suggests that the rates for severe injuries (especially fatalities) are highest in the smallest establishments. For less serious injuries, in contrast, we find somewhat lower rates in the smallest establishments. Regardless of whether the latter findings are an artifact of underreporting, the findings for deaths and severe injuries should generate concern about what is happening at smaller establishments.

Data and Methods

Our analyses examine fatality rates, i.e., the number of fatalities during a period divided by the number of worker-years of exposure during that

---

that indicated that new hire rates were about 5 percent higher at small firms than at large ones, though another survey found no differences in turnover by size (Pedersen and Sieber, 1989).

period. If an industry employs an annual average of 1,000 workers over a 10-year period, then there are 10,000 worker-years of exposure.[8]

A full discussion of our data and methods appears in Appendix B. Here, we present a brief review of our approach. We begin by describing how fatality rates were derived for our analysis, first for the numerator (the number of deaths) and then for the denominator (exposure to the risk of death). We then briefly describe the regression analyses used to add more control variables to the analysis.

Number of Fatalities (Numerator Data)

Our data on fatalities come from the OSHA Integrated Management Information System (IMIS) and are generated by the accident investigations that OSHA conducts when work fatalities (and some other serious injuries) are reported. Employers are required to telephone OSHA within 24 hours after the death of an employee. Exclusions have been made for deaths due to highway crashes, intentional violence, and some other causes. (These categories account for almost half of the deaths identified in the BLS CFOI.) On average, OSHA has investigated somewhat fewer than 2,000 deaths per year. Its investigations provide information on both the number of employees at the establishment (worksite) where the death occurred and the total employment at all worksites of the firm.

Most of our analyses focus on deaths OSHA investigated from 1992 to 2000, a sample that includes 17,481 fatalities. However, we also look at deaths back to 1985 for a subset of states for which there is continuous reporting.

Exposure to the Risk of Death (Denominator Data)

Data on the number of workers employed are needed to provide a measure of exposure to risk and thus serve as the denominator in the fatality-rate calculations. For industry employment, we relied on county business patterns (CBPs) (U.S. Census Bureau, undated[b]) and a spe-

---

[8]   Our data do not distinguish between full-time and part-time workers. This shortcoming will give rise to a tendency to overestimate rates for industries and size categories that have more employees working part time.

cial table prepared for us by the U.S. Census Bureau that distributed establishment employment by size category and industry into firm-size categories. The table tells us, for example, how many employees in meatpacking establishments with 20 to 49 workers are employed by firms with 20 to 49 workers, how many are employed by firms with 50 to 99 workers, and so on.

Regression Analyses

To see whether our conclusions about the effects of firm and establishment size might be biased due to the omission of variables with which they might be correlated, we conducted regression analyses that allowed us to control for the effects of some other variables. To examine whether unionization or metropolitan location affected death rates, we constructed a data set that included both accident investigations and programmed inspections. The latter were scheduled randomly during the period used in this analysis but were limited to establishments with more than 11 employees in industries whose lost-workday injury rates exceeded the industrywide average. So we limited the accident investigations in the same way and investigated, using Poisson regression, how the probability of a fatal accident varied with establishment size and firm size, holding other variables constant.

Findings

In this section, we review the findings of our analysis. We first provide a description of the data in terms of the number of deaths investigated over time, by industry, and by establishment and firm size. Then we examine the relationship between fatality rates and establishment size, both for various industry sectors and then for a selected set of detailed industries. Next, we consider the relationship between fatality rates and firm size at the level of the industry sector and the effects of establishment size while holding firm size constant and vice versa. We also present the results of some analyses that control for additional factors that may affect the relationship between fatality rates and firm and establishment size and will examine whether there are size-based differences in the causes of fatalities, especially in the role played by serious health and safety violations. Finally, we review trends in establishment-size fatality rates over time.

Overall Patterns in the OSHA Fatality Data

From 1992 to 2001, OSHA investigated a total of 17,481 fatalities. Nearly 39 percent of these deaths occurred in the construction sector, with manufacturing a distant second.

Table 4.3 shows the percentage distribution of deaths in different employment-size categories for both establishments and firms. A separate distribution is shown for construction because these size categories have a different meaning in construction. Even outside of construction, almost 42 percent of deaths investigated by OSHA were in establishments with fewer than 20 employees, though only 27 percent occurred in firms of that size. In contrast, only 6 percent of deaths

Table 4.3
OSHA-Investigated Fatalities in Each Establishment- and Firm-Size Category, All States, 1992–2001

Employees	Nonconstruction (N = 10,742) (%)		Construction Only (N = 6,739) (%)	
	Establishment Size	Firm Size	Establishment Size	Firm Size
<20	41.7	27.2	71.4	42.5
20–49	15.8	12.8	13.9	18.9
50–99	11.4	9.2	6.0	11.4
100–249	12.4	11.0	4.9	12.4
250–499	7.3	7.2	1.6	6.0
500–999	4.6	5.5	0.7	3.0
1,000+	6.0	26.2	0.6	4.9
Missing data	0.9	0.9	0.8	0.8
Total	100.0	100.0	100.0	100.0

occurred in establishments of the largest size category (more than 1,000 employees), but 26 percent occurred in firms of that size.

Table 4.4 shows a cross-tabulation of nonconstruction deaths from 1992 to 2001 for establishment and firm size. It indicates that most deaths occur in workplaces in which establishment and firm sizes are the same (shown in the shaded cells on the diagonal). However, it also shows that there are many deaths in the workplaces in which establishment and firm sizes differ, a necessary condition for us to be able to investigate the separate effects of firm and establishment size. The largest single cell by far, accounting for almost 30 percent of the deaths, is the one in which both the establishment and the firm have fewer than 20 employees.

The Relationship Between Fatality Rate and Establishment Size

We now examine the relationship between fatality rate and establishment size. Our data set covers all states from 1992 to 2001. Figure 4.1 shows the fatality rates for each establishment-size category for the industry sectors with the most employees: manufacturing,

Table 4.4
Nonconstruction Fatalities Investigated by OSHA, All States, 1992–2001, by Establishment and Firm Size

Establishment Size	Firm Size							
	<20	20–49	50–99	100–249	250–499	500–999	1,000+	Total
<20	3,019	405	232	271	128	109	406	4,570
20–49		975	128	146	107	70	275	1,701
50–99			628	131	82	60	323	1,224
100–249				629	117	103	481	1,330
250–499					339	60	383	782
500–999						190	304	494
1,000+							641	641
Total	3,019	1,380	988	1,177	773	592	2,813	10,742

transportation and public utilities, wholesale trade, retail trade, and services. (As described above, we omit construction here because we do not have an employment denominator for that sector that uses the same definition of *establishment* that OSHA uses.)[9]

The figure indicates that, on average, small establishments tend to have higher fatality rates than large establishments have. For every sector except retail trade, establishments with 1 to 19 employees have the highest fatality rate; in every case, this rate then falls sharply for the 20-to-49–employee size category (e.g., a 35-percent drop in wholesale trade, a 65-percent drop in manufacturing). For the manufacturing, transportation and utilities, and service sectors, the fatality rate for the

Figure 4.1
Fatality Rate, by Establishment Size

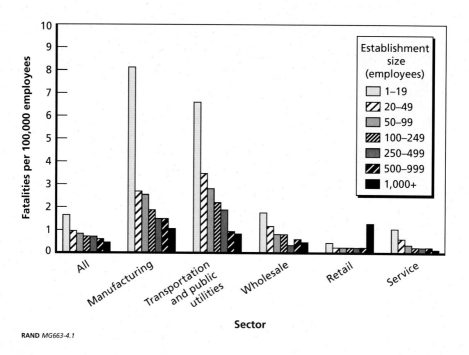

RAND *MG663-4.1*

---

[9]   Of the other industries omitted because of the few deaths investigated, agriculture and mining had high fatality rates (just below 10 per 100,000 workers) and finance had the lowest (0.18 per 100,000).

1-to-19–employee category is more than seven times that for the size category that has the lowest rate. These three sectors have the most deaths and, for all of them, the establishment fatality rates decline continuously as establishment size increases.

Looking at More Detailed Categories of Small Establishments

When we look at more detailed establishment-size categories, we find that most of the disparity in fatality rates for small establishments is driven by high rates at those with fewer than 10 employees. To perform this analysis, we used CBP data (U.S. Census Bureau, undated[b]) for establishment categories of one to four, five to nine, and 10 to 19 employees. Figure 4.2 shows that the highest fatality rate is found in establishments with one to four employees, followed by those with five

Figure 4.2
Fatality Rate, by Establishment Size: Small Establishments

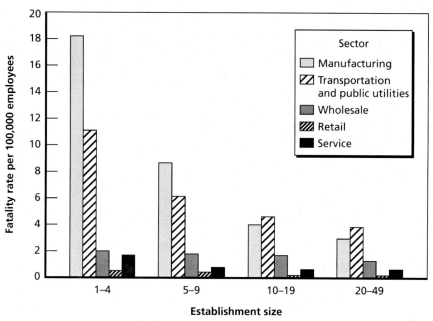

RAND *MG663-4.2*

to nine and 10 to 19 employees. Fatalities tend to decrease sharply between the one-to-four–employee and five-to-nine–employee categories and between the five-to-nine–employee and 10-to-19–employee categories; in contrast, the rate of decline tends to flatten out between the 10-to-19–employee and 20-to-49–employee categories. The fact that the highest fatality rates are found in establishments with fewer than 10 employees may be noteworthy, because OSHA exempts establishments with fewer than 11 workers from programmed inspections.

In interpreting these findings, the reader should note that the absolute rates reported here would be higher if there were full reporting. As discussed in Appendix B, the number of deaths reported through IMIS equals only about 80 percent of the total in CFOI for construction and manufacturing and 40 to 60 percent for other sectors.

Fatality Rates by Establishment Size in More Narrowly Defined Industries

The finding that smaller establishments have the highest fatality rates in industry sectors could mask different patterns in more narrowly defined industry categories. For example, if the industries that happen to have high rates also happen to be dominated by small establishments, the pattern might disappear when we look at detailed industries. To explore these issues, we examined fatality rates by establishment size for all four-digit manufacturing SICs and all nonmanufacturing three-digit SICs that had more than 70 deaths from 1992 to 2001 (results not shown).[10] We omitted establishment size categories if they had fewer than 10,000 worker-years. This left nine manufacturing industries and 20 nonmanufacturing industries.

We found that, for eight of the nine manufacturing industries (all but SIC 2421, sawmills) the smallest establishments had the highest fatality rates (although, in two of those eight industries, the differences were very small). We also found that, for 13 of the 20 nonmanufacturing industries, the smallest establishment size had the highest rate. In all 29 industries, the smallest category of establishments had a higher fatality rate than that found in the industry as a whole. In cases in

---

[10] For complete results of this analysis, see Mendeloff et al. (2006, Table 3.4).

which the smallest establishment size had the highest fatality rate of all of the size categories, the median ratio of that rate was typically five times the rate in the size category with the lowest rate for manufacturing and 10 times that in the other industries.

Although we still found that small establishments tend to have the highest fatality rates, the pattern was not as strong at this detailed level as it was at the sector level. For the manufacturing sector as a whole, for example, the fatality rate in the 1-to-19–employee establishment-size category was about 10 times higher than it was in establishments with more than 1,000 employees, and the rate declines continuously. However, for the eight detailed manufacturing industries in which the smallest establishment has the highest rate, the median ratio, from the smallest to the largest, was only five to one.

The Relationship Between Fatality Rate and Firm Size

We now examine the simple relationship between fatality rate and *firm* size, looking first at rates for various sectors. As shown in Figure 4.3, firms with 1 to 19 employees have the highest fatality rate in four of the five sectors—all except wholesale trade. In all cases, firms with more than 1,000 employees have the lowest fatality rates. There are no sectors with continuously decreasing rates, and the ratio of the highest rate to the lowest is noticeably smaller than it was for establishment rates for these sectors.

The Relationship Between Fatality Rate, Firm Size, and Establishment Size

While we have found that, on average, smaller firms have higher fatality rates than larger firms, we also know that small establishments have higher fatality rates than small firms have and that there is a strong positive correlation between firm size and establishment size. To understand the relationship between firm size and fatality rate, we need to disentangle the effects of firm size and establishment size. To do this, we assessed whether, for a given firm size, smaller establishments have higher fatality rates; and whether, for a given establishment size, smaller firms have higher fatality rates.

Figure 4.3
Fatality Rate, by Firm Size, All States, 1992–2001

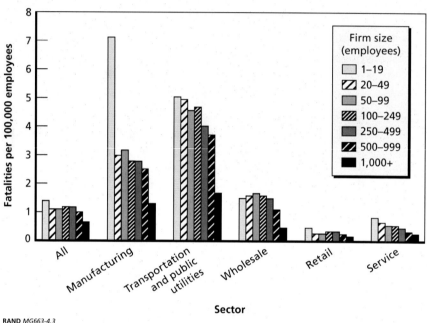

To illustrate the analysis, we first examine Tables 4.5 and 4.6, which show a cross-tabulation of the fatality rates for firm and establishment size in the manufacturing sector (with and without logging, respectively). Note that the overall fatality rate for the sector is 2.32 per 100,000 workers. For establishment-size categories, the top row shows that the rates drop from 8.13 for the smallest to 1.10 for the largest. For firm-size categories, the left column shows that they drop from 7.06 for the smallest to 1.30 for the largest. The drop is greater with establishment size than with firm size, but the difference is not large.

Next, if we look across the rows, we can see the effect of increasing establishment size within each firm size. For each firm size, the establishment rates are highest in the 1-to-19–employee category and fall sharply for the 20-to-49–employee category. For the most part, they continue to fall, although considerably less steeply, except for upturns in the largest establishment sizes within the 250-to-499–employee and

Table 4.5
Fatalities and Fatality Rate, by Establishment and Firm Size, Manufacturing Sector, 1992–2001

| Firm Size | Total | Establishment Size | | | | | | |
		1–19	20–49	50–99	100–249	250–499	500–999	1,000+
Total	2.32	8.13	2.67	2.53	1.86	1.56	1.53	1.10
	3,880	1,149	479	504	645	420	322	361
1–19	7.06	6.87						
	862	862						
20–49	2.99	33.14	2.34					
	394	80	314					
50–99	3.17	25.79	5.86	2.45				
	381	54	45	282				
100–249	2.82	21.35	4.37	2.66	2.30			
	465	57	38	50	320			
250–499	2.77	14.65	3.77	3.14	1.96	2.64		
	318	24	21	37	64	172		
500–999	2.48	22.24	3.84	3.14	1.90	1.25	2.91	
	275	28	18	32	54	36	107	
1,000+	1.30	7.71	2.29	2.39	1.42	1.21	1.23	1.10
	1,185	44	43	103	207	212	215	361

SOURCE: OSHA IMIS and U.S. Census Bureau–provided data.
NOTE: Fatality rate is fatalities per 100,000 employees.

500-to-999–employee firm sizes. If we compare the pattern among firms with more than 1,000 workers, it does not differ much from the pattern for the Total row at the top. In other words, the pattern we found when we looked at establishment size (regardless of firm size) is pretty much the one we find even after controlling for firm size.

In contrast, note the pattern in the column for establishments with 1 to 19 employees. For establishments in this size category, those

Table 4.6
Fatalities and Fatality Rate, by Establishment and Firm Size, Manufacturing Sector, Not Including Logging (SIC 241), 1992–2001

Firm Size	Total	Establishment Size						
		1–19	20–49	50–99	100–249	250–499	500–999	1,000+
Total	2.05	4.88	2.67	2.59	1.94	1.63	1.56	1.11
1–19	3.31	3.34						
20–49	2.61	21.69	2.25					
50–99	3.10	25.32	5.98	2.44				
100–249	2.87	22.64	4.66	2.77	2.36			
250–499	2.91	14.50	4.22	3.42	2.10	2.77		
500–999	2.54	21.42	4.09	3.24	1.96	1.33	2.95	
1,000+	1.36	8.17	2.51	2.51	1.50	1.26	1.27	1.11

SOURCE: OSHA IMIS and U.S. Census Bureau–provided data.
NOTE: Fatality rate is fatalities per 100,000 employees.

in the smallest firms have the lowest fatality rates. In other words, large firm size appears not to have the kind of protective effect seen for large establishments, in which fatality rates decrease steadily and strongly with size. Here, the rate for the smallest firm is the lowest, not the highest. Small establishments in medium-sized firms are the riskiest, while small, single-establishment firms (in which firm size and establishment size are the same) are among the safest. Similar results are seen for the next two establishment-size categories (establishments with 20 to 49 employees and those with 50 to 99 employees). For establishments with more than 100 employees, the smallest firm sizes have the highest rates. What stands out sharply here is the relatively low rates for single-establishment firms, e.g., establishments with 1 to 19 employees that are part of firms with 1 to 19 employees and establishments with 20 to 49 employees that are part of firms with 20 to 49 employees.

Manufacturing includes the logging industry, which is well known for having both a very high fatality rate and very small establishments and firms. To see how the rates we just examined change if we eliminate the logging industry, we show the rates without it in Table 4.6. The figures there show that the overall fatality rate in establishments with 1 to 19 employees drops almost 40 percent and the rate in establishments with 1 to 19 employees that are part of firms with 1 to 19 employees drops more than 50 percent. Thus, as we noted before, the disparity between the rate of the smallest and the largest establishment size is reduced. However, the basic findings about the relative roles of establishment size and firm size are not changed. We still find sharp drops in fatality rates as we move to larger establishments from the 1-to-19–employee category. For smaller establishment sizes, we still find the same pattern: The smallest firms have the lowest fatality rates.

An examination of other sectors found that patterns of fatality rates for establishments were quite similar to the results found in manufacturing. For all nonconstruction sectors studied, firms in these categories had a total of more than 1,100 deaths in establishments with 1 to 19 employees, an average of 114 per year.

Controls for Other Factors

We carried out a regression analysis (using the Poisson model) to see whether adding variables for nonmetropolitan location and unionization affected our estimates of establishment- and firm-size effects. Establishments in nonmetropolitan areas would be farther from trauma centers capable of providing adequate care to seriously injured workers and perhaps would have less access to information about hazards. Union status is linked with greater establishment and firm sizes and might be associated with higher risks, as other studies (Viscusi, 1983) have found. Although it might be useful to test other variables as well, these two were the only variables available in our data set.[11] To do this analysis, we had to use a different subset of the OSHA data. The data

---

[11] One reviewer did note that we could have included a variable describing the frequency of inspections in each industry and state. This would allow us to test whether a higher probability of inspection were linked to lower fatality rates. Neither the reviewer nor we believed, however, that inclusion of this variable was likely to change the size coefficients. Another possible variable could have characterized each specific establishment's OSHA inspection history. However, constructing this variable would have involved a major data-linking exercise, because the OSHA data do not include a unique establishment identifier.

set included planned inspections in manufacturing conducted randomly between 1984 and 1995 and fatality investigations in the same industries conducted during that period.

We found that, while both of these variables were associated with increases in the fatality rates (40 percent for the location variable; 12 percent for the union variable), including them did not cause changes in the estimated effects of the firm- and establishment-size variables. More information about the results of the regression analyses can be found in Appendix C.

Causes of Fatalities

Next, we consider whether the accident drivers at small establishments differ from those at larger ones. To conduct this analysis, we first looked at 1992–2001 data for establishments in all states to determine the percentage of all deaths in each sector that occurred in establishment with 1 to 19 employees. Then we calculated the percentage of deaths in that size category for each of the five most common accident event types: being struck by something, being caught in something, falling from a height, cardiovascular or respiratory failure, and electric shock. If the percentage for any one event were 10 percent higher or lower than the share in the total, we called it, respectively, *high* or *low*. If it varied by 20 percent or more, we called it, respectively, *very high* or *very low*. In other words, if the 1-to-19–employee establishment category had 40 percent of all fatalities in the sector, we labeled a particular event category *high* if its share was above 44 percent and *very high* if its share was above 48 percent. Mining and finance had no event types for these establishments that varied that much from the share in the total. For the other sectors, the event types that were distinct in establishments with 1 to 19 employees were as shown in Table 4.7.

The clearest finding in Table 4.7 is that fatalities due to cardiovascular- or respiratory-system failures comprise a relatively small percentage of the fatalities that are investigated at workplaces with 1 to 19 employees. However, this finding is probably due to reporting differences. Cardiovascular events are less obviously work-related than those

Table 4.7
The Relative Frequency of Different Events in Fatalities in Establishments with 1 to 19 Employees, by Sector

Major Event Types	Sector						
	Ag.	Mfg.	Trans. or Public Utility	Wholesale	Retail	Services	Mfg. Without Logging
Cardiovascular	Low	Very low	Low	Very low	Very low	Very low	Low
Caught in	—	Very low	—	—	—	—	—
Fall from height	High	Very low	—	Very low	Very low	—	—
Electric shock	—			—	Very high	High	Very high
Struck by	—	Very high	—	—	Very high	—	—

NOTE: Ag = agriculture. Mfg = manufacturing. Trans = transportation.

in any other category; larger workplaces may be more conscientious about reporting these deaths than very small workplaces are.

Table 4.7 shows that the manufacturing industry looks quite different if we exclude logging (which accounts for about 15 percent of manufacturing deaths). Almost all of the logging deaths are struck-by events that occur at very small establishments. Once the logging industry is removed from the sample, we find that struck-by deaths are not especially common at small manufacturing workplaces, while electric shock becomes a more prominent cause of death. Given the relatively large role of electric shock at small establishments in retail trade and services as well, further study of why electric shock fatalities are especially disproportionate there may be worth investigating.[12]

---

[12] Earlier, we had noted that some event types, such as electrocutions and explosions, were especially likely to cause deaths even though they caused relatively few injuries. We raised the question of whether these types of events were more common sources of fatal accidents at small establishments than at large establishments and thus whether that might explain why death rates were higher at smaller establishments even though rates for minor injuries were not. We do see here some support for the claim that electrocutions cause a larger percentage of the deaths at small establishments than they do at large ones. However, the largest

OSHA Violations and Establishment Size

Another possible driver of variations in fatality rates among establishments could be violations of OSHA standards. Higher fatality rates at small establishments may reflect primarily a higher rate of fatality-causing, serious violations. To examine this issue, we calculated the percentage of accident investigations of fatalities in each establishment-size category in which serious violations had been cited.

It is important to keep in mind that the issuance of a violation in these cases does not necessarily mean that the violation *caused* the death, i.e., that the death would not have occurred in the absence of the violation. The violation does not have to be a "necessary condition" in order to be issued. In general, OSHA is supposed to cite violations that contributed to the death, but it is not always possible to infer the degree to which the violation contributed.

Table 4.8 shows, for 1992 through 2001, the percentage of deaths that occurred in conjunction with serious violations, by establishment size, for the five largest sectors. The data are shown separately for OSHA states and state-plan states. Several of the latter have their own distinct sets of standards and use different codes for them.

The percentage of fatality investigations citing serious violations for 1992 through 2001 ranged from the upper 60s for construction

---

disparity was about 25 percent between the percentage of deaths at establishments with 1 to 19 employees that were caused by electrocutions and the percentage of all deaths that were in that size category. Thus, if these small establishments had 40 percent of all fatalities in a sector, they might have 50 percent of electrocutions. It is important to keep in mind that establishments with 1 to 19 employees typically have a fatality rate twice the rate for the whole sector. Thus, if the overall fatality rate for the sector were 2.0 per 100,000 employees, the rate for the 1-to-19–employees category would be 4.0. Even if the 1-to-19–employee category had 50 percent of electrocutions, the percentage of all deaths due to electrocutions never exceeded 10 percent in our data. Thus they would account for, at most, 0.4 out of a total rate of 4.0. Even if the rate for electrocutions were elevated by 25 percent, it would contribute only 0.1 to the total rate of 4.0. Thus, the higher relative frequency of accident types that (like electrocutions) contribute a larger share of deaths than of nonfatal injuries seems unlikely to explain very much of the higher death rates at small establishments.

Table 4.8
Deaths Associated with Citations of Serious Violations, by Establishment-Size Category, Selected Sectors, 1992–2001

Establishment Characteristic	Establishment Size						
	1–19	20–49	50–99	100–249	250–499	500–999	1,000+
Construction							
OSHA states (%)	68.9	67.6	65.4	59.8	50.3	35.3	48.0
N = 4,311	3,053	621	280	223	75	34	25
State-plan states (%)	65.1	62.4	63.5	65.2	68.7	42.9	62.5
N = 2,262	1,706	287	115	92	32	14	16
Manufacturing							
OSHA states (%)	72.2	78.1	77.0	69.2	73.6	67.6	53.7
N = 2,463	654	320	339	438	265	207	240
State-plan states (%)	59.5	72.1	66.5	66.2	69.8	70.8	67.2
N = 1,404	469	160	167	210	159	120	119
Transportation or public utility							
OSHA states (%)	48.3	54.7	54.3	39.2	46.6	40.6	41.5
N = 1,143	451	225	151	158	73	32	53
State-plan states (%)	42.5	51.5	49.4	44.7	52.5	40.0	35.3
N = 618	254	103	87	85	40	15	34
Wholesale trade							
OSHA states (%)	69.6	69.6	61.7	59.2	50.0	63.6	55.6
N = 637	303	135	81	76	22	11	9
State-plan states (%)	66.3	54.8	60.0	61.0	28.6	25.0	75.0
N = 358	187	73	35	41	14	4	4

Table 4.8—Continued

Establishment Characteristic	Establishment Size						
	1–19	20–49	50–99	100–249	250–499	500–999	1,000+
Services							
OSHA states (%)	52.2	58.9	53.2	51.7	48.7	39.4	43.9
N = 948	508	163	77	87	39	33	41
State-plan states (%)	47.4	47.2	40.9	46.4	43.6	30.4	50.0
N = 632	321	89	66	56	39	23	38

and manufacturing to the low 40s for retail trade and finance. The rate for services was 50.5.[13]

The findings indicate some variations between OSHA states and state-plan states. In the latter, the percentage of deaths in which serious violations were cited does not vary systematically with size. In contrast, in the OSHA states, the percentage with violations tends to be somewhat higher in the smaller-establishment size categories (although it does not decline continuously with size). The differences between the two groups of states should make us somewhat leery of drawing overarching conclusions about whether OSHA violations are likelier to contribute to deaths at smaller establishments. However, it certainly seems reasonable to conclude that fatalities at small establishments are *not less likely* to be cited for OSHA violations. This is important because, given the higher overall fatality rates at small establishments, even a finding of an equal likelihood that a serious violation contributed to the accident means that there is a considerably higher rate of deaths due to vio-

---

[13] For particular fatality event types, the shock category was most often associated with a serious violation (70.1 percent). Of the other major categories, serious violations were also often issued in cases of falls from heights (68.8 percent), caught in or between (65.5 percent), struck by (58.2 percent), and, less frequently, in cases of cardiovascular- or respiratory-system failure (36.2 percent). (Two nature-of-injury codes in the cardiovascular-event code category—asphyxia and electric shock—had percentages higher than 65 percent; few events in the "other" category, which includes most of the cases, had serious violations [18.3 percent]).

lations at these workplaces. So some part of their higher fatality rates is related to greater noncompliance.

Size Distribution of Nonfatal Injury and Accident Rates

To gain further insights into how the severity of injuries reported varies by establishment size, we looked at another source of data on non-fatal injuries. Some states that operate their own occupational safety and health programs have more extensive telephone-reporting and accident-investigation programs than OSHA does. California's is the most extensive. California requires employers to telephone OSHA about all hospitalizations (other than for observation) lasting more than 24 hours as well as for a selected set of other injuries. The IMIS reported 12,302 employee hospitalizations and 1,704 employee deaths in California from 1992 to 2001.

As Table 4.9 shows, establishments with 1 to 19 employees had 52 percent of the reported fatalities and 38 percent of the reported hospitalizations during the period covered. While not shown in this table, establishments with 20 to 49 employees show a similar decline in fatalities and hospitalizations, while larger size categories had cor-respondingly larger percentages for the less severe categories. Table 4.9 also compares these percentages to the percentage of employees in that size category.

In every sector except wholesale trade, the percentage of hospital-ized employees from establishments with 1 to 19 employees exceeds the percentage of employees in that size category. Thus, employees in that size category were at elevated risk of hospitalization. However, in every case, the percentage of hospitalizations for employees is lower than the percentage of fatalities.

Thus, we find here again the pattern that others have found. At each major step up in injury severity, the percentage of events at small establishments increases. In light of our earlier discussion of other explanations for this pattern, we see this as further evidence that under-reporting is greater for less severe injuries and that small establishments underreport more frequently than do bigger ones.

Table 4.9
Reported California Employee Deaths and Hospitalizations at Establishments with 1 to 19 Employees, 1992–2001, by Sector

Sector	Employees (%)[a]	Deaths (%)	Hospitalizations (%)
Construction	40	71	66
Manufacturing	11	32	18
Transportation or public utilities	16	41	26
Wholesale	33	40	27
Retail	33	63	44
Services	25	50	36
Agriculture	NA	60	44
Total		52	38

SOURCES: Employee data: U.S. Department of Commerce (1997). Death and hospitalization data: OSHA IMIS.

[a] Data are for 1997.

Tracking the Pattern of Fatality Rates by Establishment Size Over Time

We also considered whether the patterns of fatality rates changed over time (results not shown). To examine this issue, we divided our data into three periods: 1984–1989, 1990–1995, and 1996–2001. (As noted in our description of the data, we omitted years before 1984 because of OSHA's failure to distinguish establishment size from firm size before then.)

We found that the fatality rate for all sectors and sizes fell from 2.1 per 100,000 in 1984–1989 to 1.8 in 1990–1995 and to 1.7 in 1996–2001. The sectors showed some similarities: The fatality rates for establishments with fewer than 50 workers declined more than the rates for establishments with 50 to 499 employees. For the largest establishments, the patterns were more erratic. We did not see evidence over the period examined here that small establishments have become riskier than larger ones. If anything, they appear to have become somewhat less risky.

Implications for Policy and Research

Key Findings

Our study reinforces the growing body of literature that indicates that small establishments tend to have the greatest risks. We were surprised to find, however, that, once we controlled for establishment size, fatality rates did not also increase steadily as we went from the largest firms to the smallest. Establishment size appeared to have a substantially larger effect on fatality risks than firm size did. The finding that larger firms are safer than smaller ones appears to be largely due to the fact that larger firms tend to have larger establishments.

Our unexpected findings about the independent effect of firm size raise several possibilities. One is that financial incentives for injury prevention are not so closely related to firm size or not as powerful as our initial findings suggested. The second is that other factors are powerful enough to offset most of the preventive effects of greater firm size.

With regard to experience rating under WC, it may be important to note that our largest size category, for both establishments and firms, is 1,000 or more. For firms, this level is below what would usually be required to meet self-insurance requirements. Thus it is likely that our categorization does not give a very precise measure of risk for the very large firms that may have the strongest financial incentives to prevent injuries.

Another possible explanation for our results for firms is that the costs of injury prevention grow with firm size in ways that we have not understood. Some have speculated that higher costs to understand and coordinate activities at multiestablishment firms could undermine the possible economies of scale in providing safety. However, if economies of scale play a role in making larger establishments safer than small ones, why does this not apply to firm size as well? Unfortunately, we have no good way to test this or the other explanations suggested.

Another unexpected finding emerged when we looked at the effects of firm size for establishments of a given size. When the establishments were small, those that are within the *smallest firm-size category usually had the lowest fatality rates.* Then the rate increased with larger firm sizes until it reached firms with more than 1,000 employees, when it decreased. In contrast, for larger establishments (more than 250 employees), *those in the smallest firm-size category generally had the highest rate.* This pattern appeared in most sectors. What could explain this apparent protective effect?

Our only explanation was that this protective effect might reflect the presence of an owner on site. Admittedly, we have no prior evidence that having an owner on site does improve safety. It seems plausible that an owner might, on average, feel more responsibility than would a hired manager to run his or her plant in a way that did not injure workers. We also do not know that an owner actually is on site, though we speculate that this is likelier because these firms are small and probably consist of only a single establishment. We did confirm that, when firm size and establishment size are in the same size category, we are usually dealing with single-establishment firms.[14] (The only exception was cases in which both the establishment and the firm had more than 1,000 employees.) However, even if an owner were on the site of a single-establishment firm, the impact he or she would make on shop-floor conditions would probably be attenuated at large workplaces compared to the effect at small ones. While we find this explanation plausible, it is speculative at this point. We think that the pattern appears large enough and consistent enough to warrant further investigation.

The worst fatality rates were found at small establishments that were part of midsized firms. In manufacturing, for example, establishments with 1 to 19 employees that were in firm-size categories with 20 to 999 employees had fatality rates two to five times higher than did similar establishments in either the smallest firms or the largest firms. The other sectors showed similar patterns. For nonconstruction sectors from 1992 to 2001, establishments with 1 to 19 employees that were part of firms with 20 to 999 employees had 1,145 deaths, an average of 114 per year. If these firms could reduce their rates to those of the

---

[14] When both the establishment and the firm had 1 to 19 employees, the number of employees at the establishment equaled the number controlled by the firm in 70.2 percent of the cases. For all of the other size categories below 1,000 employees, this agreement ranged from 83 percent of the cases to 90 percent. When both the establishment and firm had more than 1,000 employees, the numbers were the same in only 40.5 percent of the cases.

smallest or largest firms, more than two-thirds of these deaths would be prevented.

A similar analysis can be conducted for establishments with 20 to 49 employees, though there the typical excess-fatality rate of firms with 50 to 999 employees is two-fold rather than three-fold. Over the 10-year period, the total number of deaths in establishments with 20 to 49 employees that were in firms with 50 to 999 employees was 451, so, if the rate for these firms could be reduced in half (i.e., to the rate of the smallest 20-to-49–employee firm or of the largest firms), about 22 additional deaths would be prevented each year.

Study Limitations

Our findings are subject to a number of possible limitations. Controlling for industry at the four-digit (in manufacturing) or three-digit (elsewhere) level does tend to reveal more diverse patterns and reduce the relatively high fatality rates of the smallest workplaces. Thus, industries with high fatality rates do tend to have a disproportionately large percentage of employment in small establishments. A further possibility is that the three- and four-digit SICs are still not refined enough to control for differences in what goes on at worksites. And it is certainly plausible that size is one proxy for these differences; for example, it is hard to believe that a steel mill (SIC 3312) that employs 50 workers is really doing the same type of work as one that employs 1,000. However, for this explanation to work, we would need to be able to explain why the higher-risk activities within these subindustries would end up, in the great majority of cases, being more concentrated among smaller establishments. Such an argument would seem to require that risk affects size as well as, or instead of, size affecting risk.

The existence of such a relationship is possible. At least one article (Ringleb and Wiggins, 1990) has argued that, at least since the 1970s, many firms have tried to spin off units that present higher risks. Their argument implies that risks should have increased at small *firms* relative to larger ones. Its relevance to establishment risks is not clear. Their study focused chiefly on risks in the form of higher expected tort-liability claims, which had increased since the 1970s. We do not find the evidence presented by Ringleb and Wiggins (1990) very compelling.

The little evidence we have on trends over time in *establishment* fatality rates does not show any tendency for a relative rise in rates at small establishments.

Another limitation concerns the accuracy of the employment and fatality data that we use to construct rates. We note in Appendix B that the employment data used (from March of each year, as reported in CBP [U.S. Census Bureau, undated(b)]) appear to understate the employment at smaller establishments. It is certainly possible that the understatement varies across industries and is largest for those that are weather-sensitive. The overall bias from using March figures reached a maximum of 15 percent for establishments with one to four employees; thus it seems unlikely that this particular bias is large enough to undermine the conclusion that small establishments typically have rates several times higher than large establishments. Our data also do not take account of hours of work exposure. As a result, if smaller establishments use more part-time workers, this would introduce a bias in our estimates of fatality rates by size.

The OSHA employment data also undoubtedly have errors, especially for firm size. However, because we are using broad size categories, these errors are unlikely to cause major problems.

As described more fully in Appendix B, our fatality numbers are lower than CFOI's, even when we exclude highway crashes and assaults. This is an area of concern, although we have argued that, if there is any bias, it is likely that it would be due to poorer reporting at smaller workplaces and thus lead us to underestimate death rates there.

Policy Options

Given the limitations of the study, more research is required to clarify its policy implications. Nonetheless, the findings are clear enough to prompt discussion of several possible policy interventions that might be considered to address health and safety problems at small establishments or firms. Each option is marked by uncertainty. Our goal, therefore, is to provide the foundation for a sound debate on policy options.

Programs Targeting Small Establishments Within Firms Employing 20 to 999 Workers. Our research suggests that it may be worthwhile for OSHA to develop programs targeting *firms* that employ 20 to 999 workers and have small establishments. As the findings showed, if a firm has between 20 and 999 employees and has small establishments (certainly below 50 and perhaps below 99 employees), the fatality rates in those establishments tend to be quite elevated compared to rates in establishments with either 1 to 19 employees or more than 999 employees. Rather than trying to work only at the establishment level, OSHA might be more effective (and use fewer administrative resources) if it began discussions at the firm level as it tries to develop an appropriate mix of tools.

OSHA Inspections of Small Establishments. Although small establishments are riskier for employees, and although the fatality rates for deaths linked to violations are also higher, it may still be difficult to justify a greater inspection effort there. For example, even if the risks per employee were five times higher at establishments with eight employees (the mean number in workplaces with fewer than 20 employees), the expected benefits in risk reduction would still be greater at a workplace with more than 40 employees (assuming that the reduction in risk was proportional to the initial risk).

Another source of caution in making the decision to redeploy inspectors to small establishments lies in the fact that there are fixed costs associated with conducting inspections, so that, for example, the time required to inspect an establishment with 20 workers is likely to be more than one-fifth the time required to inspect an establishment with 100. Moreover, the fact that death rates for establishments that have been exempted from programmed inspections declined no less over time than did rates in larger establishments casts some doubt about whether removing the exemptions would lead to increased safety performance.

On the other hand, several studies, most recently for 1992 through 1998 (Gray and Mendeloff, 2005), indicate that the effect of OSHA inspections on preventing injuries is greater (in percentage terms) at smaller establishments (those with fewer than 100 employees) and found no evidence of a preventive effect at establishments with more than 250 workers. If the latter finding is valid, then a shift toward emphasizing inspections at smaller workplaces, including those with fewer than 20 employees, might be justified. Unfortunately, the preventive effects of inspections were found only when OSHA found serious violations and assessed penalties. In their absence, inspections, on average, had no effect or a perverse one, perhaps by signaling to management that there were no problems that needed their attention.

Expansion of Existing Small-Business Consultation Programs. OSHA already conducts a consultation program that targets smaller businesses. Another policy option, therefore, would involve expansion of this program. Typically, about 25,000 consultations are conducted each year, many of which include safety training. Employers who request consultations are not cited for any violations that are found, but they do have an obligation to abate them, and consultants are supposed to make referrals to OSHA when they do not.

However, evidence on the effectiveness of consultations is sparse. Mendeloff and Gray (2001) found declines after consultations for both violations (a large effect) and injuries (a small effect), compared to establishments without consultations. However, this research could not rule out the possibility that employers who request consultations would have made the changes without the consultation. Moreover, the fact that consultation-program waiting lists are short raises questions about whether there is enough unmet demand to justify expansion of the program. In the past, big increase in demand for consultations has occurred only when employers thought they faced a much higher threat of inspection. However, it does seem that state programs have some control over the demand and that it might be possible to moderately expand the demand for consultations from smaller workplaces.

New Educational Programs. Based on the accident investigation data we reviewed, we believe that it may be worthwhile to consider a trial of a new educational program that would be targeted at small establishments. OSHA currently publishes an array of educational materials designed to assist employers in reducing hazards. The agency also carries out educational programs through cooperative activities with trade associations.

Additional information campaigns might heighten attention to safety by reminding employers about the workers in their industry in establishments like theirs who have died on the job and the factors associated with these deaths. Although workplace deaths are relatively rare, deaths may have a special salience for workers and employers alike. The infrequency of these events seems likely to make it difficult to keep much management focus on safety, especially given the multiple and conflicting demands on the time of a small-business owner. Information campaigns might be a means of raising and maintaining awareness.

Operationally, an employer in a specific industry category might get a list and description of recent deaths occurring in that industry in workplaces with fewer than 20, 50, or 100 employees. The causal factors would be described along with any OSHA violations cited as related to the deaths. These deaths would be limited to those investigated by OSHA and would exclude most highway deaths and assaults. The logic behind this approach is that employers will be more motivated to pay attention to similar issues at their own workplaces and to take action, including abating hazards that might reduce the probability of such events occurring.

The effects of such an intervention might be small, but the public costs would be small as well, probably no more than several million dollars. A crucial unknown is the level of costs that small establishments would incur in response to this initiative. If, for example, each of 1 million small establishments spent $1,000, the total cost would be $1 billion. It would probably make sense to begin with a pilot program in one or two states to identify the scope and nature of the employer response.

Future Research

As suggested in its title, this study is intended as exploratory and suggestive, not definitive. However, we believe that the findings of this study raise some interesting questions for social scientists. The finding that the smallest *firms* were relatively safe raises questions about the importance of experience rating under WC as an incentive for safety. Other studies have found strong effects of firm size on WC costs, but it is possible that many of these studies confounded firm size and establishment size.

Our finding about the different effects of firm size in small and large establishments may raise important questions for students of entrepreneurship and of organizational behavior. Some further insights may be obtained by merging IMIS data with establishment-level data from the census of manufactures (U.S. Census Bureau, 1947) and the analogous databases for other industries. That match would allow clear distinction of single-establishment firms from others.

One finding of this research was that the size patterns among establishments did sometimes vary by industry. We did not attempt to explain the reasons for these variations, but doing so might shed valuable light on the causal factors at work.

Finally, it would also be useful to try to find out whether the poorer fatality performance of midsized firms in small establishments also applied to nonfatal injuries. We are not aware of any efforts to untangle establishment-size and firm-size effects for nonfatal injuries. Any effort would need to take care to consider how underreporting would affect the results, but we believe the effort would be worthwhile.

CHAPTER FIVE

Sarbanes-Oxley's Effects on Small Firms: What Is the Evidence?

Ehud Kamar,[1] *Pinar Karaca-Mandic,*[2] *and Eric Talley*[3]

This chapter presents an overview of the regulatory regime that SOX (P.L. 107-204) created and its implications for small firms. We review the available evidence in three distinct domains: compliance costs, stock-price reactions, and firms' decisions to exit regulated securities markets.

Introduction and Background

SOX was enacted in 2002 to strengthen corporate governance and restore investor confidence after a series of financial debacles involving some of the most prominent firms in the Unites States, including Enron, Tyco, and WorldCom. SOX and the rules implementing it have transformed the reporting obligations of public firms. Most importantly, SOX requires management and an outside auditor to assess annually the effectiveness of a firm's internal controls over financial reporting. In addition, SOX tightens disclosure rules, requires management to certify the firm's periodic reports, strengthens board-

---

[1]   Associate professor of law, University of Southern California Gould School of Law.

[2]   Assistant professor, School of Public Health, University of Minnesota; associate economist, RAND Corporation.

[3]   Professor of law, University of California, Berkeley School of Law; senior economist, RAND Corporation.

independence and financial-literacy requirements, and raises auditor-independence standards.

While the intent behind SOX is clear, its ultimate effects on capital markets and economic growth are still under debate. Proponents of the act argue that it alleviates investor concerns by improving transparency and the accuracy of financial reports (e.g., Cunningham, 2003; Wagner and Dittmar, 2006; Coates, 2007). Opponents of the act argue that it unduly increases the regulatory burden associated with being a publicly traded firm (e.g., Coustan et al., 2004; Ribstein, 2002; Gordon, 2003; Romano, 2005).

For policymakers, the crux of the debate must concern SOX's *net* effects. There is no dispute that complying with SOX is costly, even though compliance costs have been going down of late. The more germane question is whether attendant benefits (public or private) justify the cost. While this question applies to all firms, it is especially salient for smaller issuers. Many SOX provisions increase accounting, audit, and other general compliance costs. Because small firms have fewer resources, enjoy lesser scale economies, and receive relatively little investor attention, they likely face higher average costs and derive lower average benefits from SOX. On the other hand, small firms (or at least their public investors) may also benefit more than others from the assurance that SOX provides; Enron, Tyco, and WorldCom aside, small companies have historically been more prone than large firms to financial fraud. Whether SOX strikes the right balance between costs and benefits can be resolved only empirically.

In this chapter, we review empirical studies of the effect of SOX on large and small firms. Because the extant studies employ different measures to define *small firms*, we will clarify the definition used in each study. Our review focuses on areas in which (1) SOX might plausibly have an impact and (2) SOX's impact is susceptible to empirical measurement: accounting and audit costs, stock prices, and exit from the market for public capital.

The evidence we review lends some support to the proposition that SOX had a disproportionately negative impact on smaller firms, at least at its initial implementation. However, the evidence is not conclusive, especially with regard to SOX's effects over the long term. More research in this area is needed.

Our analysis proceeds as follows. We first briefly review the principal reforms that the act introduced. We then explain why the act might plausibly affect small firms in a manner distinct from larger firms. Next, we summarize evidence on the accounting and audit costs associated with SOX, stock-price reactions to SOX, and changes in deregistration patterns after SOX enactment. The final section of the chapter chronicles initiatives to mitigate the effect of SOX on small firms.

Overview of the Sarbanes-Oxley Act of 2002

To situate and motivate our later discussion, we begin by reviewing the principal provisions of SOX. At the onset, it bears noting that, as a phenomenon, SOX was not a single act by Congress. Rather, the roll-out of the provisions that are now identified collectively as *SOX* was piecemeal. The multidimensionality of its constituent reforms presents a challenge for empirical study of the effects of SOX writ large. While each component of SOX might affect firms differently, researchers can often examine the effects of the provisions only as a whole, making fine-tuning of the regulatory environment difficult.

Internal Controls

The most notorious mandate that SOX introduced is a requirement for a firm's annual report to include assessments by the CEO, CFO, and an outside auditor of the effectiveness of the firm's internal controls over the accuracy of financial statements. Though a relative latecomer in the cavalcade of SOX reforms, this requirement is largely regarded as the costliest requirement in SOX. As Klingsberg and Noble (2004) note,

> Any audit committee member or general counsel will readily tell you that the most burdensome part of the Sarbanes-Oxley Act of 2002 has turned out not to be certifications by the CEO and

CFO as to the accuracy of the financial statements, the movement toward real time disclosure as most recently exemplified by new Form 8-K, or even the non-[generally accepted accounting principles] reconciliation requirement of Regulation G. Memoranda from law firms and accounting firms following the adoption of Sarbanes-Oxley and the initial SEC releases pursuant to the statute usually included only vague references to what some corporate insiders and auditors now claim has turned out to be the neutron bomb within Sarbanes-Oxley: Section 404—Management Assessment of Internal Controls. Nowadays, Section 404 is the focus and in many circles is literally synonymous with Sarbanes-Oxley.

Section 404 has been implemented slowly, and indeed it is still not fully implemented. Although the SEC received rulemaking authority in July 2002, it did not issue rules on section 404 until June 2003 (see U.S. General Accounting Office, 2003b). These rules require so-called *accelerated filers* (firms with a minimum float of $75 million and at least one year's worth of financial reporting) to include management and auditor reports on internal controls in annual reports for fiscal years ending after June 14, 2004. Other firms were required to comply for fiscal years ending after April 14, 2005. In June 2004, the SEC approved the audit standard proposed by the newly created PCAOB in connection with section 404 (see SEC, 2004b).

However, the SEC has staggered, and subsequently postponed, the start dates for compliance. In June 2004, for example, the SEC extended the compliance date to November 15, 2004, for accelerated filers and to July 15, 2005, for other firms.[4] In March 2005, the SEC extended the compliance date to July 15, 2006, for nonaccelerated filers and foreign firms (see SEC, 2005a). In September 2005, the SEC pushed back the compliance date for nonaccelerated filers to July 15, 2007 (see SEC, 2005b). In December 2006, the compliance date was

---

[4] See SEC (2004a). In November 2004, the SEC extended the deadline for filing the report by 45 days for accelerated filers with stock capitalization of less than $700 million. See SEC (2004c).

further extended to December 15, 2007, for management certification and December 15, 2008, for auditor attestation (see SEC, 2006c).

Management Certification of Financial Statements

Not all of the SOX reforms took as long to implement as the internal-controls requirement did. For example, under section 906 of the act (effective July 2002), CEOs and CFOs are required to certify the accuracy of the firm's periodic reports and are subject to criminal penalties for false certifications. In August 2002, the SEC issued a rule implementing section 302.[5]

Extended Statute of Limitations for Shareholder Lawsuits

Another immediate effect of SOX was the extension of the statute of limitations for filing shareholder lawsuits. Before SOX enactment, shareholder plaintiffs had been required to file claims within the earlier of three years of the occurrence of the fraud or one year of its discovery. Section 804 of the act increased these time limits to five years and two years, respectively.

Initially, there was uncertainty as to whether the filing deadlines were extended even for acts of fraud that preceded SOX enactment. The text of section 804 stated that the limitation extensions "shall apply to all proceedings addressed by this section that are commenced on or after the date of enactment of this Act" (P.L. 107-204, title VIII, section 804[b]). Nevertheless, trial courts initially differed on whether claims could be revived for which the pre-SOX statute of limitations had elapsed.[6] Only in 2004 was the issue resolved by the Second Circuit Court of Appeals, which ruled that section 804 did not revive

---

[5] See SEC (2002d). On June 27, 2002, the SEC ordered the CEOs and CFOs of 947 public firms with revenues exceeding $1.2 million in the previous fiscal year to file by the filing date of the first period report on or after August 14, 2002, sworn statements certifying the accuracy of period reports, immediate reports, and definitive proxy materials in the preceding year. See SEC (2002b).

[6] Compare *Roberts v. Dean Witter Reynolds* (holding that section 804 revives expired claims) with *de la Fuente v. DCI Telecomms* (holding that section 804 does not cover claims that were pending at the time of its enactment).

expired claims (see *In re Enterprise Mortgage Acceptance Co.*). The courts of appeals for the fourth and seventh circuits confirmed this ruling.[7]

Executive Compensation

SOX made immediate changes to executive compensation on several fronts. Most importantly, section 402 bans most loans by firms to directors or officers. Such loans, often made on attractive terms, were viewed as hidden compensation. In addition to the ban on loans, SOX changed executive-compensation practices in two ways. First, section 306 (effective January 2003) prevents directors and officers from trading in firm securities during pension-plan blackout periods[8] unless the trade is part of a preset trading plan.[9] Second, section 403 (effective August 2002) requires directors, officers, and 10-percent shareholders to report their trades in firm securities within two business days following the trade. Prior law allowed these reports to be delayed for 10 business days after the end of the month in which the trade took place and, in some cases, 45 days after the end of the fiscal year during which the trade took place.[10] Section 403 (effective July 2003) further provides that this report must be filed electronically with the SEC and posted on the firm's Web site.[11]

Audit Committees

Section 301 of SOX requires that all firms listed on national stock exchanges have audit committees composed exclusively of independent directors. Although audit committees had been required long before

---

[7]   The appellate courts of two other federal circuits have since followed the decision. See *Glaser v. Enzo Biochem* and *Foss v. Bear, Stearns and Co.*

[8]   A pension-plan blackout period is a period during which an employee owning the company's stock as part of his or her pension plan cannot trade in that stock.

[9]   In January 2003, the SEC issued a final rule implementing section 306. See SEC (2003a).

[10]   In August 2002, the SEC issued a final rule implementing this requirement. See SEC (2002c).

[11]   In May 2003, the SEC issued a final rule implementing this requirement. See SEC (2003e).

the enactment of SOX, the composition and duties of these committees had been mostly unregulated. In 1999, the national stock exchanges began requiring that audit committees be independent and state in their charters that the auditor is accountable to the board of directors and that the audit committee is authorized to select, evaluate, and replace the auditor. These changes, however, allowed boards to name one nonindependent director to the audit committee and exempted small businesses from the new requirements.

SOX broadly defines an *independent director* as a director who does not receive any fee from the firm other than for being a director and who is not an affiliated person of the firm or any of its subsidiaries. In April 2003, the SEC issued a rule defining an *affiliated person* as a person who controls the firm, is controlled by it, or is under common control with it.[12] Section 301 also requires firms to provide their audit committees with independent legal counsel and other advisors necessary for fulfilling their duties and requires audit committees to establish procedures to receive and investigate complaints regarding accounting and auditing matters.

In addition, section 407 of the act requires firms to disclose whether any members of their audit committees are financial experts and, if not, to explain why. In January 2003, the SEC issued a rule implementing section 407 (see SEC, 2003b). The rule required small-business issuers (firms with less than $25 million in revenues and no more than $25 million in publicly traded stock) to include the report under section 407 in annual reports for fiscal years ending after December 30, 2003, and required other issuers to include this report in annual reports for fiscal years ending after July 30, 2003.

Separation of Audit and Nonaudit Services

SOX also prohibits auditing firms from providing certain nonaudit services to the firms they audit. Section 201 of the act (effective July 2002) prohibits a firm's auditor from providing a number of other services,

---

[12] See SEC (2003d). The rule contains a safe harbor under which a person who is not an executive officer or a shareholder owning 10 percent or more of any class of the company's voting stock will be deemed not to control the company.

including financial-information system design and implementation, appraisal or valuation, internal auditing, investment banking, legal and expert services unrelated to the audit, brokerage, and actuarial services. In January 2003, the SEC issued a rule under section 208 of the act defining the circumstances in which auditors are not deemed independent (see SEC, 2003c).

The Special Case of Small Firms

Before we review the evidence, it is useful to examine why one might plausibly expect that SOX's impact on small firms may be different from its impact on their larger counterparts. The reason, in a nutshell, is that both the costs of complying with SOX and the potential benefits of SOX can be larger for small firms (see SEC, 2003c).[13]

Small firms may incur higher SOX-related compliance costs than large ones do for a number of reasons. First, they may experience a disproportionately large increase in audit fees because some of the costs associated with establishing, maintaining, and evaluating internal controls over financial reporting are fixed and because small firms often lack the staff to perform the additional accounting work in house (Wolkoff, 2005; Carney, 2006; SEC, 2006a). Doyle, Ge, and McVay (2005) find that small firms are likelier than large firms to have ineffective internal controls.

Small firms have also raised concerns about the complexity of the new audit standard. Many firms voiced displeasure with the lack of advance guidance on how to comply with the internal-control requirement. While the SEC issued final rules on this requirement in June 2003, it was not until March 2004 that the PCAOB issued the corresponding audit standard and not until May 2007 that the SEC released interpretive guidelines. Complex standards can pose a problem for all

---

[13] Prior research suggests that small firms derived a lower net benefit from being public than large firms even before SOX (Pagano and Roell, 1998; Pagano, Panetta, and Zingales, 1998).

firms, but small firms are affected more because they tend to lack in-house staff to respond to the new environment.

Third, the increased demand for accounting services following SOX enactment raised audit costs for small firms in particular. Survey results indicate that, after SOX enactment, large accounting firms stopped working with small clients, citing lack of profitability, risk, and capacity constraints, forcing these clients to seek other accountants (GAO and U.S. Senate Committee on Small Business and Entrepreneurship, 2006). The resulting imbalance in the market for accounting services could not be resolved quickly, because entry into this regulated market is slow.

While the main concern that small businesses express about SOX revolves around accounting costs, other issues have been raised as well. One concern is that some of the new rules make it difficult for firms to attract individuals to serve as directors, because these rules increase liability exposure and tighten independence standards. This concern might be greater in the case of small businesses because serving on their boards is less prestigious than serving on boards of large businesses. Linck, Netter, and Yang (2007) found that, after SOX enactment, director fees as a percentage of net sales increased significantly more for small firms than for large ones. Another concern is that preoccupation with compliance discourages taking business risks. This can be especially problematic for small firms at the start of their growth.

It is important to note that the potential benefits of SOX can also be higher for small firms. The goal of SOX was to restore investor confidence by increasing transparency. Achieving this goal can be especially beneficial to small firms because their limited accounting personnel and limited exposure to public scrutiny make their financial statements prone to inaccuracies (Doyle, Ge, and McVay, 2005).

Of course, this argument rests on the assumption that, without regulation, investors would have less information about small firms than about large firms. It is also possible that the contrary is true, namely that the regulation benefits large firms more than it does small ones because large firms' operations tend to be more complex and therefore more difficult for investors to process and distill. Ultimately, whether, on balance, SOX imposes a net loss on firms and, if so, whether the loss is larger for small firms, is an empirical question. We turn to this question next.

Evidence on Accounting and Audit Costs

Several studies document an increase in public firms' accounting and audit costs since the enactment of SOX. However, they differ about the relative impact on small firms. Asthana, Balsam, and Kim (2004) found that the average ratio of audit fees to assets increased between 2000 and 2002 and that, in particular, bigger and riskier firms and clients of the Big Four audit firms experienced a larger increase in absolute audit fees than did smaller firms and clients of other audit firms. They attributed the latter finding to decreased competition in the market for audits of multinational firms. In an analysis of the financial statements of 97 Fortune 1,000 firms, Eldridge and Kealey (2005) found a $2.3 million average increase in audit fees associated with SOX costs from 2003 to 2004. They found that SOX audit costs increase in assets, asset growth, effectiveness of internal controls, and 2003 audit fees.

Financial Executives International (FEI) surveyed public firms in January 2004, July 2004, March 2005, March 2006, and May 2007 about the cost of compliance with section 404 of SOX. Firms reported substantial and increasing costs (FEI, 2005, 2006, 2007). The 321 firms that responded in January 2004 predicted average compliance costs of $1.93 million, including $590,100 in auditor attestation fees. The 224 firms that responded in July 2004 predicted average compliance costs of $3.14 million, including $823,200 in auditor attestation fees. The 217 firms surveyed in March 2005 reported average compliance costs of $4.36 million, including $1.3 million in auditor attestation fees. While these figures show an increase in costs from January 2004 to March 2005, the study does not report how much of the difference in the results is due to the different group of firms responding to each survey. The surveys conducted in 2006 and 2007 report a 35-percent decline in total compliance costs since year one.

Several studies compare SOX costs of small and large firms. They report that section 404 implementation costs comprise a larger percentage of revenues for small firms than for large ones and that this percentage declined between the first year and the second years after SOX enactment for both small and large firms.

CRA International surveyed firms subject to SOX in March 2005, December 2005, and March 2006 (CRA, 2005, 2006). The initial survey included data on Fortune 1,000 firms with market capitalization of more than $700 million. The second and third surveys also included firms with market capitalization between $75 million and $700 million. According to the December 2005 survey, in the first year after SOX enactment, section 404 costs averaged $1.5 million for small firms (with market capitalization between $75 million and $700 million) and $7.3 million for large firms (with market capitalization greater than $700 million). Audit fees accounted for 35 percent and 26 percent of total section 404 costs for small and large firms, respectively. According to the March 2006 survey, in the second year after SOX enactment, these costs declined by 30.7 percent for small firms and 43.9 percent for large firms. During that year, audit fees accounted for 39 percent and 33 percent of total section 404 implementation costs for small and large firms, respectively. Between March 2005 and March 2006, audit fees declined by 20.6 percent for small firms and 22.3 percent for large firms. For small firms, total section 404 costs represented 0.24 percent of the average revenue in the second year after SOX enactment, compared to 0.38 percent in the previous year. The corresponding figures for larger firms were 0.05 percent and 0.11 percent of average revenue, respectively.

The surveyed auditors attributed the decline in total section 404 costs to efficiencies gained from a year's experience in implementing and assessing internal controls and from the fact that documentation that had been created in the first year did not need to be replicated. There was, however, an increase in non-404 audit fees after the first year, which auditors attributed to new non-404 audit standards, higher salaries due to increased demand for accounting personnel, and additional compliance requirements.

Hartman (2005, 2006) also reports that the average audit fees increased by a larger percentage for smaller firms than for larger ones. The studies analyze about 700 firms included in the Standard and

Poor's (S&P) 500, the S&P MidCap 400, and the S&P SmallCap 600 indexes. They find that, in 2004, average audit fees increased by 84 percent for SmallCap firms (from $1,042,000 in 2003) and 92 percent for MidCap firms (from $2,177,000 in 2003). Average audit fees of larger firms, included in the S&P 500 index, increased by a more modest 55 percent (from $7,443,000 in 2003). In 2005, average audit fees increased by 22 percent for SmallCap firms, 6 percent for MidCap firms, and 4 percent for S&P 500 firms. In total, between 2003 and 2005, average audit fees increased by 141 percent for SmallCap firms, 104 percent for MidCap firms, and 62 percent for S&P 500 firms.

GAO similarly reports that small firms have experienced a greater increase than large firms have in audit-related costs since SOX enactment (GAO and U.S. Senate Committee on Small Business and Entrepreneurship, 2006). The study finds that audit fees constituted a higher percentage of revenues for small public firms before SOX enactment than after and that this disparity increased after SOX enactment, especially for small firms that filed internal-control reports. Table 5.1 summarizes the study's findings.

Table 5.1
Median Audit Fees as a Percentage of Revenues

Market Capitalization ($ million)	Median Audit Fees as a Percentage of 2003 Revenues	Median Audit Fees as a Percentage of 2004 Revenues	
		Firms Not Filing Internal-Control Reports	Firms Filing Internal-Control Reports
0–75	0.64	0.79	1.14
75–250	0.29	0.35	0.56
250–500	0.18	0.26	0.40
500–700	0.15	0.20	0.30
700–1,000	0.13	0.12	0.25
>1,000	0.07	0.07	0.13

SOURCE: GAO and U.S. Senate Committee on Small Business and Entrepreneurship (2006).

As Table 5.1 illustrates, for firms with less than $75 million in market capitalization that filed internal-control reports, the median audit fee increased from 0.64 percent of revenues in 2003 to 1.14 percent in 2004. For firms with more than $1 billion in market capitalization that filed internal-control reports, the median audit fee increased from 0.07 percent to 0.13 percent of revenues during the same period.

GAO and the U.S. Senate Committee on Small Business and Entrepreneurship (2006) surveyed firms with less than $700 million in market capitalization and less than $100 million in revenues that filed internal-control reports in 2004. Out of 591 firms that were contacted, 158 firms completed the survey. They reported having paid consulting fees ranging from $3,000 to more than $1.4 million for assistance in meeting the new requirements. Most firms reported that they needed to make significant changes to their internal controls, and many reported expenses for hiring additional staff. Firms also reported that their CEOs and CFOs spent as much as 90 percent of their time on compliance, forcing them to defer investments.

Other SOX provisions might also have increased costs for the smaller firms. For example, 69 percent of the surveyed firms reported that the tightened auditor-independence standards forced them to pay additional fees for tax advice. In addition, about half of the firms retained outside counsel to draft charters for board committees and a code of ethics and to handle CEO and CFO certifications.

In sum, these studies provide evidence that SOX increased public firms' accounting and audit costs regardless of the company size; that before SOX passage, audit costs were already disproportionately higher for small firms; that the disparity increased after SOX enactment, especially for small firms that were subject to section 404; and that the costs declined for all firms between the first and second years after SOX enactment.

A key attraction of the accounting studies is that they provide concrete, company-specific information that is at least somewhat reflective of firms' actual compliance costs. At the same time, the accounting studies are self-limiting for a few reasons. First, they present the challenge of discerning whether the increased costs are due solely to the new regulatory terrain or also reflect preexisting costs that had previously been expended elsewhere.[14] Second, and perhaps more significantly, the accounting studies do not provide insights about the benefits of SOX. Accordingly, another area in which researchers have attempted forays is in the use of stock-market fluctuations as a reflection of whether SOX has created or destroyed economic value. It is to these studies that we now turn.

Evidence on Market Reactions and Firm Value

The evidence on abnormal stock returns around events leading to the enactment and implementation of SOX is, in a word, mixed.[15]

Several studies do not distinguish between firms according to size. Jain and Rezaee (2006) examined events occurring between June 25, 2002 (when SOX was introduced in the U.S. Senate), and July 30, 2002 (when the President signed SOX into law), finding positive returns. However, they found a positive relationship between these returns and practices SOX sought to promote: effective corporate governance, reliable financial reporting, and credible audit functions. This suggests that the firms least affected by SOX experienced higher returns. Li, Pincus, and Rego (forthcoming) cover a similar period. They find positive returns and a positive relationship between returns and earning management, a practice SOX sought to discourage. This suggests that the firms most affected by SOX experienced higher returns.

Other studies have examined the relation between firm size and returns. Engel, Hayes, and Wang (2004) studied events occurring between February 13, 2002 (when the SEC announced its intent to improve financial-disclosure regulation), and July 30, 2002 (as in Jain

---

[14] For example, even before SOX-regulated public companies were required to maintain internal financial controls under the Foreign Corrupt Practices Act (P.L. 95-213), but those controls did not have to be audited. Since SOX enactment, some of the costs of designing internal-control systems and protocols may have been (rationally) offloaded to auditors, a shift that would visibly increase audit fees, but the reduction in internal costs might not be easily detected within the company's books and records.

[15] Abnormal stock returns are the returns to a firm in excess of the returns to a market portfolio.

and Rezaee, 2006). They found that returns were negative and positively related to firm market value and stock turnover, indicating that SOX particularly harmed smaller and less actively traded firms.

Wintoki (2007) studied events occurring between January 17, 2002 (when the SEC chair proposed overhauling corporate accounting) and August 1, 2002 (when the New York Stock Exchange approved new board-independence rules). He found that returns were positively related to firm size and age and negatively related to market-to-book ratio and to expenditure on research and development.

Zhang (2005) studied events leading to SOX enactment that occurred between January 17, 2002 (as in Wintoki, 2007) and July 25, 2002 (SOX's effective date). She found negative returns. She also found that firms experienced lower returns if they purchased nonaudit services from their auditors, had complex operations, or had weak shareholder rights, suggesting that firms more affected by SOX lost more value. She did not find a relationship between returns and firm market capitalization.

Chhaochharia and Grinstein (2005) studied events occurring between November 2001 (one month before Enron filed for bankruptcy) and October 2002 (three months after SOX took effect and amendments were proposed to stock-exchange listing rules). They define *small firms* as those included in the S&P MidCap 400 and the S&P SmallCap 600 indexes (averaging $21 million in market capitalization) and *large firms* as those included in the S&P 1,500 index (averaging $1.876 billion in market capitalization). They found that small firms with less independent boards and weaker internal controls (which they assumed to be affected by SOX) underperformed small firms with more independent boards and stronger internal controls (which they assumed were unaffected). Affected large firms performed similarly to unaffected large firms and, in some regressions, performed better.

Litvak (2007a) compared the returns to foreign firms cross-listed in the United States with the returns to other foreign firms matched by market capitalization and industry. Her study period begins in January 17, 2002 (as in Wintoki, 2007, and Zhang, 2005) and October 22, 2002 (when the SEC adopted a rule requiring firms to introduce internal-control procedures). She found lower returns to cross-listed firms regardless of firm size.[16]

Overall, while the event studies provide mixed evidence regarding SOX's effect on large firms, they appear to be consistent in finding a negative effect on small firms. As noted, an advantage of these event studies over accounting studies is that they capture the *net* value that the market attaches to an anticipated regulatory change. A limitation of these studies is that they are best suited to studying sharp regime shifts and less well suited to studying a process of piecemeal regulation. With SOX, the change took shape over time, as the law was implemented. Before then, it was difficult to predict how various reforms would play out. Investors expected change but did not know what form it would take. Deregistration studies, described next, examine how the market viewed SOX a few months later, when some of the uncertainty around the new law had been resolved.

Evidence on Deregistrations

We now review the evidence concerning the relationship between SOX and firm decisions to exit the market for public capital. Section 12(g)(4) of the Securities and Exchange Act of 1934 (P.L. 73-291) provides that public firms can deregister their stock with the SEC and suspend being subject to federal securities law once they have fewer than 300 shareholders. Firms can deregister by arranging for private acquirers to buy their entire stock ("going private") or by cashing out small shareholders to reduce the number of shareholders to below 300 ("going dark").

Unlike going dark, going private can achieve a number of business goals other than avoiding securities law. For example, Michael C.

---

[16] The effect of SOX on cross-listed firms may be unique. In particular, legal change is likely to present particularly thorny obstacles to cross-listed firms because they must comply with two regulatory regimes simultaneously. Cross-listed firms also tend to be large and belong to particular industries. Litvak (2007b) found that small firms reacted more negatively to SOX when she used the same sample as in her previous study (Litvak, 2007a) but measured the effect using the post-SOX change in the ratio of the market value of the firm's debt and equity to the replacement cost of its assets.

Jensen (1989) argued that going private lowers agency costs by concentrating ownership and increasing leverage. Kaplan (1989b), George P. Baker and Wruck (1989), Lichtenberg and Siegel (1990), and Abbie J. Smith (1990) found improvements in profitability and operating efficiency in firms after going private, while Ofek (1994) found no similar improvements after failed attempts to go private. Moreover, as Kaplan (1989a) illustrates, going private can yield tax savings.

Studies of the two types of transactions suggest that going-dark transactions are more clearly related to avoiding the cost of being public, especially since SOX enactment, than are going-private transactions.

Block (2004) surveyed 110 of the 236 firms that either went private or went dark between January 2001 and July 2003 and found a link between deregistration and an interest in reducing costs, especially after SOX enactment. Among firms responding to the survey, the most common reason given for deregistering, especially among firms with low market capitalization, was the cost of being public. This reason was cited more frequently after SOX enactment, and firms reported a post-SOX increase in the average cost of being public from $900,000 to $1,954,000.

Engel, Hayes, and Wang (2004) found a modest post-SOX increase in deregistrations in a sample of 470 firms that went private or went dark between the first quarter of 1998 and early May 2005, excluding foreign firms and firms in bankruptcy or liquidation. The increase became insignificant when going-dark transactions were excluded. The study also found that smaller firms experienced higher returns at the announcement of a plan to deregister their stock in the post-SOX period than they did during the pre-SOX period, especially if they had a high percentage of inside ownership. This finding is remained when going-dark transactions were excluded.

Leuz, Triantis, and Wang (2006) compared a group of 436 firms that went private and 484 firms that went dark between January 1998 and December 2004 to firms that remained registered. They found that firms that went dark were smaller than firms that went private, had lower past returns, were more distressed, and had poorer accounting quality. In addition, they found an increase in the number of going-dark transactions per month after SOX enactment and through May

2003, followed by a decrease, but found no change in the number of going-private transactions per month. They also found that, before the enactment of SOX, distress was a predictor of going dark, while, after SOX enactment, agency costs were a predictor of going dark.

GAO and the U.S. Senate Committee on Small Business and Entrepreneurship (2006) analyzed deregistrations by U.S. firms between 1998 and 2005. The study excluded firms that deregistered as a result of liquidation, reorganization, or bankruptcy. It found that the number of deregistrations increased from 143 in 2001 to 245 in 2004. It also reported the reasons that firms cited for deregistering. Table 5.2 provides a summary.

Table 5.2 shows an increase between 2001 and 2004 in the percentage of firms deregistering due to costs. The percentage of firms citing direct costs as the primary reason for deregistering increased from 32.2 percent in 2001 to 53 percent in 2004, while the percentage of firms citing indirect costs as the primary reason increased from 13.3 percent to 25.7 percent. Across all years, market and liquidity issues were important factors in deregistration decisions and were cited more often than indirect costs of being public. Firms also cited advantages of being private, such as reduced pressure to generate quick profits and the ability to avoid disclosing information that could benefit competitors.

Table 5.2
Primary Reasons Cited for Deregistration

Year	Direct Costs of Being Public (%)	Indirect Costs of Being Public (%)	Market or Liquidity Issues (%)	Benefits of Being Private (%)
2001	32.2	13.3	31.5	23.8
2002	44.4	13.9	35.4	22.9
2003	57.8	27.5	38.5	21.3
2004	52.7	25.7	28.6	15.9

SOURCE: GAO and U.S. Senate Committee on Small Business and Entrepreneurship (2006).

NOTE: Firms may cite more than one primary reason for deregistering.

The multitude of factors affecting the decision to deregister makes it difficult to isolate SOX's effect on deregistration. For example, financial-market liquidity around the time that SOX was enacted could have increased the willingness of private investors to pursue acquisitions independent of SOX.[17] Similarly, the weakness of the public capital market at that time could have independently encouraged firms to exit this market. Maupin, Bidwell, and Ortegren (1984), for example, reported that financial officers commonly cited undervaluation by the market as a reason for going private.[18] Lerner (1994) and Pagano, Panetta, and Zingales (1998) found that the likelihood of an initial public offering decreased when stock prices were low. Benninga, Helmantel, and Sarig (2005) developed a model in which going public is positively related and going private is negatively related to stock prices.

There is reason to believe that the weakness of the public capital market around the time of SOX enactment increased the pressure on firms to go private. According to Block (2004), almost 40 percent of firms that deregistered after SOX enactment cited the absence of liquidity in the public capital market and the absence of opportunity for a secondary market as one of the primary costs of being public.[19] Indeed, *The Economist* (2003a, 2003b) notes that dwindling profits and low stock prices induced going-private transactions around the time that SOX was enacted not only in the United States but also worldwide.

Kamar, Karaca-Mandic, and Talley (2006) separated SOX's effects from the effects of other, contemporaneous factors using foreign firms as a control group. Defining *small firms* as firms in the sample's bottom quartile of market value (less than $15 million), they found that, in the first year after SOX enactment, the probability that small public firms undergoing acquisitions will be bought by private acquir-

---

[17] Holstein (2004), MacFadyen (2002, 2003, 2004), and Carney (2006), for example, reported that the ready availability of private-equity financing around the time of SOX enactment fueled going-private transactions.

[18] Whether the belief held by financial officers of firms that go private that the market undervalues their firms is founded is a separate matter. D. Scott Lee (1992) found no evidence to support it.

[19] The appendix provides examples of rationales that firms gave for their decisions to go private or to go dark after SOX enactment.

ers (rather than by other public firms) increased for U.S. firms by 53 percent (from 43 percent to 66 percent) and is attributable to SOX. The study found no effect among large firms or in the second year after SOX enactment and interpreted the latter finding as indication that maladapted firms went private immediately to avoid initial compliance with the new requirements, leaving behind public firms that were better suited to the new regulatory environment.

While the comparison to foreign firms screens out the effects of market changes, it does not separate SOX's effects from the effects of other forms of scrutiny that tightened in the United States around the same time. Passage of SOX was not the only response to the corporate scandals of the late 1990s. Courts, regulators, stock exchanges, and investors intensified their scrutiny of public firms in additional ways.[20] Each of these non-SOX changes could have raised the cost of being public. Therefore, the study compared the combined effect of SOX and these related changes to contemporaneous trends abroad. Moreover, the study focused on public firms that were acquired. It does not measure the effect that SOX may have had on public firms that were not acquired or its effect on private firms' decisions to go public.

---

[20] For example, numerous scholars have documented how the scandals that precipitated SOX caused judges in corporate cases to be more sympathetic to allegations of mismanagement than ever before (Strine, 2002; Marcus, 2003; Loomis, 2003; Subramanian, 2003). Moreover, roughly simultaneously with the passage of SOX, Congress dramatically increased the budget of the SEC (Rogers, 2002). The SEC, in turn, intensified its market-monitoring activity, leading Loomis (2003) to report "record numbers of high-profile enforcement actions" in 2003 by the SEC and the U.S. Department of Justice. The year 2003 also saw a proposal by the SEC to allow shareholders to nominate directors in firm proxy statements. The national stock exchanges similarly toughened their corporate-governance standards in 2003, requiring listed firms to have a majority of independent directors. See SEC (2003f, 2003g). The changes were made at the SEC's prodding. See SEC (2002a). In 2004, the IRS announced its intent to routinely audit executive compensation in public firms based on findings from auditing large public firms since the beginning of 2003 (Lublin, 2004 [describing the decision]; McKinnon, 2005 [describing implementation]). Also in 2004, the U.S. Sentencing Commission tightened the sentencing guidelines for noncompliance with corporate programs. See U.S. Sentencing Commission (2004, Appendix C).

Proposals to Mitigate Sarbanes-Oxley's Effect on Small Firms

Since SOX's enactment, the SEC has taken several actions to address the concerns of small firms. First, it repeatedly extended the section 404 compliance deadline for nonaccelerated filers. The most recent extension is still in force as of this writing. Second, in March 2005, it formed an advisory committee to assess SOX implications for small firms. In April 2006, the committee presented its final report, in which it recommended scaling down the requirements under section 404 for firms whose stock-market capitalization is between $128 million and $787 million (small-cap firms) and further scaling down these requirements for firms whose stock-market capitalization is less than $128 million (microcap firms).[21] Alternatively, the report recommended exempting from section 404 small-cap firms with less than $250 million in annual revenues but more than $10 million in annual product revenue and microcap firms with between $125 million and $250 million in annual revenue.

The SEC rejected the idea of creating special carve-outs for small firms. Instead, in May 2006, it announced that it would prepare interpretive guidelines on how to comply with section 404, work with the PCAOB to improve its audit standard, and ensure that PCAOB auditor inspections focus on efficiency. The SEC also announced that it would postpone enforcing the section 404 requirements for nonaccelerated filers until the guidelines and audit standard are released. In December 2006, the SEC set the compliance deadline as the end of 2007 for management certification of internal controls and as the end of 2008 for auditor attestation. In May 2007, the SEC adopted interpretive guidelines to section 404 premised on scaling internal controls to firm size, materiality to financial results, and risk of misstatement, and the PCAOB adopted a companion audit standard to replace the standard from 2004.

---

[21] Microcap firms comprise 1 percent of stock-market capitalization in the United States, and small-cap firms comprise another 5 percent. Together, however, they account for 78.5 percent of the number of U.S. public firms.

Conclusion

In this chapter, we reviewed the evidence on the effects of SOX on small firms and large firms in three areas: accounting and audit costs, stock prices, and deregistration decisions. Table 5.3 offers a concise summary of the literature as it now stands.

Three factors make comparison of the studies difficult. First, the studies define *small firm* differently. Second, the studies examine different periods and—except for CRA (2005, 2006); Leuz, Triantis, and Wang (2006); and Kamar, Karaca-Mandic, and Talley (2006)—do not distinguish between short-term effects and long-term effects. Third, the studies differ in design and in the degree to which they control for factors other than SOX that may have affected their results.

There is ample evidence that SOX increased public firms' accounting and audit costs. Before the passage of SOX, audit fees had already constituted a higher portion of revenues for smaller firms than for larger ones. This disparity between small firms and large firms increased after the enactment of SOX, especially for small firms that complied with section 404. Comparing audit fees, however, is only the first step toward evaluating the effect of SOX on small firms. The question is whether the higher costs that small firms bear are matched by higher benefits.

Event studies analyzing SOX's impact on firm value represent one method of attempting to answer this question. These studies provide mixed results, which seem to depend on the choice of events and control variables. Nevertheless, almost all studies that distinguish between firms based on size find that SOX has affected small firms more adversely than it has large firms and that its effect on small firms has been negative.

Studies of firm deregistrations are another way of capturing the net effect of SOX. They too produce mixed results. Most studies find that SOX increased the number of going-dark transactions, with moderate or no impact on going-private transactions. However, these studies do not separate the effect of SOX from that of contemporaneous factors, such as financial-market liquidity, which could have increased the rate of deregistration. Kamar, Karaca-Mandic, and Talley (2006) used a control group of foreign firms to address this problem. They

Table 5.3
Summary of the Studies Reviewed

Study	Period Studied	Small Firm Definition	Primary Outcome	Finding
Asthana, Balsam, and Kim (2004)	2000–2004	No distinction	Audit fees	Average ratio of audit fees to assets increased between 2000 and 2002.
FEI (2005, 2006, 2007)	Surveys in January 2004, July 2004, March 2005, March 2006, and May 2007	No distinction	$404 costs	$404 costs increased from January 2004 to March 2005.
Eldridge and Kealey (2005)	2003–2004	Only Fortune 100 firms included	Audit fees	Audit fees increased from 2003 to 2004.
CRA (2005, 2006)	First and second years after SOX became effective (July 2002)	Firms with market capitalization between $75 million and $700 million	$404 costs	$404 costs were higher for small firms in the first year after SOX became effective. Costs declined for all firms in the second year.
Hartman (2005)	FY 2003 and FY 2004	S&P SmallCap 600 firms	Audit fees	Audit fees increased disproportionately for small firms between FY 2003 and FY 2004.

Table 5.3—Continued

Study	Period Studied	Small Firm Definition	Primary Outcome	Finding
Hartman (2006)	FY 2005	S&P SmallCap 600 firms	Audit fees	Percent increase in audit fees was higher for small firms than for large firms in FY 2005.
GAO and U.S. Senate Committee on Small Business and Entrepreneurship (2006)	1. 2003 and 2004 for audit fees. 2. 1998–2005 for deregistrations.	1. Less than $75 million in market capitalization. 2. Less than $700 million in market capitalization and less than $100 million in revenues.	Audit fees, deregistrations	1. In 2003 and 2004, audit fees represented a larger share of revenues for small firms than for large firms. 2. The increase in deregistrations between 2001 and 2004 was due to costs. No evidence of distinction by firm size.
Jain and Rezaee (2006)	February 14, 2002–July 30, 2002	No distinction	Abnormal stock returns	SOX is associated with positive returns. Returns are higher for less affected firms.
Li, Pincus, and Rego (forthcoming)	February 13, 2002–July 25, 2002	No distinction	Abnormal stock returns	SOX is associated with positive returns.
Engel, Hayes, and Wang (2004)	1. February 13, 2002–July 30, 2002, for abnormal stock returns. 2. 1998–2005 for deregistrations.	Market value is a control.	1. Abnormal stock returns 2. Deregistrations	1. SOX is associated with negative returns. Returns are lower for small and less liquid firms. 2. There was a modest increase in going-dark transactions, especially for small firms.
Zhang (2005)	January 17, 2002–July 25, 2002	Market value is a control.	Abnormal stock returns	SOX is associated with negative returns regardless of firm size.

Table 5.3—Continued

Study	Period Studied	Small Firm Definition	Primary Outcome	Finding
Wintoki (2007)	January 17, 2002–August 1, 2002	Market value is a control.	Abnormal stock returns	Returns associated with SOX are lower for small, growth firms than for other firms.
Chhaochharia and Grinstein (2005)	November 2001–October 2002	S&P SmallCap 600 firms	Abnormal stock returns	SOX reduced the value of small firms. It had no effect, or a positive effect, on the value of large firms.
Litvak (2007b)	January 17, 2002–October 22, 2002	Market value is a control.	Abnormal stock returns	SOX reduced the value of cross-listed firms regardless of firm size.
Litvak (2007a)	Year-end 2001–year-end 2002	Market value is a control.	Cross-listing premium	SOX reduced the value of cross-listed firms, especially if they were small.
Block (2004)	January 2001–July 2003	Market value	Deregistrations	Small firms are likelier than large ones to cite the cost of being public as reason for deregistering. This reason is cited more often since SOX went into effect than before it went into effect.
Leuz, Triantis, and Wang (2006)	January 1998–December 2004	Market value is a control.	Going dark and going private	The rate of going-dark transactions increased during the first 10 months after SOX went into effect, especially for small firms. Since SOX went into effect, agency costs have been a predictor of going dark.
Kamar, Karaca-Mandic, and Talley (2006)	January 2000–December 2004	Bottom quartile of market value (less than $15 million)	Going private	The rate of going-private transactions increased for small firms in the first year after SOX went into effect. There was no effect on large firms or in the second year after SOX went into effect.

found that, in the first year after the enactment of SOX, the rate of going-private transactions in small public firm acquisitions increased in the United States more than abroad. In contrast, they did not find a negative effect among large firms.

Overall, the evidence offers qualified support for the view that SOX has had a negative effect on the value of small firms, at least initially. This evidence should be interpreted with caution, however, for at least three reasons.

First, other hypotheses unrelated to the wisdom of SOX as a policy vehicle might also be consistent with these findings. For example, the event studies measured the effects of SOX by looking at investor beliefs (as capitalized in stock price) at notable moments surrounding the enactment of SOX. But given the novelty of the requirements that SOX introduced and the delegation its provisions made to regulatory bodies and stock exchanges, investors could easily have been wrong about the future effects of SOX.

Second, one must account for the possibility that increasing compliance costs for small firms was warranted. For example, the deregistration studies suggest that SOX tipped the scales for some small firms in favor of exiting the public capital market. While, on first blush, this appears undesirable, it is possible that the exiting firms were opaque, risky, or prone to financial misstatements and that the firms that remained public benefited from SOX more than the exiting firms lost.

Finally, both the event studies and deregistration studies examined the initial period following SOX's enactment. It is important to understand the extent to which those initial effects represented one-time issues versus recurring ones. The decline in compliance costs since the enactment of SOX has already been noted, and the recent interpretive guidelines and audit standards may further decrease costs. Consequently, the puzzle surrounding the overall effect of SOX is far from over. Additional empirical studies will almost certainly inform the policy debate for years to come.

CHAPTER SIX

Do the Owners of Small Law Firms Benefit from Limited Liability?

John A. Romley, Eric Talley, and Bogdan Savych

Legal liability is a significant concern for the owners of businesses that supply legal, accounting, and other professional services.[1] Adverse judgments or settlements against a professional firm might be so costly as to put the firm out of business, and the costs of resolving disputes alone can seriously impact a firm's bottom line. Moreover, professional errors and omissions ("malpractice") represent a unique and significant source of liability exposure for professional-service firms. Everyday experience and a vast body of research attest to the importance of malpractice liability to professionals generally.[2] Legal liability, furthermore, can pose a threat not just to the viability of the professional business itself but also to the personal assets of the owners. In a professional partnership, the owners' personal assets can be called on, without limit, to satisfy a legal judgment.

Beginning in the 1990s, new limited-liability organizational forms became available to an important group of professional-service firms, namely, law firms. These LLPs and LLCs shield each owner from vicarious liability for the firm's obligations, including those arising from the malpractice of other owners.

While existing evidence indicates that exceptionally large law and accounting firms have embraced these forms, much less is known about

---

[1] Medicine, architecture, and engineering are further examples of services that are typically viewed as professional in character.

[2] See, for example, Chandra, Nundy, and Seabury (2005).

their take-up among smaller firms, which represent a significant segment of the professional-service sector of the U.S. economy, and how reorganization affects subsequent performance. This chapter examines reorganization of law-firm partnerships as LLPs and LLCs during the 1990s, as well as the growth of firms that did and did not reorganize.

Importance of Liability for Small Professional Firms

Small firms represent a significant segment of the professional-service sector of the U.S. economy.[3] However, the definition of *small* varies with the professional service. In 1999, the SBA proposed that law firms and CPA firms be defined as *small* if their receipts did not exceed $5 million and $6 million, respectively (*Federal Register*, 1999). Figures 6.1 and 6.2 indicate that law firms with receipts of less than $5 million earned collectively almost $65 billion in 1997 and employed 591,000 people (U.S. Census Bureau, 2000a).[4] These figures comprise almost half of the total industry receipts and almost 60 percent of its employment. CPA firms with receipts of less than $5 million earned collectively about $17 billion and employed 224,000 people.[5]

Legal liability is a significant concern for small professional businesses. Direct impacts on a firm's welfare can include adverse judgments or settlements as well as the costs of resolving disputes. Concern about the potential for litigation has also heightened the need for professional firms to carry liability insurance. Indeed, in a recent survey,

---

[3] Receipts in this sector totaled $751 billion in 1997, while employment totaled 6.8 million people (U.S. Census Bureau, 2000a; 2000b). These statistics include the two-digit sector 54 (professional, scientific and technical services) in the 1997 North American Industrial Classification System (NAICS), as well as the six-digit industry 621110 (offices of physicians). This simple definition is arguably narrow. For example, offices of dentists (NAICS industry 621210) are excluded. Thus these statistics may be conservative.

[4] Law and CPA firms correspond to NAICS industries 541110 and 541211, respectively. These statistics include taxable establishments with payroll operating the entire year.

[5] Because the 1997 Economic Census (U.S. Census Bureau, 2000a) defines firm size only by ranges of receipts (e.g., $5 million to $10 million), information on CPA firms with receipts of less than $6 million is unavailable. Therefore, these statistics underestimate the importance of small CPA firms.

Figure 6.1
Total Revenues of Law and Accounting Firms in 1997, by Firm Revenue

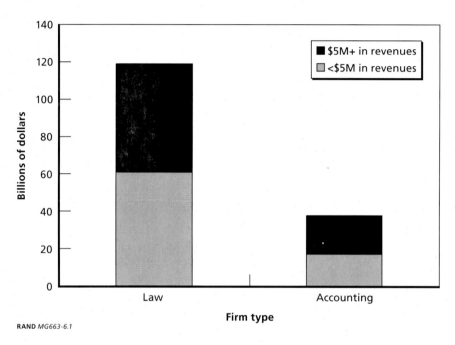

RAND *MG663-6.1*

small professional businesses ranked the cost and availability of liability insurance third on a list of 75 concerns, after HI costs and federal taxes (Phillips, 2004).

Potential Value of LLP and LLC Forms to Small Professional Firms

The new LLP and LLC organizational forms may help address liability concerns among small professional firms by shielding owners from vicarious liability, at least with respect to the malpractice of other owners. Concern over malpractice suggests that firms with more than one owner may find these new forms especially attractive.[6]

---

[6] An owner remains personally liable for his or her own malpractice and that of those he or she supervises.

Figure 6.2
Employees of Law and Accounting Firms in 1997, by Firm Revenue

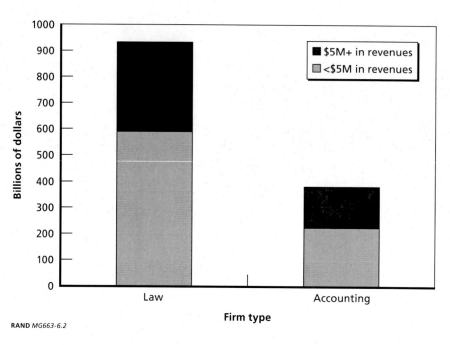

RAND *MG663-6.2*

Anecdotal evidence suggests that vicarious liability can be a significant concern among law firms in general. As one attorney remarked, "You would have to be out of your mind to be a partner in a law firm these days" (Reuben, 1994). When this attorney's firm went bankrupt, 260 partners were required to pay a total of $40 million. He then became a partner at another firm, which subsequently was required to pay $41 million for the conduct of a few partners relating to a failed savings and loan. After the firm's insurance was exhausted, 109 partners were personally responsible for the remaining $16 million.

This example, from the 1990s, provides a reminder that the availability of the LLP and LLC forms owes much to the savings-and-loan crisis, during which federal regulators sought to recover their financial losses from lawyers and accountants affiliated with the failed financial institutions (Ciccotello and Grant, 1999). The LLP form was first authorized for professionals in Texas in 1991.[7]

But do these new organizational forms tend to provide the greatest benefit to large or small firms? At least for law firms and perhaps accounting firms, the preceding anecdote and the historical context suggest that big businesses may be the primary beneficiaries of a limitation on vicarious liability. Ribstein (1998, 2001) has argued that vicarious liability imposes a disproportionate burden on large law firms, constraining them from operating at their efficient scale and scope. In a formal model, Romley and Talley (2005) found that limited liability strengthens the bargaining position of relatively large firms with respect to their clients. If these accounts are correct, large firms might have more to gain than small firms from the limited-liability organizational forms.

Others, however, have stressed the importance of the LLC and LLP forms for small businesses. For example, the president of the Chicago Bar Association advocated the authorization of the LLP form for law firms with a hypothetical example that illustrates the potential importance of this organizational form for small firms:

> The scenario is this: a small firm with three partners, each with a different area of practice. Partner one makes an error and the firm is sued for malpractice. Judgment is entered against the firm and all the firm's insurance and assets are used to pay the judgment. But it is not enough, and partner one has very few personal assets, so partners two and three, the non-acting, innocent partners, lose their homes to satisfy the judgment. (Nijman, 2003)

When the Supreme Court of Illinois gave its approval to authorize LLPs, the same observer remarked, "This is very good news for any law firm in Illinois, but especially for small firms" (Vock, 2003, quoting Nijman). She explained that smaller firms are asset-poor and less likely

---

[7]   The LLC form was created in the late 1970s with small businesses in mind (Ciccotello and Grant, 1999). As we discuss in Chapter Two, law firms were permitted to organize as LLCs beginning only in the 1990s.

than large ones to carry enough insurance, thus jeopardizing owners' personal assets.[8]

It is possible that limited (vicarious) liability is attractive to professionals irrespective of firm size. A chair of the American Bar Association subcommittee on limited-liability companies remarked, "I think every law firm in the country is probably looking at this in one way or another. . . . It's clearly the hottest topic in the law today, at least when it comes to practice management" (Reuben, 1994).

Existing Evidence on the LLP and LLC Forms Among Professional Firms

There is some evidence concerning take-up of the new organizational forms in the legal-service industry.[9] Two studies have analyzed the prevalence of the LLP and LLC forms on the basis of firm size, as defined by a firm's number of lawyers.[10]

Scott Baker and Krawiec (2005) investigated New York City–based firms with at least 25 lawyers. They found that 67 percent were LLPs and 1 percent were LLCs.[11] Among these firms, there was no apparent relationship between size and organizational form.[12]

---

[8] The evidence on the malpractice experience of law firms by size is limited. In Florida, from 1988 to 1994, insured law firms with two to five lawyers experienced 38.5 percent of all the malpractice claims while employing 19.3 percent of lawyers (Ramos, 1995).

[9] Ciccotello and Grant (1999) investigate the prevalence of professional-service firms among businesses registering as LLPs and LLCs. Law, medicine, and accounting comprised 70 percent of LLP registrants. Emerging professions (such as consulting) are prominent among LLCs. These data are not directly informative about the prevalence of the new forms within (versus across) industries. Nor did the authors investigate the sizes of firms that opted for the LLP versus LLC forms.

[10] While the SBA defines small law firms on the basis of receipts, the studies discussed here lacked access to such data. Our view is that the number of lawyers is likely to be highly correlated with receipts.

[11] The timeframe for these statistics appears to be 2003.

[12] The authors abstract from LLCs in this particular analysis.

Hillman (2003) considered all U.S. law firms. He found that, among firms with 50 or more lawyers in 2002, 48 percent were LLPs and 9 percent were LLCs. Among all firms, these statistics were 9 percent and 7 percent, respectively. Therefore, the respective shares of LLPs and LLCs among firms with fewer than 50 lawyers must have been less than 9 percent and 7 percent. Thus, this study found that firms with fewer than 50 lawyers were thus much less likely to be organized under the new limited-liability forms than were firms with 50 or more lawyers.

This evidence is relevant to the issue of whether small law firms benefit from the LLP and LLC forms and, in particular, their liability shields. Owners presumably tend to choose the organizational form that is best for their firms. Given this premise, we can conclude from the findings of these studies that many larger firms (defined as having either 25 or more or 50 or more lawyers) have benefited from the new forms. However, because the studies to date have not looked specifically at firms with fewer than 25 lawyers, the existing evidence does not speak to the relationship between organizational form and size among small firms, which comprise the vast majority of firms in the United States (see Chapter Three).

Focus of This Chapter

This chapter analyzes the relationship between the number of lawyers in a firm with unlimited liability and its decision to reorganize as an LLP or LLC. We also examine the performance of firms subsequent to reorganization. We did so by creating a unique data set on the number of lawyers and organizational form of U.S. law firms between 1993 and 1999, when many states first permitted law firms to organize as LLPs and LLCs. While we would like to assess whether liability limitations are beneficial to the owners of small firms in a variety of professional-service industries, appropriate data on the size and organization of professional firms are generally unavailable. Thus, we focus on the legal-service industry.

Our research strategy rests on two assumptions. First, we postulate that a law firm whose owners are vicariously liable reorganizes as an LLP or LLC if and only if their benefits, particularly their liability shields, outweigh their costs, particularly the costs of reorganization. Take-up by small multiowner law firms would then indicate that these firms benefit. Second, we postulate that growth subsequent to reorganization is a further indicator of benefits from limited liability.[13]

While others have investigated the relationship between limited liability and firm growth (Harhoff, Stahl, and Woywode, 1998), to our knowledge, we are the first to do so in the context of professional services.

This chapter therefore addresses the following questions:

- Did small, multiowner law firms whose owners were vicariously liable reorganize as LLPs or LLCs? Did take-up by these firms differ with their size?
- Did the number of lawyers at those firms that reorganized subsequently grow? Did such firms grow faster than firms that did not reorganize?

Our analysis has limitations. First, we do not address the impact of limited liability on the *creation* of small law firms. While the LLC and LLP have come to be the forms of choice among small start-ups (Miller, 1997), new firms cannot be identified reliably in our data set. Second, we do not analyze the impact of limited liability on consumers of legal services. Critics have argued that lawyers benefit at their clients' expense (McWilliams, 2004).[14] This important concern lies beyond the scope of the present effort.

---

[13] Romley and Talley (2005) formally derived related hypotheses from a theoretical model relating the benefits of limited liability to firm size.

[14] On the other hand, Ribstein (2001) argued that vicarious liability harms the clients of large law firms.

Organizational Forms for Multiowner Law Firms

This section describes the history of the organizational forms under which multiowner firms have practiced law and characterizes those features that seem likely to influence owners' decisions about form during the study period of 1993–1999.

General Partnership

A general partnership (GP) is a form of business organization under which owners (that is, partners) share equally in firm profits and losses. Historically, a multiowner firm could not operate as a corporation, only as a GP. A variety of motives accounted for this prohibition, including the view that lawyers should be accountable to their clients for malpractice (Hillman, 2003). The corporate form generally limits owners' vicarious liability.

As Table 6.1 indicates, the most important feature of a multiowner GP is that each owner is vicariously liable for the firm's obligations, including those arising from the malpractice of other owners. Other features of the GP seem likely to influence owners' choices among organizational forms. First, partnership income is taxed only once. The partnership itself pays no taxes but passes income through to its owners. The owners then pay personal taxes on the income. Corporations, in contrast, can face double taxation. Second, the GP is very flexible. We will describe some of the restrictions on firms that render other forms less flexible and therefore less attractive, all else being equal.

Professional Corporations and Professional Associations

Under the GP form, law firms could not avail themselves of certain benefits conferred by the Internal Revenue Code on corporations. For example, neither a corporation nor its employees pays taxes on pension contributions (Gilson, 1991). Professionals challenged this disparate treatment in the courts. In 1954, the IRS was compelled to treat business associations of professionals that had the "primary characteristics" of a corporation as such. The IRS complied but required that such associations be allowed the characteristics of corporations under state law. In response, states began, in the 1960s, to enact statutes

Table 6.1
Important Features of Organizational Forms for Multiowner Law Firms from an Owner's Perspective

Form	Vicarious Liability	Taxation	Flexibility
GP	Yes	Firm passes income through to owners without paying taxes	Most flexible
Profesional corporation (PC) or professional association (PA)	To some extent for other owners' malpractice, none for other obligations	Pensions and other benefits are treated more favorably than under GP; corporate income is taxed (unless S corporation)	Probably least flexible
LLP	None for other owners' malpractice, maybe for other obligations	Firm passes income through to owners without paying taxes	Flexible
LLC	No	Firm passes income through to owners without paying taxes	Flexible

permitting law firms to incorporate. As of 2004, every state had done so (Donn, 2004). Following Hillman (2003), we label these forms PCs and PAs.

PCs and PAs differ from general partnerships in several respects. First is the issue of liability. Organization as a PC or PA has generally constrained an owner's vicarious liability for a firm's obligations, although, during the study period, some such firms continued to face liability for other owners' malpractice. State courts, exercising their inherent authority to regulate the legal profession, in some instances, invalidated statutory prohibitions on such liability (Hillman, 2003). In other states, such liability was merely capped (SBA and Government Contracting Institute, 2000). In any case, an owner remains liable for his or her own malpractice and that of the employees he or she supervises, as is true for all organizational forms (SBA and Government Contracting Institute, 2000).

PCs and PAs also differ from other organizational forms in terms of tax treatment and flexibility. The income of a PC or PA is taxable unless the firm opts for S-corporation status. The S-corporation form, however, imposes significant restrictions on firms. For example, the number of owners (i.e., shareholders) is capped at 75, and each owner must be a U.S. citizen. S-corporation status also restricts certain tax deductions (Ciccotello and Grant, 1999).

Limited-Liability Partnerships and Limited-Liability Companies

More recently, a law firm's organizational options have broadened to include LLPs and LLCs. The authorization of these forms has not been straightforward. In a previous study, we described the significant events in each state and our conclusions about the timing of authorization (Romley and Talley, 2005). As Figure 6.3 illustrates, a large number of states authorized the LLP and LLC forms for law firms during the study period.

The LLP and LLC forms generally combine some of the attractive features of a partnership with those of a corporation. Under both forms, vicarious liability is limited. However, in some instances, an LLP or LLC must carry liability insurance (Ciccotello and Grant, 1999; SBA and Government Contracting Institute, 2000). Furthermore, business income is passed through to the owners. Finally, the LLP and LLC forms are more flexible than the PC and PA forms but perhaps less so than the GP form. For instance, an LLP or LLC may be required to have a finite lifetime, whereas a GP is not (Ciccotello and Grant, 1999).

LLPs and LLCs differ from each other in potentially important respects. Some of these differences favor the LLP. For example, owners of law firms appear to prefer the title "partner" under an LLP to that of "shareholder" under an LLC (Hillman, 2003), and some practitioners reportedly fear that LLCs may eventually face regulation under securities law. On the other hand, owners of an LLP remain vicariously liable for business obligations unrelated to malpractice in some states (SBA and Government

Figure 6.3
States Authorizing LLP and LLC Forms for Law Firms, by Year

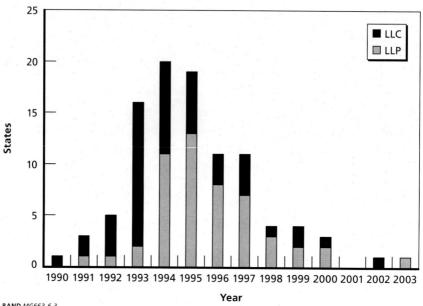

RAND *MG663-6.3*

Contracting Institute, 2000), and the potentially finite lifetime of an LLP may create management challenges (Ciccotello and Grant, 1999).[15]

The LLP and LLC forms may be attractive to partners in an existing GP. Owners will weigh the benefits of reorganizing against the costs. The limitation on vicarious liability is the crucial benefit of these new forms relative to the GP. To the extent that the new forms are less flexible than the GP, GPs would be less likely to reorganize, obscuring the benefit of limited liability to their owners. As to other costs of reorganization, registering as an LLP or LLC is a modest expense that sometimes increases with firm size (Bromberg and Ribstein, 2003). The reordering of relationships among owners may be more problematic (Scott Baker and Krawiec, 2005). We believe that these costs are,

---

[15] In some states, firms owned by one person may organize as LLCs (Ciccotello and Grant, 1999.) Our focus here is on multiowner firms.

if anything, likely to increase with firm size, making smaller firms likelier than larger ones to reorganize, all else being equal. If large firms are likelier than small ones to reorganize, the reason must therefore be that the limited-liability form is especially beneficial for these firms.

We would expect that the new forms are less attractive to PCs and PAs than to companies of other forms. Such firms may incur significant tax liabilities through reorganization (SBA and Government Contracting Institute, 2000). Moreover, in some jurisdictions, the owners of these firms have not been vicariously liable for other owners' malpractice.

Data and Methods

In this section, we first discuss the process used to create the data set and present some descriptive results concerning the organizational structure of the legal-service industry in the 1990s. We then describe our methods for analyzing the relationships among size, reorganization, and growth.

A New Data Set on U.S. Law Firms in the 1990s

Our data set derives from the Martindale-Hubbell® (MH) Law Directory. MH describes its directory as the "most complete, widely used, and trusted source of information on the worldwide legal profession" (Martindale-Hubbell Law Directory, 2003). While appearance in the directory is voluntary, an MH representative has estimated that 80 to 90 percent of law firms are included (Hillman, 2003).

We used computer-readable versions of the fall 1993 and fall 1999 editions of the directory to create the data set. The remainder of this section describes this complex process. Our previous study elaborated on these tasks (Romley and Talley, 2005).

The data set was constructed in four steps. First, each law firm and its offices were identified. Office listings were linked to firms based on firm names. These names typically included the surnames of prominent lawyers and, in many cases, information on the firm's organizational form, e.g., "Professional Corporation" or "P.C." For each law firm, a main or home office was identified. Whenever the directory did not designate the home of a multioffice firm, we designated the office with the most lawyers as the home office.

Our algorithm identified 65,620 firms and 74,966 offices for 1993.[16] In the second step, we identified the number of lawyers at each firm. Each lawyer listing was linked to an office and thus to a firm. For 1993, we were unable to link any lawyers to 4,231 firms. For an additional 852 firms, no owner could be identified on the basis of lawyers' titles.[17] Firms for which we could not identify an owner were excluded from the sample.

The number of lawyers appears to be largely accurate among remaining firms. The number of lawyers at such firms averaged 5.41 in 1993. In comparison, the average was 2.96 in the 1992 Economic Census (U.S. Census Bureau, 1995, 1996).[18] Furthermore, George P. Baker and Rachel Parkin (2006), also using the directory, were able to identify 284,729 lawyers in firms with five or more lawyers in the United States in 1999; we could identify 270,746 such lawyers.[19]

In the third step, we characterized the organizational form of law firms. We relied exclusively on firm names, which typically contained some information about form. Hillman (2003) classified each state's forms of business organizations as LLPs, LLCs, or PCs or PAs based on

---

[16] Our description of the data focuses on 1993 because our analysis focuses on law firms that operated as GPs in 1993.

Matching on firm names mischaracterized some unaffiliated offices as a single firm and some affiliated offices as distinct firms. A crude estimate is that as many as 1,143 firms may have been mischaracterized as distinct firms in 1993. Furthermore, our sample likely excludes some firms operated by lawyers for whom no institutional affiliation was reported. These are likely one-person firms.

[17] The directory identified a lawyer with an ownership interest by the title of "Member" in 1993 and 1999. The number of owners of a firm was obtained by counting the number of lawyers with the title "Member."

[18] This statistic includes sole practitioners, partners, and associate lawyers in establishments with payroll subject to federal income tax. The larger size of firms in our data set is consistent with our exclusion of some sole practitioners and the apparent exclusion by the U.S. Census Bureau of attorneys with an ownership interest in certain firms (e.g., PCs and PAs).

[19] This discrepancy, while not negligible, does not strike us as problematic.

a review of state policies. For example, Arkansas firms were permitted to organize as a professional limited company. This form, which is akin to an LLC, may be abbreviated as PLC. Therefore, Hillman designated an Arkansas firm with PLC in its name as an LLC.[20] We followed this approach. The directory also includes sole proprietorships (SPs), which are law firms owned by a single lawyer. We adopted Hillman's classification of all remaining firms as GPs or SPs according to the apparent ownership of the firm, as inferred from the firm name.[21]

In the final step, we identified firms operating in both 1993 and 1999. We again matched on the basis of firm names and locations. Because a firm could reorganize, names were stripped of information about form prior to matching. If firms matched on name, we further verified that the city and state of an office in 1993 matched those of an office in 1999. This algorithm may have mischaracterized some firms. For example, a law firm in 1993 may fail to match a firm in 1999 due to a merger, spin-off, or other change in ownership that entails a change in name. Firms could also fail to match due to discrepancies in spelling or punctuation across years. To the extent that the failure to match was systematically related to firm size as well as reorganization, our findings could be confounded. We have no reason to believe this is true,

---

[20] Furthermore, a firm was classified as a PC or PA if its form designator did not appear in Hillman's (2003) list of PC or PA designators for its home state, yet the designator always corresponded to a PC or PA elsewhere. For example, a chartered Arkansas firm was classified as a PC/PA.

Based on Bromberg and Ribstein's (2003) review of state regulation of firm names, it appears nearly universal that LLPs must include LLP (or some variant thereof) in their name. We do not know whether this is true of LLCs, PCs, or PAs. In any case, Hillman (2003) suggests that some firms may not include information about their organizational form in their names within the directory. Thus, the number of LLPs, LLCs, PCs, or PAs may be undercounted. We are unaware of any reason that such undercounting would be related to firm size, thus potentially biasing our results.

[21] Hillman (2003) classified any firm with one lawyer or the word "associates" in its name as an SP. For the remaining unclassified firms, those with multiple surnames in their name were classified as GPs. Where Hillman did this by visual inspection, we did this by counting the number of words in the firm name, once any designators for organizational form had been removed. Because GPs can have a single surname in their name, this general approach may undercount GPs.

yet we cannot preclude the possibility. In any case, there was no feasible alternative to our approach.

Organizational Structure of the U.S. Legal-Service Industry, 1993 and 1999

Figure 6.4 illustrates the organizational structure of the U.S. legal-service industry in 1993 and 1999. In 1993, GPs were the leading form, with 40.6 percent of firms. PCs and PAs were next most common, with 32.9 percent. The combined share of LLPs and LLCs was a negligible 0.4 percent. By 1999, the share of PCs and PAs had risen to 47.7 percent, while that of GPs fell to 30.2 percent. The shares of LLPs and LLCs grew to 7.2 percent and 3.7 percent, respectively.

Approximately 40 percent of all law firms and 50 percent of GPs operating in 1993 were matched to a firm in the 1999 directory. A crude estimate is that 61 percent of law firms survived from 1993 to 1999.[22] This estimate suggests that we may have failed to match as many as 20 percent of GPs.

Approximately 17 percent of GPs in 1993 that were matched in 1999 had reorganized as LLPs, LLCs, PCs, or PAs. As Figure 6.5 illustrates, more than half of these reorganizers (10 percent out of 17 percent) became LLPs. Almost 25 percent became LLCs.[23] Among law firms that had reorganized as LLPs or LLCs as of 1999, the vast majority had been GPs in 1993.[24] Figure 6.6 reveals that 96 percent of firms that became LLPs had been GPs. Eighty-seven percent of LLCs had been GPs (see Figure 6.7).

---

[22] Eight percent of law offices (as distinct from firms) "died" from 1995 to 1996 (U.S. Census Bureau, 2006). Applying this rate to the period 1993–1999 implies that almost 40 percent of offices would have died [100%–(100%–8.0%)^6=39.4%]. The rate for offices may be a reasonable approximation of the rate for firms, as 89 percent of firms in our 1993 sample had only one office.

[23] To give a sense of the number of reorganizations, 1,229 of the 11,954 GPs we analyze in the next section became LLPs. Another 314 became LLCs, while 526 became PCs or PAs.

[24] Some have suggested that unlimited liability could economize on the cost of monitoring attorney conduct (Carr and Mathewson, 1990). None of the 262 LLPs or 26 LLCs in 1993 reorganized as a GP as of 1999. To the extent that these firms did not fully account for monitoring costs in deciding to be an LLP or LLC, their failure to reorganize as GPs suggests that monitoring may be of modest importance.

Figure 6.4
Share of Law Firms, by Organizational Form in 1993 and 1999

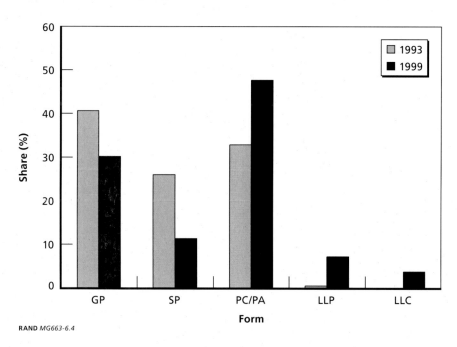

These descriptive findings are consistent with the view that unlimited vicarious liability can be a significant concern for the owners of many GPs. The LLP and LLC forms shield owners from such liability. While it is possible that, in some instances, these forms offer benefits beyond limited liability, the limitation of liability is the crucial difference between these forms and the GP form. Thus, the partners in GPs will reorganize as an LLP or LLC only if their benefits, mainly consisting of limited liability, outweigh the costs of reorganization, potentially including a decrease in organizational flexibility. For the nearly four-fifths of GPs in 1993 that remained GPs through 1999, the benefits of reorganization apparently did not justify the costs.

Analysis of Size and Reorganization Among General Partnerships

We analyzed whether small GPs in 1993 had reorganized as LLPs or LLCs as of 1999 and, moreover, how take-up changed with firm size. A variety of measures of firm size seem intuitive—for example, receipts,

Figure 6.5
Organizational Forms of 1993 General Partnerships in 1999

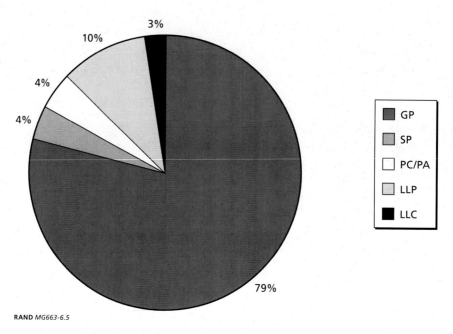

RAND *MG663-6.5*

profits, number of lawyers, and number of owners. However, data on receipts and profits are not widely available. While our account of the value of limited liability centers on the number of owners in a firm, we measured firm size by the number of lawyers for the sake of consistency with existing evidence. The correlation between the numbers of lawyers and owners exceeds 0.90, in any case.

As the preceding subsection explains, our data set tracks the sizes and organizational forms of U.S. law firms between 1993 and 1999.[25] All of our analyses group GPs into size classes according to number of lawyers in 1993. These classes are defined as follows: two to four lawyers, five to nine, 10 to 14, 15 to 24, 25 to 49, and 50 or more.[26]

---

[25] In contrast, Scott Baker and Krawiec (2005) tracked firms based in New York City with 25 or more lawyers. Hillman's (2003) data set on U.S. law firms in 2002 includes firm size only for firms with 50 or more lawyers.

[26] A GP always has more than one lawyer.

Figure 6.6
Organizational Forms of 1999 LLPs in 1993

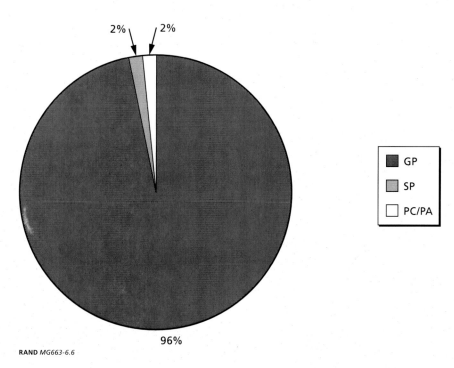

RAND *MG663-6.6*

Under this approach to firm size, the relationship between firm behavior (such as reorganization) and size in different classes is fairly flexible. This flexibility may be valuable. Figure 6.8 shows the share of GPs in 1993 in each size class. Seventy-two percent had two to four lawyers. Ninety-six percent had fewer than 25 lawyers.

Our analysis of the relationship between reorganization and firm size took two approaches. First, we computed the average rate of reorganization observed in our data set for each size class. Under the view that firms reorganize when the benefits of doing so outweigh the costs, we have argued that these rates reveal the extent to which some firms of a particular size benefited from limitations on liability. These rates are not informative, however, about the nature of the benefits.

In our second approach, we assessed whether the benefits from limitations on liability under the new forms flow directly from firm

Figure 6.7
Organizational Forms of 1999 LLCs in 1993

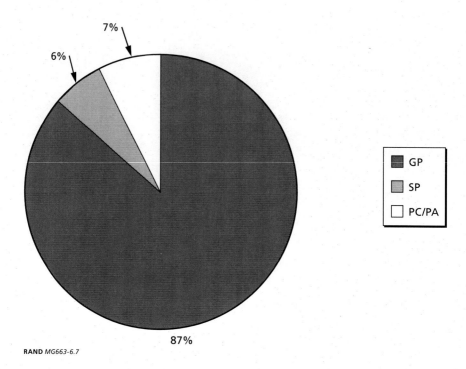

RAND *MG663-6.7*

size. In a previous study, we investigated the optimal size and organizational form of law firms (Romley and Talley, 2005). The model developed for that study predicts that larger firms will adopt a limited-liability form so as to improve their economic position vis-à-vis their clients. The fundamental assumption is that a lawyer's performance is important for legal outcomes (e.g., victory at trial) but is difficult to monitor. Lawyers therefore assure clients of good performance by sharing in the financial reward of good outcomes (such as a favorable judgment at trial) and forfeiting some of their personal wealth in the event of adverse outcomes. Liability for professional misconduct is one means by which lawyers can be punished for poor outcomes. Such incentives must be stronger at large law firms, because each lawyer must share the rewards with more colleagues. Large-firm clients are willing to provide stronger incentives than small-firm clients to the extent that their

Figure 6.8
Share of General Partnerships in 1993, by Size Class

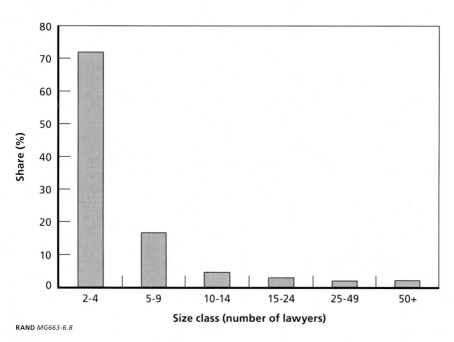

financial stakes in good outcomes are greater. The model predicts, and the real world suggests, that large firms tend to have high-stakes clients. Because lawyers with high-stakes clients have only so much wealth to forfeit as punishment, clients strengthen lawyers' incentives by increasing the reward for good outcomes. Limiting liability lowers available wealth and therefore further strengthens the position of large-firm lawyers.

The rates analyzed under our first approach might confound an assessment of the causal relationship just described, because factors other than size may affect the incentive to reorganize. We therefore specified and estimated a multinomial-logit model that accounted for factors in addition to firm size (McFadden, 1974). Under this model, the probability of the jth outcome for the ith GP was as follows:

$$Pr(i, j) = \frac{\exp\left(u_{i,j}\right)}{\sum_{j'} \exp\left(u_{i,j'}\right)}.$$

(6.1)

A GP in 1993 might remain a GP in 1999, reorganize as an LLP (if permitted), reorganize as an LLC (if permitted), reorganize as a PC or PA, become a SP, or not be matched to any law firm in the 1999 data. For purposes of this analysis, the small proportion of firms that became SPs were grouped with GPs in 1999. Rather than changing their legal form, these firms merely shrank in size. Our benchmark specification thus included GP (or SP), LLP, LLC, and PC/PA as outcomes in 1999. PCs and PAs are included to ease comparisons between the model's predictions and the patterns observed in the directories and existing studies. Unmatched firms were excluded from the analysis for the same reason.[27]

The $u_{i,j}$ terms in Equation 6.1 incorporated the firm-specific factors that determine outcomes. We specified these terms as follows:

$$u_{i,j} = \beta_{j,0} + \sum_{k \neq 1} \beta_{j,1,k} size93_{k,i} + \beta_{j,2} numberofstates93_i$$
$$+ \sum_{k \neq 1} \beta_{j,3,k} home93_{k,i} + \varepsilon_{i,j}.$$

(6.2)

$size93_{k,i}$ is a variable that equals 1 when the ith firm belongs to the kth size class and 0 otherwise. For example, at a GP with six lawyers, $size93_{2,i} = 1$ and $size93_{3,i} = 0$.[28] $numberofstates93_i$ is the number of states in which a firm had an office in 1993. The difficulty or cost of reorganizing may be greater for a GP that operated in multiple states. For example, Illinois was a late adopter of the LLP form, so a national firm operating in Illinois would have had to divest its Illinois operations to become an LLP elsewhere (Hillman, 2003).

---

[27] It is possible that some GPs changed their names as well as reorganized under one of the new forms. Such firms would be unmatched in 1999. We were unable to accommodate this potential problem.

[28] Because Equation 6.2 includes the constant $\beta_{j,0}$, the summation is taken over $k \neq 1$.

Finally, $home93_{k,i}$ is a variable that equals 1 when a firm's home office is located in state k and 0 otherwise. As we discussed in Chapter Two, the various forms (including LLPs and LLCs) differed across states in their particulars. Thus, the jth form may have been more or less attractive than its alternatives in certain states. Consistent with this possibility, Figure 6.9 plots the average rate of reorganization under either of the new limited-liability forms within each state and against the year in which one of the forms was first authorized.[29] The negative relationship between reorganization rates and year of authorization is open to a variety of interpretations. For example, early-adopting states may have created LLP or LLC forms that were especially appealing. Some firms may have opted to reorganize as a PC or PA in late adopting states, then chosen not to reorganize again as an LLP or LLC because of the tax costs. Finally, some firms may have simply waited to reorganize.[30] Unfortunately, these home-state effects could not distinguish among these explanations. In any case, these effects also controlled for the fact that the LLP or LLC form had not been authorized in certain states as of 1999. Our sample here and throughout our analyses excluded GPs based in Kentucky and Nebraska. Neither the LLP nor the LLC form had been authorized in these states as of 1999.

The relationship between any particular factor and an outcome j can be assessed by simulation of predicted outcomes as the factor changes. We describe the results of such simulations in the next section.

Analysis of Size, Reorganization, and Growth

We also analyzed growth among small GPs that did and did not reorganize under the new limited-liability forms. This analysis excluded GPs that reorganized as PCs or PAs. Following Harhoff, Stahl, and Woywode (1998) and Scott Baker and Krawiec (2005), we defined

---

[29] Our versions of the Martindale-Hubbell Law Directory were issued in fall 1993 and fall 1999. We therefore defined *year of authorization* as the first year in which a form was available prior to September 1.

[30] Firm size may also be correlated with $home93_{k,i}$. Equation 6.2 distinguishes these factors.

Figure 6.9
Average Rates of Reorganization of General Partnerships Under New Limited-Liability Forms Within States and by Year of First Authorization

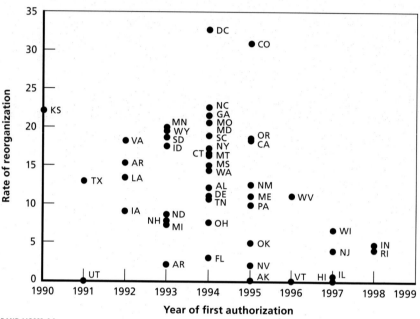

growth as the annualized rate of growth—in particular, in the number of lawyers between 1993 and 1999.[31]

First, we computed the average growth rate observed in our sample for firms that reorganized and those that did not within each size class. Next, the following regression was estimated:

$$Growth_i = \beta_0 + \beta_1 LL99$$
$$+ \sum\nolimits_{k \neq 1} \beta_{2,k} size93_{k,i}$$
$$+ \sum\nolimits_{k \neq 1} \beta_{3,k} LL99 \times size93_{k,i} + \beta_4 \# states93_i$$
$$+ \sum\nolimits_{k \neq 1} \beta_{5,k} home93_{k,i} + \varepsilon_i.$$

$$(6.3)$$

---

[31] Growth is necessarily undefined for GPs in 1993 that were unmatched in 1999.

This regression accounts for size class as before. *LL99* is a variable that equals 1 for a GP that reorganized under one of the new limited-liability forms as of 1999 and 0 otherwise. *LL99* also interacted with each size class. Finally, we again included controls for a firm's home state and number of states with offices in 1993.

As we have discussed, Romley and Talley's (2005) model of law-firm size and organizational form predicts that large firms are likelier to benefit from having limited liability. The model further predicts that, for firms that reorganize under limited-liability organizational forms, relatively small firms should grow, if any firms do. Under unlimited liability, the personal wealth of small-firm lawyers may not have constrained punishment for poor outcomes. If so, these firms must grow after reorganizing to force clients to offer stronger incentives to perform well and provide good outcomes. By growing enough under limited liability, wealth becomes constrained, and clients must turn to increased rewards for good outcomes, leaving a firm's owners better off. On the other hand, larger firms may (but need not) shrink in size, decreasing the necessary reward for good outcomes and thus ensuring that their clients remain willing to pay for good performance.

Under an assumption that reorganizers would have grown at the rate of similarly sized firms that did not reorganize, *growth* is defined as growing faster than this benchmark. Hypotheses about the relationship among size, reorganization, and growth can then be stated in terms of the parameters in Equation 6.3. The interactions between *LL99* and each $size93_{k,i}$ term allowed growth to vary with both reorganization and size class. $\beta_{3,2} > 0$ would mean that reorganizers with five to nine lawyers grew, i.e., grew faster than firms with five to nine lawyers that did not reorganize. Our model would then predict that reorganizers with two to four lawyers must grow, i.e., grow faster than firms with two to four lawyers that did not reorganize, so that $\beta_1 > 0$. The model does not make clear predictions about differences in growth (i.e., differences in differences). For example, it need not be the case that $\beta_1 > \beta_{3,2}$.

We emphasize that alternative accounts of growth are consistent with our theory's predictions, despite our best efforts to control for other factors. For example, two equally sized firms might have differed in their plans for expansion as of 1993. The firm that grew might have decided that having limited liability was now worthwhile. Under this account, obtaining limited liability would be associated with, but not the cause of, growth. Ideally, the business form and size of firms would be regularly observed between 1993 and 1999, but this is not the case.[32] Therefore, we must be cautious in our interpretation of the results about limited liability and growth.

Results

In this section, we present the findings of our analyses. We first discuss the relationship between firm size and reorganization, then look at the relationships among size, reorganization, and growth.

Size and Reorganization Among General Partnerships

The analysis of firm size and reorganization is consistent with the interpretation that small GPs, and particularly the smallest firms, were significantly less likely to benefit from the new forms' liability shields than were large firms.

Average rates of reorganization under the LLP and LLC forms are illustrated in Figure 6.10. GPs of all sizes were likelier to reorganize as LLPs than LLCs. Firms with two to four lawyers in 1993 were unlikely to convert to either form. Just over 3 percent became LLPs, while 1.1 percent became LLCs. Among firms with five to nine lawyers, the rates are 15.3 percent and 4.9 percent for LLPs and LLCs, respectively.

The likelihood of reorganizing increased with size among firms smaller than 25 lawyers, especially for LLPs. The rate of reorganization under the LLP form was 40.6 percent for firms with 15 to 24 lawyers; the rate for the LLC form was 12.4 percent. As Figure 6.8 illustrated,

---

[32] We thank Scott Baker for offering this example.

Figure 6.10
Rate of Reorganization of General Partnerships Under the LLP and LLC Forms, as of 1999, by Number of Lawyers in 1993

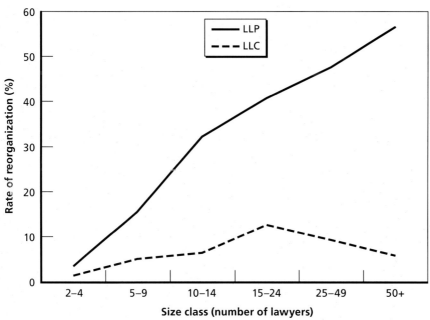

these firms comprised only 3 percent of the sample. GPs with two to four lawyers comprised 72 percent of the sample.

The reorganization rate under the LLP form continued to increase with size, while the rate for LLCs decreased. For firms with 25 to 49 lawyers, these rates were 47.4 percent and 9.1 percent for LLPs and LLCs, respectively, while, for firms with 50 or more lawyers, the rates were 56.4 percent and 5.6 percent. Thus the rate of reorganization under either of the new limited-liability forms increased from 53.0 percent at firms with 15 to 24 lawyers to 56.5 percent at firms with 25 to 49 lawyers to 62.0 percent at firms with 50 or more lawyers.

These rates of reorganization among firms with 25 or more lawyers are roughly similar to those found in previous studies. Scott Baker and Krawiec (2005) found that, in 2003, the shares of LLPs and LLCs among all New York City firms with 25 or more lawyers were 67 percent and 1 percent.[33] Hillman (2003) found that, in summer 2002, 48 percent of all U.S. law firms with 50 or more lawyers were LLPs, and 9 percent were LLCs.

Table 6.2 reports the results for the multinomial-logit model that accounted for factors other than firm size. The estimated parameters on firm size are highly statistically significant.[34] To interpret the impact of firm size, we performed a thought experiment based on these estimates. For each firm, we use the results shown in Tables 4.1 and 4.2 in Chapter Four to predict how the likelihood of reorganizing as an LLP or LLC would have changed if the firm had, in fact, been large enough to belong to the next size class up. We isolated the impact of size by leaving all other firm characteristics unchanged in the thought experiment. To give an example, for a GP operating in Missouri and Illinois with two to four lawyers, we compared the predicted likelihood that the firm would reorganize as an LLP or an LLC, given its actual size, with the predicted likelihood that the firm would have reorganized if

Table 6.2
Results for Multinomial-Logit Model of Organizational Form in 1999

Covariate	Parameter Estimate	Standard Error
LLP		
Constant	−28.186[a]	1.074
5–9 lawyers in 1993	1.878[a]	0.095
10–14 lawyers in 1993	2.978[a]	0.120
15–24 lawyers in 1993	3.642[a]	0.137
25–49 lawyers in 1993	3.822[a]	0.157
50+ lawyers in 1993	4.533[a]	0.166
Number of states in 1993	−0.282[a]	0.0625

---

[33] The denominators in these shares include any new firms or conversions from the PC or PA form. We believe there are few such firms.

[34] Throughout our analyses, we used variance-covariance estimators that were robust to heteroscedasticity of unknown form (Wooldridge, 2002).

Table 6.2—Continued

Covariate	Parameter Estimate	Standard Error
LLC		
Constant	−28.34[a]	1.042
5–9 lawyers in 1993	1.819[a]	0.160
10–14 lawyers in 1993	2.488[a]	0.224
15–24 lawyers in 1993	3.852[a]	0.219
25–49 lawyers in 1993	3.571[a]	0.269
50+ lawyers in 1993	3.587[a]	0.305
Number of states in 1993	−0.340[b]	0.140
PC or PA		
Constant	−2.182[a]	0.753
5–9 lawyers in 1993	0.637[a]	0.122
10–14 lawyers in 1993	1.195[a]	0.187
15–24 lawyers in 1993	1.243[a]	0.238
25–49 lawyers in 1993	1.311[a]	0.295
50+ lawyers in 1993	1.225[a]	0.337
Number of states in 1993	−0.249[c]	0.131
All forms		
Controls for home state in 1993	Yes	
Other statistics		
Observations	11,954	
McFadden's R-squared	0.2464	

NOTE: Sample included GPs in 1993 matched in 1999 and not based in Kentucky or Nebraska in 1993. GP is the excluded category in the analysis. Standard errors are heteroscedasticity-robust.

[a] Statistically significant at the 1-percent level.

[b] Statistically significant at the 5-percent level.

[c] Statistically significant at the 10-percent level.

the firm had instead had five to nine lawyers. We predicted the change in the likelihood of reorganizing for each firm in our sample and averaged the predictions.

Figure 6.11 illustrates the results of this experiment. GPs with two to four lawyers would have been 4.8 percent likelier, on average, to reorganize as an LLP and 1.5 percent likelier to become an LLC if there had instead been five to nine lawyers at these firms. The magnitude of these impacts is large in relation to the actual rates of reorganization among firms with two to four lawyers. The rate of reorganization under *either* of the new forms increased with the number of lawyers for firms of all sizes. While firms with 15 to 24 lawyers would have been slightly less likely to reorganize as an LLC if they were larger, the impact of size on the likelihood of reorganizing as an LLP is larger in magnitude. On balance, these firms would have been likelier to reorganize under

Figure 6.11
Predicted Effect of Increasing Size Class on the Rate of Reorganization, by Number of Lawyers in 1993

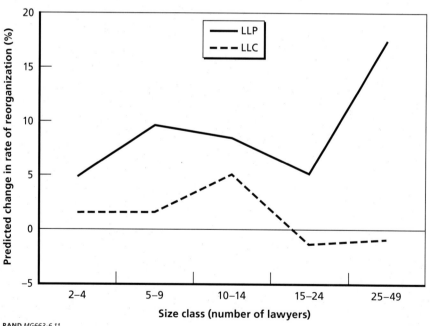

a limited-liability form. A similar observation applies to firms with 25 to 49 lawyers.[35]

These findings for the multinomial-logit analysis are broadly similar to those based on the observed reorganization rates. However, under the multivariate model that distinguishes the effect of firm size from the effects of other factors, the likelihood of reorganization increased much more for firms with 25 to 49 lawyers than for firms with two to four lawyers.[36]

Thus, our findings suggest that reorganization has been modestly beneficial for relatively small law firms. Under our argument that having limited liability is the principal benefit of the LLP and LLC forms as well as our model of reorganization (Romley and Talley, 2005), the results of the multinomial-logit analysis are consistent with the interpretation that large firms strategically exploited limited liability to improve their economic position but that the vast majority of (smaller) firms were unable to do so. While reordering relationships among owners might have been a substantial impediment to reorganization, our view is that this cost is likely to increase with firm size, making large firms less likely to reorganize.

Size, Reorganization, and Growth

Our analysis of size, reorganization, and growth supports the interpretation that small GPs that reorganized under one of the new limited-liability forms benefited. Large firms also benefited.

Figure 6.12 illustrates the annual growth rate of GPs according to their reorganization under a new limited-liability form as of 1999 and

---

[35] Simulation of predicted outcomes also revealed that firms with offices in more states were less likely than other firms to reorganize under any form. The number of states averaged 1.07 in 1993, with a standard deviation of 0.39.

[36] The parameter estimates of the number of states in which a firm operated in 1993 imply that the probability of reorganizing as an LLP, LLC, PC, or PA relative to remaining a GP decreased with the number of states. As we noted in Chapter Two, the LLP and LLC forms were not available in every state between 1993 and 1999. A firm that operated in multiple states might therefore have to restructure to avail itself of the LLP or LLC forms where permitted. The finding with respect to these forms is consistent with this observation.

Figure 6.12
Growth, by Reorganization Under New Limited-Liability Form as of 1999
and Size Class in 1993

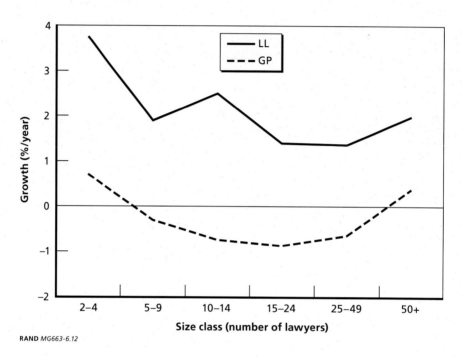

number of lawyers in 1993.[37] The figure shows that, for firms with 50 or more lawyers, reorganizers grew, i.e., grew 1.5 percent faster per year in the number of lawyers than firms with 50 or more lawyers that did not reorganize. Our model then predicts that smaller reorganizers grew faster than firms of the same size that did not reorganize. For firms with two to four lawyers, the growth gap is almost 3 percent. Growth rates tended to decrease with size among small firms. Firms with 25 to 49 lawyers grew about as fast as those with 15 to 24 lawyers.

Table 6.3 presents the results of the regression that accounted for factors other than reorganization and size. The results are illustrated in Figure 6.13 for firms based in New York. The relationships among size,

---

[37] This analysis excluded the small proportion of firms that reorganized under the PC and PA forms.

Table 6.3
Results for OLS Regression of Growth

Covariate	Parameter Estimate	Standard Error
Constant	1.214	0.871
Limited liability in 1999	3.154[a]	0.342
5–9 lawyers in 1993	−1.025[a]	0.189
5–9 lawyers in 1993[b], limited liability in 1999	−0.847[b]	0.509
10–14 lawyers in 1993	−1.474[a]	0.418
10–14 lawyers in 1993[b], limited liability in 1999	0.121	0.640
15–24 lawyers in 1993	−1.682[a]	0.640
15–24 lawyers in 1993[b], limited liability in 1999	−0.765	0.822
25–49 lawyers in 1993	−1.431[b]	0.868
25–49 lawyers in 1993[b], limited liability in 1999	−1.011	1.006
50+ lawyers in 1993	−0.309	0.853
50+ lawyers in 1993[b], limited liability in 1999	−1.381	0.976
States in 1993	−0.190	0.163
Controls for home state in 1993	Yes	
Other statistics		
Observations	11,428	
R-squared	0.0279	

NOTE: Sample included 1993 GPs operating as GPs, LLPs, or LLCs in 1999 and not based in Kentucky or Nebraska in 1993. Standard errors are heteroscedasticity-robust.

[a] Statistically significant at the 1-percent level.

[b] Statistically significant at the 10-percent level.

Figure 6.13
Predicted Growth of New York Firms, by Reorganization Under New Limited-Liability Form as of 1999 and Size Class in 1993

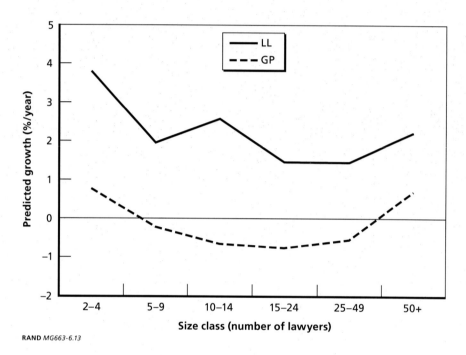

reorganization, and growth in other states parallels those in New York, because home state shifted the intercept of the growth regression.

As with the preceding analysis of firm size and reorganization, the results are similar under the two approaches. Firms that reorganized grew more than those that did not. This gap narrowed with size; the difference for the smallest firms is statistically significantly larger than that for the largest firms. Under further assumptions, this finding is consistent with Romley and Talley's (2005) theoretical prediction that smaller reorganizers should grow faster than larger ones.[38] The gap for the largest firms is nonetheless positive at standard levels of statistical significance.

---

[38] Romley and Talley (2005) did not model the dynamics of firm growth. One would have to assume that firms that reorganized would have grown at the same rate as firms that did not (on average, and conditional on size) had the former firms not opted to reorganize.

This evidence is open to the alternative interpretation that better-managed firms were likelier both to reorganize and to grow. Under this view, reorganization is an effect of growth rather than a cause. Similarly, it is possible that firms grew for reasons unrelated to limited liability, then opted to reorganize.

Conclusion

This study has investigated whether the owners of relatively small law firms have benefited from limited liability under the LLP and LLC forms. Our research strategy rested on two assumptions. First, we postulated that a GP reorganizes as an LLP or LLC if and only if the benefits of those forms, particularly their liability shields, outweigh their costs, particularly the costs of reorganization. Take-up by small, multiowner GPs would then indicate that these firms benefit. Second, we postulated that growth subsequent to reorganization is a further indicator of benefits.

We therefore analyzed the relationship between firm size and the reorganization and growth of GPs under the new forms. Using a new data set on the number of lawyers and organizational form of U.S. firms during the 1990s, we found that smaller firms were much less likely than larger ones to reorganize. Indeed, while 62 percent of GPs with 50 or more lawyers reorganized as an LLP or LLC between 1993 and 1999, only 4.3 percent of GPs with two to four lawyers did so. We also found that, comparing GPs with similar numbers of lawyers in 1993, firms in each size class grew faster than those that did not.

One may wonder why so few small firms reorganized, if having limited liability causes growth among small law firms and growth is good. One explanation is that some other factor causes both reorganization and growth. In Romley and Talley's model (2005), firms with high-stakes clients can improve their bargaining position by reorganizing under a limited-liability form, yet small reorganizers may have to grow to do so. The model predicts, and the real world suggests, that larger firms tend to have high-stakes clients. Thus, while our data and analysis are subject to limitations, our empirical findings suggest that having limited liability is modestly beneficial to the owners of small law firms organized as GPs.

Whether the new forms have served their purpose is unclear. Some advocates asserted their likely benefits to small firms. If our findings are disappointing, policy might target the benefits of limited liability to firms below some size threshold. The LLP and LLC forms are presently available to law firms of any size. Indeed, if smaller and larger firms compete, these forms might favor large firms by lowering their costs relative to small firms (Ribstein, 2001). In other contexts, policymakers have imposed maximum size limits on policies intended to help small businesses and minimum size thresholds (i.e., small-business exemptions) on policies that impose costs on firms (Keefe, Gates, and Talley, 2005).

More generally, the impact of limiting liability on consumers of legal services is an important policy issue. The generalizability of this study's findings to other professional services also merits further investigation.

CHAPTER SEVEN

Data Resources for Policy Research on Small Businesses

Amelia Haviland and Bogdan Savych

Historically, data collected on U.S. businesses have focused almost exclusively on large firms (typically those with at least 250 employees). As a result, researchers interested in small businesses and entrepreneurship have been strongly constrained in their ability to carry out empirical, policy-related research. Ongoing concerns about the lack and quality of data on small firms led to a conference on data sources related to entrepreneurship (the Kauffman Symposium on Entrepreneurship Data, November 10–11, 2004) and to the creation of a National Academy of Sciences panel on federal business statistics, which issued its final report in 2007 (Haltiwanger, Lynch, and Mackie, 2007). Such efforts have been part of a recent trend to increase the number, quality, and richness of data sources on small firms. While data sources continue to improve, information on the uses, availability, and limitations of these sources is scattered among the multitude of governmental and private organizations that collect and own the data.

Policy-relevant research on small businesses is typically concerned with questions of how a particular policy has influenced or will influence small firms. It is thus concerned with changes in outcomes for small businesses over time, as well as with comparisons between small and larger businesses. As a result, data relevant for small-business research are typically data that are relevant for research on businesses more generally, with the added requirement of the availability of information on the size of the businesses.

Empirical research on small businesses and entrepreneurship must begin with a definition of what constitutes a small business. The simplest definition, and the one most frequently used by the SBA, is a firm with fewer than 500 employees.[1] However, policymakers at the federal, state, and local levels use a wide variety of approaches to define a small business, either to include businesses in special support programs or to exempt them from specific regulations. These definitions may be based on a variety of firm characteristics and often depend on the specific nature of the policy or regulatory issue under consideration. For example, for the purposes of employment and HI regulations, size is typically defined in terms of the number of employees in the firm. On the other hand, economic regulation often classifies small businesses based on market capitalization or organizational form.

Assessing Data Set Value

Once the proper definition of *small business* has been identified, researchers must assess the extent to which available data allow for the measurement of firm size and other outcomes of interest in a way that is faithful to that definition. If a necessary data set does not yet exist, researchers may instead need to carry out their own data collection using an appropriate sampling frame of firms or establishments. Ideally, this sampling frame would provide enough information to identify units of interest without screening. In assessing the value of a particular data set, researchers need to consider several issues: available firm-size measure (establishment or firm), source of data (employee or firm), access to data, data quality, and the ability to link data longitudinally.

Available Size Measures
In addition to different measures of size, researchers may be interested in the sizes of different business units: establishments or firms. From

---

[1]   The definition of what constitutes a small business differs among industries. The SBA provides a complete list of small-business size standards matched to the NAICS. The size standard is expressed in average annual receipts, average number of employees, or, sometimes, in physical volume of output. For more information, see SBA (undated[a]).

a policy perspective, the relevant unit of analysis for small-business issues is typically the firm. However, many existing data sets collect data at the level of establishment or worksite. An establishment is an economic unit that produces goods or provides services, such as a factory, store, or mine. Usually, it is a single physical location engaged in predominantly one economic activity (see BLS, 1997). Although it is common for researchers to use establishment-level data to study small-business issues, it is crucial to recognize the differences between firms and establishments. At one extreme, a firm may be comprised of a single establishment that is the same size as the firm. At the other extreme, a firm of 1,000 employees may be comprised of 1,000 establishments with one employee each. As illustrated in the work of Mendeloff et al. (2006), described in Chapter Four, firm size and establishment size can have different relationships to outcomes of interest. Researchers must take care to clearly understand the unit of analysis of data and how well matched it is to the definition of *small business*.

Source of Data: Employer or Firm

Data on a workplace can be obtained either from the employees or from the employer or firm. Each source of information has advantages and disadvantages, and these will vary depending on the specific policy question under consideration.

Access to Data

Researchers are concerned about ease of access to data. If data are publicly available, is there a fee associated with this access? If they are not publicly available, how long and involved is the process for accessing these data? If the data set is not publicly available, researchers may use aggregated tables created from the data. Most agencies provide tables that are aggregated by geography or industry.

Data Quality

How reliable and accurate are the data? If data are based on a survey, what are the sampling frame and the response rate to the survey? If data are based on administrative records, how complete and reliable is the recording process?

Ability to Link Data Longitudinally

Studies of small businesses are often concerned with questions of entry and exit, as well as firm growth, prompting the question, did a particular policy force small firms out of the market or impede their growth relative to that of larger firms? To study these issues, it is crucial for researchers to be able to link data over time to identify when new firms enter the data and when firms leave the data and to determine the growth trajectory of firms. A key consideration is therefore whether it is possible to link data longitudinally and, if so, for how long.

This chapter briefly describes the main government and private data sources currently available or under construction that could be used for research on small businesses and entrepreneurship. It provides a general overview of the data sets, how they have been used to address small-business issues, and a discussion of how they might be used. Individuals interested in more detail about one or more of these data sets are referred to Haviland and Savych (2005). That paper provides detailed information on each data set, including the collection method, coverage, main variables and limitations, and data uses.

This chapter is organized into five sections. The first three sections discuss government data sources: BLS, the U.S. Census Bureau, and other government sources. The fourth section describes private data sources. The final section concludes.

U.S. Bureau of Labor Statistics Data Sources

A multitude of government agencies collects information relevant to small-business research. This section focuses on several data sets created by BLS. BLS is the principal federal agency that collects data in the field of labor economics and statistics. BLS's mission is to collect, process, analyze, and disseminate "essential statistical data to the American public, the U.S. Congress, other Federal agencies, State and local governments, business, and labor" (BLS, 2001). Its goal is to provide timely, consistent, and high-quality data on a range of issues including employment, wages, and workers' benefits.

To achieve its mission, BLS maintains several data sets. Those include the Quarterly Census of Employment and Wages (QCEW), Business Employment Dynamics (BED), Current Employment Statistics (CES), and National Compensation Survey (NCS). The QCEW and BED data are closely related. QCEW is a comprehensive set of data on establishment-level employment and payroll information derived from administrative records. The BED data link QCEW data at the establishment level over time to create longitudinal histories. Although the data in QCEW and BED reflect establishment-level information, researchers have used the employer identification number (EIN) to aggregate information to the firm level. The CES and NCS data are based on establishment-level, BLS-conducted surveys on employment, employee characteristics, hours, benefits, earnings, and organizational characteristics. These surveys supplement the employment and payroll information available through QCEW and BED. Because they reflect a sample rather than the universe of establishments, there is no way to aggregate the data to the firm level. However, with full data access, it should be possible to link the records from these surveys to QCEW data, and then one could control for firm size in examining the establishment-level data. A key limitation of all four of these data sets is that they are not publicly available. Researchers interested in using these data must submit an application to BLS, and restrictions may be imposed on the analytical outputs. These data can provide a cross-sectional and dynamic picture of local labor markets and employment patterns. BED in particular can be used to study within-establishment changes over time and across location, job creation, job destruction, and changes in establishment and firm sizes over time.

BLS also cooperates with the U.S. Census Bureau to collect data for the Current Population Survey (CPS), a household-level survey. The survey gathers demographic and labor-market information, as well as information on a variety of specific topics such as education, HI, and pensions. Because it is a household-level survey, it captures information on self-employed individuals; however, firm-level information is extremely limited. Households are surveyed several times over the course of two years; thus, it is possible to create a short longitudinal series for individuals. Among other things, this allows researchers to identify new business owners. The coverage of the CPS makes it a particularly useful tool for the analysis of the self-employed and new entrepreneurs. Unlike the other data sources described in this section from BLS, CPS data are publicly available.

Quarterly Census of Employment and Wages

QCEW provides cross-sections of administrative data for a limited number of variables covering nearly the entire the universe of establishments. So far, there is little research using cross-sections from QCEW. Access to data is a major constrain that researchers face in using the full records. Assuming that a researcher has obtained access to the data, the records collected through the QCEW program can be used in a number of situations. These confidential records include the address of the business, which can be used to compare regional policies or compare effects of the policies in the affected and unaffected regions, counties, ZIP codes, or other geographic areas. Modern mapping software may provide a way to aggregate available data to some geographic area, as described in Konigsberg, Talan, and Clayton (2005). In addition, BLS links these cross-sectional records to produce a longitudinal database of establishments. Researchers can gain access to a longitudinal data set of establishments and firms through the BED program discussed below. The Census Bureau also draws upon these data to supplement various multilevel business databases. In addition, this database can be used as a sampling frame for further surveys and to produce denominators for other research, if access issues are resolved.

Some researchers may also take advantage of the aggregated tables that are publicly available. These tables can be used to examine effects of the state-level policies on the distribution of the establishments, by establishment-size category. Unfortunately, these tables are not provided at the firm level, and there is no information about entrance or exit from the market.

Business Employment Dynamics

Data from the BED program can help provide a dynamic picture of local labor markets. It is an important new database that includes the universe of longitudinal establishment data. As such, these data make it possible to study within-establishment changes over time and across locations. For example, Faberman (2001, 2002, 2004) used these data to study different aspects of job creation and job destruction, job flows, and labor dynamics. In addition, these data can be used to answer basic questions about changes in establishment and firm sizes over time. For instance, it is possible to study growth in firms and establishments by employment-size categories recorded at different points in the year. This information is currently unavailable and could change inferences based solely on March employment or average annual employment. These changes can be connected to various state-, county-, or even city-level policies, so that researchers can use geographic variation in polices over time to examine their effects.

Researchers can also use aggregated tables that provide statistics derived from BED microdata. These series provide information about gross job gains and losses, expansions and contractions, and job openings and closings by establishment-size categories. This information is publicly available aggregated to the state level. These records are provided at both firm and establishment levels. For a detailed description of how these statistics were developed, see Butani et al. (2006).

Current Employment Statistics

To date, most of the work that used CES did not consider issues relating to firm size. Also, most of the research has relied on the publicly available national-level data not stratified by establishment size. These studies have often been concerned with employment and wage trends in selected industries (see, for example, Krantz, 2002; Hatch, 2004; Strople, 2006). Other studies have also been concerned with the trends in hours of work (Kirkland, 2000; Hetrick, 2000; Kropf and Getz, 1999). None of these studies, however, considers these issues from the point of view of small businesses.

If researchers obtain access to the full CES, they can use the information to examine a variety of policy-relevant issues. Even though CES is based on a survey sample rather than on administrative records, it provides information that is not available in QCEW and that could be important for tracking economic development. In particular, CES provides information on reasons for changes in the number of employees, the number of women, and the number of production workers. Some researchers may use CES to examine effects of various policies on the development of the firms. For example, these data allow researchers to examine whether firms react to policies by increasing the hours that current employees work or by hiring additional workers.

National Compensation Survey

NCS data have been used to examine factors that determine low-wage labor (Bernstein and Gittleman, 2003), incidents of provision of health benefits (Barsky, 2004), and trends in employer-provided prescription-drug coverage (Dietz, 2004). Each of these topics could be addressed by establishment-level employment-size categories. With these data, it would also be possible to evaluate the relationship between employer-provided health benefits and establishment or worker characteristics by establishment size.

Current Population Survey

CPS's overall advantages are large sample sizes, long time series, quick access to timely data, a very large built-in comparison group of non-entrepreneurs, and a wide range of topics in the supplements. CPS's coverage makes it an important tool for the analysis of the self-employed and new entrepreneurs. Several papers use CPS to analyze issues that are relevant for small businesses. For example, Berger et al. (1999) used March 1999 CPS data to examine the distribution of low-wage workers by firm employment-size categories and investigate effects of the minimum wage. Labor economists have used CPS extensively to analyze the relationship between a firm's employment size and wages (see Idson and Feaster, 1990; Mellow, 1982; Bowlus, Kiefer, and Neumann, 1995; Pearce, 1990; Card, 1996; Charles Brown and Medoff, 1989; Antos, 1983; Hirsch and Schumacher, 1998; Weiss and Landau, 1984; Evans and Leighton, 1989). Other studies have included analyses of the prevalence of formal on-the-job training (Loewenstein and Spletzer, 1997); factors that explain differences in turnover between large and small firms (Even and Macpherson, 1996); effects of having HI on hours worked (Cutler and Madrian, 1998; Gruber and Poterba, 1994); effects of employment protection (Oyer and Schaefer, 2002); earnings broken down by racial or ethnic characteristics (Agesa, Agesa, and Hoover, 2001; Carrington, McCue, and Pierce, 2000; Trejo, 1997); patterns of entrepreneurship (Evans and Leighton, 1989); gender differences in earnings (Sorensen, 1990; Macpherson and Hirsch, 1995); evidence of labor-market cycles for the self-employed (Carrington, McCue, and Pierce, 1996); transitions among full-time and part-time employment and retirement (Peracchi and Welch, 1994); WC (Hirsch, Macpherson, and DuMond, 1997); patterns of self-employment among older U.S. workers (Karoly and Zissimopoulos, 2003); and access to computers and the decision to become self-employed (Fairlie, 2005).

CPS can be used to support further studies of self-employment and entrepreneurship, including patterns of HI coverage, human capital, and education among the self-employed. CPS can also be used to examine patterns of self-employment and entrepreneurship among recent immigrants or other demographic groups of interest.

U.S. Census Bureau Data Sources

The Census Bureau is the leading source of quality data about the nation's people and economy. In addition to the widely known decennial population census, the Census Bureau collects and maintains data sets that provide information on businesses. These include the Business Register (BR), Business Information Tracking System (BITS), Characteristics of Business Owners (CBO) survey, Integrated Longitudinal Business Database (ILBD), Economic Census (EC), Company Organization Survey (COS), Survey of Women-Owned Business Enterprises (SWOBE), Survey of Minority-Owned Business Enterprises (SMOBE), and Survey of Business Owners (SBO). These data sources vary in terms of how comprehensive they are, how often they are updated, and whether it is possible to create longitudinal series on the basis of these data.

BR provides a comprehensive roster of each known establishment and company. It covers both employer and nonemployer businesses. The data set draws its information from administrative records (e.g., IRS and SSA records) and surveys (e.g., EC and COS). The detailed, cross-sectional data are available for each year since 1975. BR contains information on establishment and firm employment, payroll, revenues, full address, firm affiliation, and industry classification.

CBP aggregates BR data to the level of county for establishments with paid employees. Some industries that are represented in the BR data are excluded from the CBP roll-up. In particular, the coverage excludes some agricultural industries; railroads; postal service; private households; large pension, health, and welfare funds; and public administration. Yearly tables are provided for data from 1964 to the present. The CBP tables are often used to derive denominators for employment as well as the number of establishments in a particular establishment-size category by county.

Two longitudinal databases based on the BR data are available. These longitudinal data sets are particularly useful to researchers who want to study the emergence and dynamics of small businesses because they allow for an examination of entry, exit, and gross job flows by establishment or firm employment size. The Longitudinal Business Database (LBD) is created by linking information on all establishments included in BR across years. BITS links information longitudinally for those establishments included in the annual CBP data. There are several key differences between LBD and BITS. First, BITS has more restrictive coverage of industries, since it uses the same coverage as CBP. In addition, LBD has longer panels. While BITS goes back only until 1988, LBD links establishments back to 1976. On the other hand, BITS currently includes both firm and establishment data, while both levels of data are not yet available for LBD.

Two census-survey efforts feed into the underlying BR data: COS and EC. These surveys are used to gather up-to-date company affiliation, location, and operating information for establishments that are part of multi-establishment companies in BR. Such information may be relevant for researchers interested in special topics. COS surveys all multiple-unit firms with more than 250 employees every year and smaller multiple-unit firms on a rotating basis. EC covers all establishments of multi-unit companies, all single-unit employers larger than the industry size cut-off (usually three employees), and a sample of smaller single-unit employers. It gathers data on revenue, payroll, address, and ownership type, as well as other sector- and industry-specific information.

Three related surveys, the samples of which are drawn from the BR data frame, are SMOBE, SWOBE, and SBO. These surveys supplement BR and related databases with more detailed information on business owners. These data can be linked with firm-size information from BR to compare characteristics of owners of small versus large businesses and to understand how these surveys cover key features of business operations for large and small businesses.

Current efforts in the Census Bureau are directed at developing integrated databases that include employer and employee characteristics by extending LBD along two dimensions. These data have great potential for studying dynamic changes in establishments and firms and connecting these to owner and worker characteristics. The first extension integrates nonemployer data, making it possible to track transitions to and from employer to nonemployer status.[2] The data set including both employee and nonemployee businesses is called ILBD. The second extension is to include information from the Longitudinal Employer-Household Dynamics (LEHD) files, which provide person and business identifiers for all workers and businesses covered by UI in 30 states. The person identifiers can then be used to match workers to information in other person-level census products, such as the Survey of Income and Program Participation (SIPP) or the long-form census.

A major limitation of all these data sources is that they are not publicly available. In most cases, researchers can apply for access to the microdata at the Census Research Data Centers.[3] The Census Bureau publishes tables based on the underlying data, and, in many cases, researchers can request that the Census Bureau produce additional tables summarizing information on specific variables of interest. Researchers can combine many of these sources to provide more detailed information about the small-business universe. Next, we sum-

---

[2]   In 2002, there were approximately 16 million nonemployer businesses. Approximately 14 million do not have EINs but are uniquely identified by the owner's social security number, and the other 2 million have EINs (Davis et al., 2006).

[3]   For a detailed description, see U.S. Census Bureau (undated[a]).

marize the way in which each of these resources could be or have been used.

Standard Statistical Establishment Listing or Business Register

BR provides underlying records that form a number of statistical databases within the Census Bureau. For example, LBD and BITS connect some of the records from BR over time to create longitudinal databases of establishments. In addition, BR serves as a sampling frame for a number of surveys conducted by the federal government.

Longitudinal Business Database

LBD is useful to researchers who want to examine entry, exit, and gross job flows by establishment or firm employment size. The data allow researchers to study changes over a long period within establishments. In the past, the data set was used to examine entry and exit of firms in specific industries (Jarmin, Klimek, and Miranda, 2004) and establishment and employment dynamics (Foster, 2003). This data set can be connected to other Census Bureau products.

County Business Patterns

The CBP data set is a standard reference source of local economic data. The CBP tables are often used to derive denominators for employment and number of establishments in a particular establishment-size category (numerator data typically come from other sources). These tabulations can be used to examine effects of state- and county-level policies on establishments of varying sizes and in different industries.

Business Information Tracking System

Using this longitudinal database, it is possible to identify establishment births, deaths, expansions, and contractions. Most census products can be connected to each other using an EIN or permanent plant number (PPN). Therefore, a researcher could use information from the other census products to identify a type or category of establishments and from BITS to track those establishments over time. Several studies used BITS data to examine issues that may be important for small businesses. The data were used to examine the persistence of new jobs

(Armington and Acs, 2004); job-flow dynamics (Acs and Armington, 1999; Armington and Acs, 2004); survival of firms in various industries, including start-ups (Headd, 2001; Boden, 2000a, 2000b); and mergers and acquisitions (White, 2002; Armington and Robb, 1998).

Economic Census and Company Organization Survey

As we have stated, EC and COS serve as two of the main surveys that add data to BR. The type-of-ownership and organizational-form data could be compared across firms of different size using employment, payroll, and revenue-based size definitions. In addition, researchers can make use of the detailed industry information collected in EC. For example, Garicano and Hubbard (2005a, 2005b, 2005c) used data from the 1992 Census of Service Industries (U.S. Census Bureau, 1995) to study specialization within and among law firms.

Surveys of Women- and Minority-Owned Business Enterprises, Characteristics of Business Owners, and Survey of Business Owners

These data sources provide a rich and unique set of information on the characteristics of small- and large-business owners and their sources of financing. The researchers often use confidential records from the CBO survey to study factors that affect entrepreneurship. For example, Fairlie and Robb (2005a, 2005b) used the 1992 CBO survey to examine how family and human-capital factors affect sales, profits, employment size, and survival probabilities of minority-owned businesses. Holmes and Schmitz (1992) used the 1982 CBO survey to examine how the failure and sale of a small business depends on the characteristics of its managers. Bates (1995) used the 1987 CBO survey to examine the effect of state and local government managerial, technical, and procurement assistance on the survival of small businesses.

One of the benefits of this survey is that it can be connected to the other census products that have longitudinal information on employment and revenues. Using the 2002 SBO, one can also examine characteristics of firms that have federal and local public agencies as their main consumers.

Integrated Longitudinal Business Database and Longitudinal Employer-Household Dynamics

This data set has great potential for studying dynamic changes in establishments and firms and connecting these to owner and worker characteristics. The data set includes more data elements than found in business owner surveys and covers an important part of the small-business universe, such as nonemployer businesses. Current research is using LEHD to study the impacts of new technologies on firms and workers (Abowd et al., 2001); to measure the relationships between human capital and a firm's technology (Abowd et al., 2002); and to examine the relationship between employer provided HI, worker mobility, and wages (Stinson, 2003). The data are also used in the recent book *Economic Turbulence* (Brown, Haltiwanger, and Lane, 2006), which examines the impact of economic volatility on workers and businesses. For other papers that have used LEHD, see U.S. Census Bureau (2007a).

Other Government Sources of Data

The census and BLS data described in the previous sections of this monograph have distinct strengths and weaknesses. Because the data are derived from administrative records or compulsory surveys, they are extremely comprehensive and gathered in a relatively consistent way over time. As a result, they are useful for providing a cross-sectional overview of business characteristics, making comparisons among businesses of different sizes, and for examining changes in such characteristics over time. Researchers have some ability to link records over time and use these data to study firm dynamics, entry, and exit. However, the fact that most of these data are derived from administrative records also means that the type of information available is limited to fairly basic characteristics. Several government efforts survey firms to gather more detailed information on specific topics. We describe these efforts in this section.

The survey efforts described in this chapter address business finance, HI, and medical expenditures. They provide detailed information from a random sample of businesses, including small businesses.

As such, the data can support research on specific topics that compares large and small businesses. In general, the data are available to researchers, though researchers may be required to submit a proposal and pay a fee to use the data. Survey response rates can be quite low, and data are not always collected on a regular or continuing basis. This may compromise the generalizability of any research results and limit the ability to engage in longitudinal analysis.

Survey of Small Business Finances

In addition to these census and BLS sources of data, the Federal Reserve Board sponsors a survey of small firms. The Survey of Small Business Finances (SSBF) was conducted in 1987, 1993, 1998, and 2003. SSBF contains information from more than 3,500 firms with fewer than 500 employees. It oversampled African-American–, Asian-American–, and Hispanic-American–owned firms. The sampling frame for SSBF is the DUNS® Market Identifier (DMI) file,[4] which is described below. Unlike most of the government data sources described here, full public data sets for each of the first three years of SSBF are available from the Federal Reserve. This survey appears to have been well designed, and the sampling plan and implementation are well documented.

Researchers have used this survey to examine financial constraints that firms face (Lel and Udell, 2002; Robb, 2002); adoption of computers (Bitler, 2001); use of financial services (Bitler, Robb, and Wolken, 2001); borrowing experience by gender, race, and ethnicity of firm owners (Coleman, 2002a, 2002b, 2003); and the decision to become a public firm (Helwege and Packer, 2003). For a description of some studies that have used SSBF, see Federal Reserve Board (2006).

National Employer Health Insurance Survey

Some federal agencies collect data related to the provision of HI. For instance, in 1994, the Centers for Disease Control and Prevention (CDC) conducted the National Employer Health Insurance Survey (NEHIS). The survey was designed to produce estimates on employer-sponsored HI data in the United States for establishments of different

---

4   DUNS® is a registered trademark of Dun and Bradstreet.

sizes (see CDC, 2007b). It served as a precursor to the insurance component of the Medical Expenditures Panel Study (MEPS), described below.

Due to confidentiality restrictions, this survey is available to researchers only though the National Center for Health Statistics Research Data Center (RDC) (see CDC, 2007a). Prospective researchers must submit research proposals to RDC. In addition, there are costs associated with working in the center ($500 per month for remote access and $1,000 per week of on-site access).

Medical Expenditures Panel Survey

MEPS, conducted by the Agency for Healthcare Research and Quality (AHRQ), also contains information on the HI offerings of businesses of different employment sizes. MEPS includes four components that provide an important overview of access to HI and care. It includes a household component (HC), nursing-home component (NHC), medical-provider component (MPC), and insurance component (IC). HC and IC provide some information valuable to small-business researchers. MEPS collects data on health services used by Americans, frequency of use, cost of services, and method of payment. In addition, data are collected on the cost, scope, and breadth of private HI held by and available to the U.S. population (see HHS, undated). Yearly surveys have been conducted since 1996.

Several studies have used MEPS. For example, Gresenz, Rogowski, and Escarce (2005) used the data to study access to care among the uninsured. This data set can also be used to study characteristics of firms that provide HI coverage for workers. For example, Zawacki and Taylor (2005) used MEPS-IC to examine characteristics of establishments that paid 100 percent of HI premiums for their workers. In addition, the data set can be used to study workers' responses to different types of insurance provided by a firm (e.g., the selection of workers into different firms based on HI coverage, compensation for workers who secure HI from other sources). Some of the component data sets allow for analysis of the self-employed, costs of providing insurance for small firms, and the impact of changes in federal and state health-care policies. Within the Census Bureau RDCs, the MEPS data can be matched to the records obtained from EC. For discussion of linking algorithms and possible issues that arise, see McCue and Zawacki (2005).

Private and Commercially Available Data Sources

Although government administrative data sets and surveys provide a wealth of information on small businesses, there are two important reasons for also considering private data sources. The first reason is that few of the government data sources, longitudinal data sources, or potential data frames of all businesses are publicly available. The second reason is that, as with all data sources, the information collected by government sources typically seeks to address a particular question or mandate and may not include the information necessary to address other timely policy questions on particular populations of interest.

The private data sources described here are publicly available but may carry considerable cost. In addition, the needs of researchers may not have been the primary concern for those collecting the data. Thus, these sources can raise a variety of other data issues such as coverage, representation, and for survey sample sources, response rates.

DUNS Market Identifier

The private data source most widely used by both government and private organizations for research on small businesses is Dun and Bradstreet's (D&B's) list of U.S. businesses, the DMI file. While the Census Bureau and BLS use separate master files of U.S. businesses as sampling frames for their own surveys, they do not make these lists available to other government agencies or private organizations due to confidentiality concerns. For these agencies and organizations, DMI is currently the most complete listing of businesses from which to draw a potentially nationally representative probability sample.

DMI includes measures of firm and establishment employment (*employment* includes owners or unpaid family members who are workers, which differs from the definition used by government data sources) and annual sales. In addition, the listing provides detailed location data: telephone number, location, and owner name. Data are also collected for owner minority status, industrial classification, firm's start year, and legal status.

The data are most commonly used as a sampling frame for new surveys of firms. DMI data are available for purchase from D&B, which makes the listing more accessible than other sources.

Kauffman Firm Survey

The Kauffman Firm Survey (KFS) is a new survey commissioned by the Ewing Marion Kauffman Foundation to provide publicly available longitudinal data on new firms. Researchers currently have completed two rounds of pilot data collection and the first full panel. Data from the baseline survey are not available as of this writing. The goal of KFS is to longitudinally track new firms with an emphasis on financial-development, high-technology, and women-owned firms. Two cohorts of new firms will each be followed for multiple years. The first cohort of approximately 5,000 firms, new in 2004, will be followed for three additional years and the second panel of 5,000 firms, new in 2006, for one additional year. KFS is using listings from DMI with a 2004 start year as the sampling frame for the first cohort and are oversampling high-technology and female-owned firms.

The first stage of sampling includes a 10-item screener for new firms. This screener includes questions about the timing of first paying UI taxes, payment of social-security taxes, submission of a Schedule C for business income or losses, and application for an EIN. This information could be used to determine when new firms are recorded in government data sources (BITS and BED) that use one or more of these indicators to mark firm births. In addition, the screener collects information on possible forms of a firm's legal status (there are seven options including SP, limited partnership, and LLC).

The full survey collects information about firm employment, including number of full- and part-time workers. In addition, the survey collects information about the proprietor's work behavior and demographics, characteristics of the firm, business strategy and use of innovation, business organization, human-resource benefits, and detailed information on finances.

Research Data Set Derived from the Martindale-Hubbell Law Directory

In recent years, researchers have synthesized databases from various listings and directories. One example is a research database of law firms extracted from the MH Law Directory. MH is the leading reference on the U.S. legal-service industry. MH publishes listings for almost the entire universe of lawyers and law firms, but the underlying data for each firm are not available. However, researchers can use directory listings to synthesize the database.

As described in Chapter Six, Romley and Talley (2005) extracted the listings of all lawyers and law firms from the MH directory for 1993 and 1999. A matching mechanism was used to create a firm-level database with information on each establishment within a firm. There are approximately 65,000 law firms included in each year, and firms are connected between years. The authors used this longitudinal data set to examine effects of the availability of new organizational forms for law firms of different employment sizes. More generally, researchers can use this data set to examine the effects of different policies on access to and quality of lawyers as well as their specializations within the legal profession.

The Henry J. Kaiser Family Foundation/Health Research and Educational Trust Employer Health Benefits Surveys

There are also private databases with information about small firms and HI offerings. One such data source is KFF/HRET Employer Health Benefits Surveys, which have been fielded annually since 1999. Previous versions of the survey were sponsored by the Health Insurance Association of America from 1987 to 1990 and by KPMG from 1991 to 1998. The nationally representative sample was drawn from D&B's list of the nation's employers with three or more workers, stratified by firm employment.

Researchers used these data to examine effects of HI regulations on firm size. For example, as described in Chapter Three, Kapur et al.

(2006) used repeated cross-section samples from 1993, 1996, and 1998 surveys to examine how small-group HI reforms affected firm size.

Conclusion

Great strides have been made in recent years to create data sources useful for conducting research on small businesses and their policies. Of particular importance are new longitudinal data sets created by the Census Bureau and BLS, which allow for the study of business entry and exit (which is especially relevant to small-business policy) as well as changes within establishments and firms to be studied over time.

In creating administrative longitudinal databases, progress has been made on three problematic issues: connecting establishments to parent firms, matching establishments and firms over time, and identifying firm inception dates and closures. This substantial work made it possible to create the data sets described in this chapter; however, challenges in using these data remain. At present, there continue to be significant challenges involved in obtaining longitudinal data, data that include information at several organizational levels, and appropriate sampling frames. Two of the main problems are lack of availability due to cost or confidentiality concerns and the poor quality of linkages, either within units over time or between establishments and firms. Other important concerns for longitudinal data sources include the point in time at which a new firm or establishment is identified to enter a database, the point in time at which it is determined that a business has closed and should be removed, and the point in time at which the size of the business, whether based on number of employees or some other criterion, is measured.[5] Researchers need to carefully consider how well the three issues were addressed in each data source and whether the resulting quality of the data might impact their research.

Researchers interested in studying small-business issues need to be aware of whether a data set's size measures reflect establishment size or firm size. Although some of the data sets described in this discus-

---

[5] For information on how size-class measurement timing can matter, see Okolie (2004).

sion allow for the linking of establishments and firms, many of them provide information on one but not the other. Although it is common for researchers to use establishment size as a proxy for firm size, the work of Mendeloff et al. (2006) described in Chapter Four illustrates that there are substantive differences between the two. Policy research on small-business issues must be careful to determine the unit of analysis that is critical to the policy under investigation and ensure that the data are, in fact, capturing that unit of analysis.

Most of the data sets described in this monograph are based on surveys of or information on businesses. Such data are useful for examining many different issues. CPS, a household survey, provides a rich and widely used data resource for studying entrepreneurship and new-business formation; however, it is not possible to study business growth, success, and failure with this data set. Firm-level data are needed to address the latter issues. Although longitudinal firm-level data needed to address such issues are available from the Census Bureau, particularly BITS and BED, only a handful of research studies have used these sources. Indeed, officials at the Census Bureau have voiced interest in more researchers making use of these. In his presentation at the Kauffman Symposium on Entrepreneurship Data in November 2004, John Haltiwanger strongly encouraged researchers both to submit proposals for using the data at Census Bureau RDCs and to continue to support the Census Bureau's use of BED as a frame for survey samples through which more detailed and specific information can be collected and made publicly available.

The most notable gap in current small-business data sources is the lack of a *publicly available* source of longitudinal data. In the next five years, this gap will be at least partially addressed by the KFF firm survey of new businesses. Information on this survey is available now, and researchers can work now to design research studies that would take advantage of the information when it becomes available.

Table 7.1 provides a summary reference concerning the data sets described in this report, including information on collection method and coverage, main variables, periodicity and dates available, unit of observation, employment definition, and major limitations.

Table 7.1
Summary of the Available Data Sets

Data Set (Source)	Collection Method and Coverage[a]	Topic, Main Variables[b]	Periodicity, Dates Available, Longitudinal Links[c]	Unit of Observation[d]	How Employee Is Defined[e]	Major Limitations[f]
QCEW, also known as ES-202 (BLS)	Administrative records. Includes all establishments covered by UI and UCFE, about 8.4 million establishments.	Employment, wages, full address (both mailing and physical location)	Quarterly, cross-section; 2001 forward (NAICS basis); 1975–2000 (SIC basis)	Establishment, can be aggregated to the firm level using EIN	Everyone on payroll	Not publicly available.[g] Some aggregated tables are available.[h] Excludes self-employed, unpaid family members, and elected officials. UI coverage is different by state.

Table 7.1—Continued

Data Set (Source)	Collection Method and Coverage[a]	Topic, Main Variables[b]	Periodicity, Dates Available, Longitudinal Links[c]	Unit of Observation[d]	How Employee Is Defined[e]	Major Limitations[f]
BED (BLS)	Connects 6.4 million establishments from QCEW over time using SESA-ID and probability matching.	Monthly employment, wages, job gains and losses, full address	Quarterly, panel, 1992 forward	Establishment, can be aggregated to the firm level using EIN	Everyone on payroll	Not publicly available.[a] Some aggregated tables are available. Excludes government employees, private households, and establishments with zero employment. UI coverage differs by state and may change over time.
CES (BLS)	Monthly sample survey of about 160,000 businesses and government agencies covering about 400,000 establishments	Employment, hours, and earnings, industry detail, full address	Monthly, cross-section, 1990–present; some series are available since 1939	Establishment	Everyone on payroll	Not publicly available.[g] Some aggregated tables are available.[i] Establishments are not connected over time. Nonresponse.

Table 7.1—Continued

Data Set (Source)	Collection Method and Coverage[a]	Topic, Main Variables[b]	Periodicity, Dates Available, Longitudinal Links[c]	Unit of Observation[d]	How Employee Is Defined[e]	Major Limitations[f]
NCS (BLS)	Survey, sampling frame is QCEW, three-stage design: regions, establishments, and occupations. About 19,000 establishments. Large firms are likelier than small ones to be selected.	Benefits and wages, firm employment	Yearly, cross-section	Occupations within an establishment	Everyone on payroll	Not publicly available.[g] Change in methodology in 1999.
CPS (BLS, Census Bureau)	Monthly sample survey of approximately 60,000 households. Rotating sample design, respondents are in for 4 months, out for 8 month and in for an additional 4 months.	Firm employment, business ownership, self-employment, some characteristics of small-business employee	Monthly, 1962–ongoing. Respondents are in for 4 months, out for 8 months, and in for an additional 4 months.	Household, family, person	Not explicitly discussed	Categorical size count; matching over time is imperfect.

Table 7.1—Continued

Data Set (Source)	Collection Method and Coverage[a]	Topic, Main Variables[b]	Periodicity, Dates Available, Longitudinal Links[c]	Unit of Observation[d]	How Employee Is Defined[e]	Major Limitations[f]
SSEL or BR (Census Bureau)	List of all establishments and companies with paid employees; 180,000 multiunit companies, representing 1.5 million affiliated establishments, 5 million single-establishment companies, and nearly 14 million nonemployer businesses. Administrative data from IRS and SSA. Also compiles data from economic censuses and current business surveys.	Employment, revenues, business full address, organization type, industry classification, operating data, EIN.	Yearly, cross-section, 1974–2001	Establishment and firm	N/A	Not publicly available.

Table 7.1—Continued

Data Set (Source)	Collection Method and Coverage[a]	Topic, Main Variables[b]	Periodicity, Dates Available, Longitudinal Links[c]	Unit of Observation[d]	How Employee Is Defined[e]	Major Limitations[f]
LBD (Census Bureau)	Matched records from SSEL over time using PPN, using CFN and EIN, or using name and address match. Covers all nonfarm private economy and some public-sector activities. 4.5 million to 7.1 million records per year.	Establishment age and tenure, payroll, employment, firm affiliation, full address	Yearly, panel, 1974–1999, ongoing	Establishment and firm	Everyone on payroll	Not publicly available.[j]

Table 7.1—Continued

Data Set (Source)	Collection Method and Coverage[a]	Topic, Main Variables[b]	Periodicity, Dates Available, Longitudinal Links[c]	Unit of Observation[d]	How Employee Is Defined[e]	Major Limitations[f]
BITS, also known as LEEM (Census Bureau)	Links SSEL establishments over time using PPN, CFN, or EIN. Includes establishments with positive payroll. 13 million establishments. Same industry coverage as CBP.	Employment, firm employment, payroll, firm ownership, firm affiliation, census geography, primary industry, starting year, CFN	Yearly, panel, 1989–present	Establishment and firm	Everyone on payroll	Not publicly available.[j]
CBP (Census Bureau)	Aggregated tables derived from SSEL, excludes some agriculture, rail transportation, private households, and public administration.	Employment, payroll, total number of establishments, county	Yearly, cross-section, 1977 forward	Establishment and firm	Everyone on payroll	Aggregated tables; some industry-level data are not disclosed.
ILBD (Census Bureau)	Connects establishment data from LBD to statistics of nonemployers.	See LBD	Yearly, panel, 1992–2001	Establishment	Everyone on payroll	Not publicly available.[j]

Table 7.1—Continued

Data Set (Source)	Collection Method and Coverage[a]	Topic, Main Variables[b]	Periodicity, Dates Available, Longitudinal Links[c]	Unit of Observation[d]	How Employee Is Defined[e]	Major Limitations[f]
LEHD (Census Bureau)	Connects establishment data from LBD to household data. 4 million establishments for about 20 states.	See LBD; also, employer human capital, workforce indicators	Yearly, panel, 2003	Establishment	Everyone on payroll	Not publicly available.[j]
EC (Census Bureau)	Covers 5 million establishments with more than five employees and a sample of the rest.	Employment, labor costs, measures of output, expenses, city identifiers	Years ending in 2 and 7	Establishment and firm	Everyone on payroll	Not publicly available.[j]
COS, also known as Report of Organization (Census Bureau)	Surveys 40,000 multiunit companies with more than 250 employees, and approximately 10,000 smaller multiunit companies on rotating basis.	Establishment operational status, payroll, employment, controlling interests held by other domestic or foreign-owned organizations	Annually since 1974, cross-section; survey coverage and content vary during the census year	Establishment and firm	Everyone on payroll	Not publicly available.[j]

Table 7.1—Continued

Data Set (Source)	Collection Method and Coverage[a]	Topic, Main Variables[b]	Periodicity, Dates Available, Longitudinal Links[c]	Unit of Observation[d]	How Employee Is Defined[e]	Major Limitations[f]
SWOBE and SMOBE (Census Bureau)	Sample from BITS data frame, part of EC	Organizational form, sales and receipts, employees and annual payroll	1992, 1997, 2002, cross-section	Establishment	Everyone on payroll	Not publicly available.[j]
CBO (Census Bureau)	Sample from BITS data frame, 78,000–115,000 records for establishments and 117,000–128,000 observations for owners file, part of EC	Legal form of organization, receipts, sources of capital, employment, whether the business is home based or not	Yearly, 1982, 1987, 1992; combined with the SMOBE/SWOBE in 2002 to form SBO, cross-section	Establishment and individuals	All employees reported on a firm's payroll during specified pay periods	Not publicly available.[j]
SBO (Census Bureau)	Sample from BITS data frame, 78,000–115,000 records	Legal form of organization, receipts, sources of capital, employment, whether the business is home based or not	Yearly, cross-section, 2002, for other years see SMOBE and SWOBE	Establishment	All employees on payroll	Not publicly available.[k]

Table 7.1—Continued

Data Set (Source)	Collection Method and Coverage[a]	Topic, Main Variables[b]	Periodicity, Dates Available, Longitudinal Links[c]	Unit of Observation[d]	How Employee Is Defined[e]	Major Limitations[f]
SOI (IRS)	Stratified probability samples of master file of all tax returns	Tax-related issues, business receipts, selected deductions, payroll, and net income	Yearly, cross-section, 1990–2002	Firm	All employees on payroll	Not publicly available.
SSBF (Federal Reserve Board)	Sampling frame is the DMI file. Firms with fewer than 500 employees. About 3,500 businesses.	Firm's use of credit, firm's assets, liabilities, income, revenues, profits, expenses, employment, owners' characteristics	1987, 1993, 1998, cross-section	Firm	Employees on payroll or not, family members on payroll	Only 33% response rate.

Table 7.1—Continued

Data Set (Source)	Collection Method and Coverage[a]	Topic, Main Variables[b]	Periodicity, Dates Available, Longitudinal Links[c]	Unit of Observation[d]	How Employee Is Defined[e]	Major Limitations[f]
NEHIS (CDC)	National probability-sample survey of business establishments, governments, and self-employed individuals with no employees and no other locations. 34,604 completed interviews (70% response rate).	Health-insurance offerings, employment	1994, cross-section	Establishment	All employees on payroll	Not publicly available.[j]
Research data set derived from MH Law Directory	Directory of lawyers and law firms. Complex algorithms can be used to extracts and match records of lawyers to establishments and firms.	Size of firm, specialization, ratings, full address	1993, 1999, panel	Law firm, law office	Lawyers or supporting personnel affiliated with the firm	Not publicly available.

Table 7.1—Continued

Data Set (Source)	Collection Method and Coverage[a]	Topic, Main Variables[b]	Periodicity, Dates Available, Longitudinal Links[c]	Unit of Observation[d]	How Employee Is Defined[e]	Major Limitations[f]
KFF-HRET Employer Health Benefits Surveys (KFF/HRET)	Survey of public and private employers, sampled from DMI; about 3,262	Employer health plans coverage, costs, enrollment patterns, health-plan choice, employee costs, employment	Annually since 1999; before that, the survey was conducted by KPMG from 1991–1998 and by Health Insurance Association from 1987 until 1991.	Establishment	Not explicitly discussed	Not publicly available. Categorical definition of firm size.

Table 7.1—Continued

Data Set (Source)	Collection Method and Coverage[a]	Topic, Main Variables[b]	Periodicity, Dates Available, Longitudinal Links[c]	Unit of Observation[d]	How Employee Is Defined[e]	Major Limitations[f]
MEPS (AHRQ)	HC: panels of 5 rounds of interviews over 30 months. IC: annual survey of establishments from SSEL sample frame, 27K establishments. Also sample of establishments with workers from prior-year HC.	HC: health status, access to care, income, employment, employment status, eligibility for private and public insurance coverage, health-care use and expenses. IC: types of plans provided, number of workers covered, employment (total, by gender, by age over 50, and by earnings).	Annual, 1996–present. HC: panel. IC: cross-section	HC: household IC: establishment	Everyone on payroll, not including temporary workers	Not publicly available.[k]
DMI (D&B)	Extension of D&B credit database	Information about owners, sales, employment and legal status, full address	Yearly, ongoing; panel can be created using D&B identifiers	Establishment and firm	Everyone on payroll plus unpaid family members.	Is available for a fee.

Table 7.1—Continued

Data Set (Source)	Collection Method and Coverage[a]	Topic, Main Variables[b]	Periodicity, Dates Available, Longitudinal Links[c]	Unit of Observation[d]	How Employee Is Defined[e]	Major Limitations[f]
KFS (KFF)	Survey of new businesses from DMI listing sample frame. About 5,000 firms.	Owner's characteristics, employment, business organization and benefits, and business finances	Annual, 2005, panel	Owner		Will be publicly available; data have not yet been released.

Table 7.1—Continued

NOTE: UCFE = Unemployment Compensation for Federal Employees. SESA-ID = state employment security agency identification number. SSEL = Standard Statistical Establishment Listing. CFN = census file number. LEEM = Longitudinal Establishment and Enterprise. SOI = Statistics of Income.

[a] Information about the origin and sources of the data. Note that some of the entries refer to tables aggregated from the actual data set. Unless stated otherwise, the number of observations includes the most recent date for which the data are reported.

[b] The most important variables in the data set as well as information on the most precise geographical identifiers available (region, state, county, ZIP code, city, full address).

[c] Range of years for which data are available. This column also indicates whether the data are cross-sectional or whether the underlying units of observation are connected over time into a panel.

[d] Units for which data are gathered and any linkages to higher levels of observation (e g., establishment-level data aggregated at the firm level).

[e] Typically defined as the number of people on payroll in the pay period that includes the twelfth of the month.

[f] The main limitations of the data set.

[g] Researchers can apply for the access to the confidential microdata. For details, see BLS (2007).

[h] See, for example, BLS (undated [b]).

[i] See, for example, BLS (undated [a]).

[j] Researchers can apply for access to confidential data; see U.S. Census Bureau (undated[a]).

[k] Researchers can apply for access to confidential data; see CDC (2007a).

CHAPTER EIGHT

Conclusions

In this book, we have examined what is currently known about the effect of government regulation on small businesses in four key regulatory areas: corporate securities, environmental protection, employment, and HI. In examining these general areas, and specific topics in depth, we have gleaned new insight into the implications of public policy for small businesses and entrepreneurship.

There is general recognition that public policy can have both intended and unintended effects on small businesses and that the effects of policies may differ by firm size. This recognition has led to a variety of special considerations for small businesses in the regulatory sphere. Overall, we have some understanding of the different ways in which regulation affects small businesses and how that differs from its effect on large businesses. However, our understanding of the effectiveness of special policy treatment received by small businesses is less well understood. Across the board, there has been little evidence as to whether the special consideration offered by policymakers to small businesses in the regulatory context makes sense from a cost-benefit perspective, whether regulations designed to benefit small businesses achieve their intended aims, whether programs designed to assist small businesses comply with regulations are well targeted and well utilized, and whether thresholds that define exemptions from regulations are based on a careful consideration of the relative costs and benefits of regulation. The research presented in this book begins to shed light on some of these issues.

In summarizing the findings of these studies, we focus on three key issues. First, we observe that laws and regulations designed specifically to benefit small businesses do not always achieve that aim. Second, we provide additional support for the idea that regulations affect the way in which businesses behave and may affect small and large businesses differently. In particular, our research provides evidence of a regulatory "threshold" or "notching" effect. Finally, we found the definition of a *small business* to be a moving target.

Policies Designed Specifically to Help Small Businesses Do Not Always Have the Intended Effect

Policymakers often design regulations or policies with the specific intention or stated purpose of helping small businesses. However, such policies often fail to meet their stated goals—either because they end up benefiting large businesses as much as (or even more than) small businesses or because they fail to meet their objectives entirely. This monograph provides evidence of both types of policy failure.

In Chapter Six, Romley, Talley, and Savych show that new organizational forms (LLPs and LLCs) advocated, in part, because of their supposed benefit for small firms, have not been adopted by small law firms to the extent that they have been by larger firms. The authors show that, in the 1990s, law firms that adopted these new forms experienced higher rates of growth than those that did not adopt them, suggesting that the new options were, in fact, desirable. However, the authors also found that larger law firms were much likelier to adopt the new organizational forms than were smaller firms. On the one hand, because the larger law firms in the study tended to have fewer than 500 employees, one could view the new legal forms as having helped small businesses. However, to the extent that policymakers are interested in assisting smaller law firms, they might be concerned that smaller firms are less likely to adopt the new forms. Additional research is needed to understand why more small firms have not adopted these forms. If it turned out that small law firms were not adopting the forms due to lack of knowledge or some cost involved in the process, then outreach and support might help more small firms take advantage of these options.

Gates, Kapur, and Karaca-Mandic report a similar finding in Chapter Three with regard to the adoption of CDHPs and other HI options among small firms. Although CDHPs have been advocated as a way to expand HI among small businesses, their adoption has been much higher among larger firms. The research found even more discouraging results regarding the effects of state HI mandates that were designed to expand access to HI to small businesses through regulation of the small group market. The study found no evidence that these policies increased the propensity of small firms to offer HI or that they reduced premiums. When research indicates that regulations are not having the intended positive effect, modifications can be made to the regulation or support programs can be introduced to improve the outcomes. In the case of CDHPs, additional research is needed to understand why small firms are less likely to adopt these plans and precisely what types of support could expand access among small businesses.

When research suggests that regulations designed to help small businesses are having unintended consequences or not achieving intended aims, the results raise questions as to whether the regulation should be rescinded.

The Regulatory Environment's Effect on Small-Firm Behavior Differs from Its Effect on Large Firms

Many regulations are designed to influence firm behavior, but most of these are not designed specifically with small firms in mind. As discussed in the introduction to this book, there is longstanding concern among policymakers that the behavioral response of small firms to regulations might differ from that of larger firms and that this difference might put small firms at a competitive disadvantage. This concern is well grounded theoretically and has been empirically documented in a number of contexts. Generally speaking, the specific ways in which the behavioral response of small firms differs from that of large firms depend largely on the regulatory context. The research presented in this book provides additional evidence of these differing responses in several regulatory contexts.

In some cases, size thresholds designed to exempt small businesses from the effects of regulation or to help them comply have instead appeared to hinder firm growth. As emphasized in the introduction to this book and detailed in Appendix A, it is common for government regulation to provide an alternative regulatory regime for smaller businesses or even to exempt them entirely from regulation. Typically, such special treatment, or "tiering," is accorded to firms on the basis of their size as measured by the number of employees (a number that might range from 11 to 100), although other metrics are also used, including dollar value of gross sales, volume of toxic materials released, or value of shareholdings. Common sense suggests that the thresholds used to determine whether firms are or are not subject to a regulation could affect firm growth, although there has been no prior research documenting such an effect in the United States. In Chapter Three, Gates, Kapur, and Karaca-Mandic demonstrate such a "threshold effect" in the context of state HI mandates. The authors provide evidence that firms near the threshold for exemption from the regulated HI market adjust their size to avoid the more highly regulated market. Interestingly, this chapter identifies an *avoidance* threshold effect in the case of regulation that was *specifically designed to help* small firms. One might expect to see even stronger threshold effects in instances in which the regulation is not intended to benefit small firms. This negative, unintended effect (along with an absence of intended positive effects) suggests that greater effort is required to evaluate the effect of regulations whenever possible.

As noted above and discussed further in Chapter Two, regulatory thresholds vary dramatically across regulations. Given concerns about the complexity of the regulatory environment, policymakers might ponder whether it would make sense to align the thresholds by applying the same threshold to all (or many) regulations. However, the finding that regulatory thresholds appear to influence firm growth suggests that such an alignment might actually be a bad idea. Such regulatory alignment would likely create a focal point for businesses that could lead to significant effects on firm-growth decisions at that one threshold point. Baumol, Litan, and Schramm (2007) discussed the implications of stringent European labor laws (which tend to apply to firms with more than 10 to 15 employees) on firm growth. Although certainly complex and confusing for firms, the variation in thresholds across regulations means that no one decision leads to a dramatic increase in a firm's regulatory burden.

We also provide additional evidence that small firms respond differently than large firms to the substance of regulation. Kamar, Karaca-Mandic, and Talley (Chapter Five) provide evidence that small firms may have responded differently to SOX implementation. Specifically, they found that the probability that small firms were acquired by private (compared to public) acquirers increased by more than 50 percent in the first year after SOX implementation, whereas there was no effect for larger firms. However, they did not find an effect in the second year after enactment. This suggests that, even when small firms respond differently to the regulatory environment, the different behavioral effect may be short lived. When examining the effect of new regulation on small businesses, researchers need to be sure to distinguish short-run from long-run effects and resist drawing long-run conclusions based on behavioral responses that immediately follow regulatory implementation.

The findings also raise interesting issues for policymakers to consider. From a policy perspective, a disproportionate short-run effect on small firms may, in some cases, be acceptable or even desirable. In the case of SOX, it is possible that this short-run effect was due to the fact that some small firms were inadequately prepared to comply with the new policy environment and therefore exited the market quickly, while other small firms (i.e., those that remained in the public market) were not affected. On the whole, however, there is simply not enough evidence available yet to assess whether the different behavioral response to SOX is a good thing (in the sense that the regulation is primarily pushing small firms with financial problems out of the public market). Since none of the studies to date separately identifies the costs and benefits of SOX, it is not possible to reach a conclusion as to whether granting small firms regulatory relief from SOX is a good idea.

In some cases, the research suggests possible directions for future policy that achieve a better balance between the interest in restricting firm behavior through regulation and the desire to encourage small businesses and entrepreneurs. For example, small establishments have long posed a special regulatory challenge for federal agencies. Although it has been well documented that workplace injury and fatality rates are higher at smaller establishments, it is extremely costly to monitor compliance with health and safety regulations at thousands of small establishments, and the cost-benefit trade-off has thus pushed agencies to focus attention on larger establishments. The research presented in Chapter Four suggests that there might be more efficient and effective ways to target those small establishments that are of most concern. In this chapter, Mendeloff et al. provide evidence that small, single-establishment firms have different workplace-safety outcomes from those at small establishments that are part of larger firms. The authors conjecture that the owners of small, single-establishment firms might take a stronger interest in workplace safety than would individuals who manage a small worksite for a larger firm. They suggest ways in which enforcement policies might respond to these real behavioral differences between small and large firms, by, for example, targeting small establishments that are part of medium-sized firms (with 20 to 999 employees). Clearly, much more research would be needed to identify and fully understand such differences and craft appropriate policy responses.

What Exactly Is a Small Firm?

The studies described in this monograph indicate that both policymaking and research could benefit from more consistency in the definition of *small firms* or *small businesses*. Chapter Two (Dixon et al.) discusses the different ways in which firms are identified as small in various regulatory spheres. The characterization of firms as small or large varies quite dramatically across policy areas. As described in Appendix A, the definition of *small firm* as articulated in laws or regulations can be based on a number of factors ranging from employment size and revenue to asset value and output. However, even within a specific policy area, there can be a lack of consensus regarding what constitutes a small firm. This is particularly true when there is (as yet) no special regulatory provision for small firms. For example, in Chapter Five, Kamar, Karaca-Mandic, and Talley review the various definitions of *small firms* used to assess the effect of SOX on small firms.

As we mentioned earlier, it is common for government regulations to provide an alternative regulatory regime for smaller businesses or even to exempt them entirely. Such exemptions are typically accorded to firms on the basis of their size—as measured by the number of employees. As such, employment size at the firm level appears to be a particularly useful way to distinguish large firms from small ones for the purposes of policy analysis.

However, Chapter Seven reveals that many data sources collect information on establishments rather than firms. As a result, policy researchers often use establishment-level data to examine the effects of regulations on firms, assuming that small establishments are a reasonable proxy for small firms. The work of Mendeloff et al. (Chapter Four) reveals that this assumption is not necessarily a good one. Research that blindly uses data on establishments to assess the effect of policy on small firms may miss some critical differences between small and large firms. The key issue is that small establishments may be small firms or may be part of larger firms. Empirical findings based on differences between large and small establishments may be driven by those between large and small establishments within large firms. Policy analysis should bear this issue in mind and, ideally, strive to match the unit of analysis to the policy question at hand.

Further Research Is Needed to Support Entrepreneurship Public Policy

Over the past 40 years or so, regulations have proliferated; research as to the effects of these regulations has improved but has not kept pace. A careful assessment of the costs and benefits of a regulation that distinguishes between its effects on small and large businesses is the ideal approach to regulatory analysis. Such analysis is highly context-dependent. It is perhaps unrealistic to expect that it can be achieved for all regulations at all levels of government. However, we find that this standard of analysis is rarely achieved, even at the federal level.

A systematic comparison of the costs and benefits of regulations and policies is a promising avenue for research in several areas. For example, researchers might be able to get a handle on the benefits of regulation in the realm of workplace health and safety regulations. Existing research on workplace fatalities sheds light on the potential benefits of health and safety regulation, but the focus of that research has been on establishment size rather than firm size. Similarly, information needs to be synthesized concerning the environmental damage caused by small (as opposed to large) firms and the benefits of reducing this damage. Information on these cost-benefit trade-offs could help policymakers design more effective policy.

Corporate and Securities Law

Although corporate and securities law does not typically receive attention in the study of small firms, it is clearly deserving of such attention. There are several interesting and researchable policy questions related to the differential impact of corporate and securities law on small businesses compared to large ones.

First, there is a need to develop an empirical understanding of the differences in the risk profiles of closely held firms and publicly traded firms. To the extent that smaller firms tend to remain unincorporated, another possible business or legal distinction between large and small companies concerns the jurisdictional landscape they face. A disproportionate number of large companies incorporate in the state of Delaware and are subject to its laws. In contrast, unincorporated firms (and perhaps some smaller incorporated ones) are likelier to be subject to the business-organization laws of the states in which they do business. Another interesting area of research, then, might be to consider whether a "Delaware effect" (such as that identified for firm value by Daines [2001]) carries over to other operational- and business-risk components of firms' profiles.

The implications of personal-bankruptcy reform for entrepreneurs is another promising area for future research. There are differing views regarding whether the reforms are a good or bad thing for small businesses. In this book, we have discussed the possible chilling effect on entrepreneurship of the increased difficulty for businesses to make a fresh start. However, if the law makes business opportunities riskier, it might drive some bad risks out of the market, resulting in a more robust set of small-business entries that will be less vulnerable to failure. In addition, a more procreditor bankruptcy regime might benefit small businesses that are creditors to individuals and other small businesses. The net implications are unclear and worthy of future research.

There are many other, related public-policy issues that are not specifically regulatory in nature but that are potentially relevant to small businesses. For example, in the late 1990s, California considered a major reform to its unfair-competition law, which allows private rights of action by citizens (as private attorneys general) to seek enforcement. To date, there has been virtually no research on the effects of this statute. Anecdotal accounts, however, suggest that small businesses and large businesses are subject to very different kinds of suits, in which plaintiffs seek equitable relief in the former and significant damages in the latter. The divergent conditions under which plaintiffs seek redress in these cases may also be pertinent to whether the statute achieves its overall policy goals.

Environmental Regulation and Policy

While the existing body of research on environmental protection in the business context is extensive, further research is needed to better understand how recent trends in environmental regulation, enforcement, and liability are affecting businesses along size dimensions. Better information is also needed concerning which aspects of environmental regulatory and liability policy cause the greatest problems for small firms. A better understanding is also needed of the environmental damage caused by small firms and the benefits of reducing this damage.

Major environmental initiatives have initially focused on large firms, and some believe that the regulations were formulated with large firms in mind. There is a need to understand whether a different approach to source control, pollution prevention, compliance assistance, and enforcement is necessary to deal with the lean operations of small firms. There also needs to be a more thorough evaluation of how small firms have utilized different initiatives, such as the Common Sense Initiative and self-auditing programs, and what types of modifications to these programs would make them more attractive to small firms. Large firms are motivated to participate in environmental initiatives partly by concerns about their image in the communities in which they operate or their image with their customers. More research is needed to determine the types of concerns that would motivate small businesses to address the effects of their operations on the environment.

Employment Law and Regulation

In the employment area, many federal statutes protect individuals against discrimination or a hostile or unsafe workplace environment and prevent employers from terminating employees in specific, protected classes for specific reasons. Many of these federal rules are applied using size thresholds, such that the regulations do not cover businesses with small numbers of employees. Similar laws that exist at the state and local levels supplement these federal statutes. Because these regulations increase the risk of legal action by establishing a government agency with the authority to investigate firm behavior and take legal action, the very small firms that fall below the employment-size threshold for a regulation may face a lower risk of legal action in this area. An analysis of the distribution of firms by size could shed light on the issue of whether firms avoid adding employees when they are close to the employment-size threshold for particular regulations. Because some states and localities have lower thresholds than related federal regulations have, there is substantial variation to explore in this area.

The legal and regulatory system appears, on its face, to be neutral toward small firms when it comes to enforcing contractual limitations on employee behavior. However, research suggests that small businesses bear a disproportionate share of litigation costs in general. Because noncompete and trade-secret agreements can be enforced only through litigation, a small business may face a greater burden in enforcing such a clause and thus may be on a closer-to-equal footing with larger firms in states that limit the use of such agreements. Moreover, noncompete agreements may affect labor supply in a way that has a particularly strong impact on entrepreneurship or small businesses. For example, people who recently worked for a larger company in the same industry may staff start-ups. On the other hand, small businesses may have more to lose in the event that one of their employees violates such an agreement. There is empirical evidence to support the notion that labor mobility is higher in the high-technology industry clusters in California (Fallick, Fleischman, and Rebitzer, 2006). An empirical examination of the relationship between the stringency of state-court enforcement of noncompete and trade-secret agreements and the level of entrepreneurship could help inform the debate as to whether these agreements are an overall positive or negative for small businesses.

There are interesting questions to be studied regarding WC. WC policy varies significantly across states and, to a lesser extent, over time. This provides useful variation with which to analyze different policies that involve firm size directly—e.g., through size thresholds—or indirectly—e.g., through self-insurance requirements or two-tiered benefit programs. This variation could be used to test the effect of these and other policies (and policy changes) on a number of important outcomes. Perhaps the most obvious question is whether WC affects the distribution of firm size.

Health-Insurance Regulation

Finally, HI remains a critical issue to small businesses. In this rapidly changing area, research on the impact of recent reforms could help inform the development of new HI regulations or options.

Concluding Thoughts

The list we provide here is by no means an exhaustive one. Our understanding of the impact of regulation on entrepreneurship could be greatly expanded by further exploration into these and related topics of interest.

An improved understanding of the effects of regulation on small businesses could benefit policymakers at all levels. The federal RFA (P.L. 96-354) and related legislation in many states require government agencies to assess the potential effect of proposed regulations on small businesses. In effect, this requires agencies to use available research evidence to inform regulatory policymaking. However, because the required assessment occurs before the regulations take effect, research evidence is typically not available when key decisions are being made. While it is possible for policymakers to glean insight from an analysis of the implementation of similar regulations in other contexts (i.e., a different regulatory area, a different country, or a different state), there is much more to be learned from a retrospective analysis of the effect of a regulation after it has been implemented. The gold standard of such retrospective analyses would begin with a clear documentation of the regulation and the implementation process. It would consider both intended and potential unintended effects and would assess costs as well as benefits of regulation. Finally, it would distinguish specific characteristics of regulatory effects (i.e., long run versus short run or the effects on large versus small businesses). Such retrospective analyses could be used to revise and improve existing regulations and would ultimately provide agencies with information that could be used in a prospective analysis of the potential effects of similar regulations in the future. Although the federal RFA requires agencies to reevaluate regulations periodically, currently, the preimplementation reviews receive the most attention. Stakeholders often close the book on a regulation once it has been implemented and move on to a different issue. More research on the effects of regulation could alter this reality and foster effective change to existing regulations.

Criteria Used to Define *Small Business* in Determining Thresholds

Ryan Keefe, Susan M. Gates, and Eric Talley

This appendix reviews federal workplace, environmental, and economic regulations. It describes the purpose of and requirements associated with the regulations, any penalties associated with regulatory violations, and how requirements or penalties differ for small and large firms. It also describes programs designed to support small businesses and the firm characteristics that determine eligibility for such programs. This review reveals that, in the regulatory sphere, there is no single definition of *small business* that applies across policy areas. Businesses that might be considered small for the purposes of one regulation may be considered large for the purposes of another.

Criteria Used to Define *Small Business* in Determining Thresholds

There is no one definition of size used to determine when an organization is a small business, but separating the applicable federal statutes into broad categories does provide some general guidance as how the threshold for defining *small business* is applied. We have divided the relevant federal statutes into four broad categories:

1. Workplace regulations
2. Environmental regulations
3. Economic regulations
4. Programs providing support to small businesses.

The federal statutes within each of these categories use a variety of criteria to define *small business* for the purpose of determining whether the statute applies. This appendix provides a list of federal statutes that regulate firm behavior by category and a summary of statutes specifically designed to support small-business operations. We use these four categories to structure the appendix. Workplace regulations are regulations that govern employer behavior vis-à-vis current or potential employees. They cover a wide range of issues including discrimination, wages, working conditions, workplace health and safety, and HI. Small businesses are exempt from most workplace regulations. The threshold for exemption in this area is typically defined in terms of the number of employees, and the specific threshold varies widely from 11 to 100. In general, workplace regulations that have been enacted more recently have higher thresholds.

Environmental regulations govern firm behavior related to hazardous or toxic substances that may be generated in the course of business operations. Firms are not exempt from such regulations based on firm size. Economic regulations govern the relationship between firms and their customers, shareholders, or other stakeholders. The scale of the economic activity being regulated typically defines these thresholds. The final category addresses programs designed to benefit small businesses or to help them to comply with regulations. All programs in this category have thresholds that determine eligibility. The definition of these thresholds is industry- and context-specific. Each entry includes a brief summary of regulatory requirements and potential penalties, along with information on the threshold for inclusion or coverage under the statute. These descriptions are not intended to be comprehensive or exhaustive in either case, as many statutes carry several pages of specific requirements and penalties. It is also worth noting that all of these regulations are federal, and individual states may have stricter regulations in some cases, to which small firms could still be subject.

Exemption from Federal Workplace Regulations

Many federal workplace regulations provide an exemption from the application of these regulations for small businesses. For workplace regulations, the number of employees within a firm typically defines the threshold for exemption. The specific number of employees that determines whether a business is a small business varies by statute. For example, certain provisions, such as the record-keeping requirements of the OSH Act (P.L. 91-596), do not apply to a firm with fewer than 11 employees. At the other extreme, firms with fewer than 100 employees are exempt from the Worker Adjustment and Retraining Notification (WARN) Act (P.L. 100-379). Generally, more recent workplace regulations have higher thresholds. In at least one case, the Fair Labor Standards Act (P.L. 75-718), a small business is defined for the purpose of exemption by the volume of gross sales per year ($500,000).

Family and Medical Leave Act (P.L. 103-3, 1993)

Intent of Statute. To entitle employees to take reasonable leave for medical reasons; the birth or adoption of a child; and the care of a child, spouse, or parent who has a serious health condition.

Requirements. Employers covered by this regulation must

1. allow eligible employees to take up to a total of 12 work weeks of leave during any 12-month period for medical reasons; to bond with a new child; or to care for a seriously ill child, spouse, or parent.
2. upon return from such leave, restore the employee to his or her position or an equivalent position with equivalent employee benefits, pay, and other terms and conditions of employment.
3. maintain records that document compliance.

An eligible employee is defined as an employee whom the employer has employed for at least 12 months and for at least 1,250 hours of service during the previous 12-month period.

Penalties. Any employer that violates the rights that this statute guarantees is liable to any eligible, affected employee

1. for damages equal to
   a. the amount of any wages, salary, employment benefits, or other compensation denied as a result of the violation
   b. in a case in which leave is not granted and so wages, benefits, and so on are not lost, any actual monetary losses the employee sustained, such as the cost of providing care, up to a sum equal to 12 weeks of wages or salary for the affected employee
   c. the interest on damages.
2. for equitable relief, including employment, reinstatement, and promotion.

Both affected employees and the U.S. Secretary of Labor may bring action in any court to recover these damages.

Thresholds That Provide Exemptions. Firms employing fewer than 50 employees within a 75-mile radius are exempt (29 U.S.C. 2611[2][B][ii]).

Americans with Disabilities Act (P.L. 101-336, 1990)

Intent of Statute. To provide enforceable standards addressing discrimination against individuals with disabilities. The term *disability* means, with respect to an individual,

1. a physical or mental impairment that substantially limits one or more of the individual's major life activities
2. a record of such an impairment
3. being regarded as having such an impairment.

Requirements. Employers may not discriminate against potential employees with disabilities and are required to make reasonable accommodations to existing employees with disabilities. The term *reasonable accommodation* may include

1. making existing facilities used by employees readily accessible to and usable by individuals with disabilities

2. job restructuring; part-time or modified work schedules; reassignment to a vacant position; acquisition or modification of equipment or devices; appropriate adjustment or modifications of examinations; training materials or policies; the provision of qualified readers or interpreters; and other, similar accommodations for individuals with disabilities.

Penalties. A charge may be filed by an aggrieved individual or by a representative of the EEOC. After conducting an investigation, if the EEOC findings support the claim, restitution may be sought in court. The court may require the employer to alter existing employment practices, to reinstate or hire an employee with or without back pay (up to two years, payable by the responsible employer), or undertake other equitable relief.

Thresholds That Provide Exemptions. Firms are exempt that meet any of the following criteria (42 U.S.C. 12111[5][A]):

- employed fewer than 15 employees for more than 32 weeks in each of the prior two calendar years
- are owned by native tribes
- are tax-exempt, private membership clubs.

Legislative Note. The original threshold defining *small business*, as specified in the statute, was 25 employees. This threshold was legislated to be in effect for the first two years of this statute, after which the current threshold of 15 employees became the standard (in 1994).

Worker Adjustment and Retraining Notification Act (P.L. 100-379, 1988)

Intent of Statute. The purpose of the WARN Act is to ensure that workers and their communities receive advance notice of their loss of employment in the context of plant closings or mass layoffs so that they may begin searching for other employment or obtain training for another occupation.

The term *mass layoff* is defined as a reduction in force that

1. is not the result of a plant closing

2. results in employment loss at the single site of employment during any 30-day period for
   a. at least 500 employees (excluding part-time employees).
   b. at least 50–499 employees, provided that they make up at least 33 percent of the employer's active workforce (excluding part-time employees).

Requirements. At least 60 days before a plant closing or mass layoff, an employer must serve written notice to

1. each representative of the employees affected as of the time of the notice or, if there is no such representative at that time, to each affected employee
2. the state or entity designated by the state to carry out rapid-response activities under 29 U.S.C. 2864(a)(2)(A) and the chief elected official of the unit of local government within which such closing or layoff is to occur.

Penalties. Any employer that orders a plant closing or mass layoff without providing this advance notice shall be liable to each aggrieved employee who suffers an employment loss as a result of such closing or layoff for

1. back pay for each day of violation
2. benefits under an employee-benefit plan (either welfare or pension) including the cost of medical expenses incurred during the employment loss that would have been covered under an employee-benefit plan if the employment loss had not occurred.

Such liability shall be calculated for the period of the violation up to a maximum of 60 days but, in no event, for more than half the number of days the employer employed the employee.

Thresholds That Provide Exemptions. A firm with fewer than 100 full-time employees or a firm with 100 or more employees who work an aggregate of fewer than 4,000 hours per week is exempt (29 U.S.C. 2101[a]).

Consolidated Omnibus Budget Reconciliation Act (P.L. 99-272, 1986)

Intent of Statute. To ensure that individuals have continued access to their current HI in spite of an event that would otherwise lead to a termination of coverage. Qualifying events include

1. the death of the covered employee
2. the termination (other than by reason of such employee's gross misconduct) or reduction of hours of the covered employee's employment
3. the divorce or legal separation of the covered employee from the employee's spouse
4. the covered employee becoming entitled to benefits under title XVIII of the Social Security Act [42 U.S.C. 1395 et seq.]
5. a dependent child ceasing to be a dependent child under the generally applicable requirements of the plan
6. a proceeding in a case under title 11, commencing on or after July 1, 1986, with respect to the employer from whose employment the covered employee retired at any time.

Requirements. The group health plan must provide written notice to each covered employee and spouse of the employee of the rights provided by this act.

1. The employer must maintain records with respect to notifications, payments made by and correspondence with beneficiaries, and COBRA administration procedures.
2. The employer must notify the plan administrator of a qualifying event within 30 days.
3. The coverage must extend for at least the period beginning on the date of the qualifying event and ending not earlier than the earliest of
   a. 18 months for termination or reduction in hours worked
   b. 36 months for multiple qualifying events and qualifying events other than employee termination, reduction in hours, and employer bankruptcy

c. the date on which the employer ceases to offer the employee-benefit plan

d. the date on which the beneficiary fails to make timely payment of any necessary coverage premium.

Penalties. The Technical and Miscellaneous Revenue Act of 1988 (TAMRA) (P.L. 100-647) authorizes the IRS to assess excise taxes for failure to follow COBRA rules. Internal Revenue Code §4980B sets out the IRS's COBRA provisions and incorporates the excise-tax penalties as they have applied to violations since 1988. In general, the amount of tax imposed on any failure with respect to a qualified beneficiary is $100 for each day the employer is in noncompliance (with a $200 per-day limit for families with more than one qualified beneficiary).

Penalties for an employer may be as high as $2,500 for each beneficiary affected by the failure to comply or the total amount based on the length of the noncompliance period, whichever is less. If the IRS finds a violation that it considers to be more than minimal, the employer may be subject to a penalty of as much as $15,000. In the case of a plan other than a multiemployer plan, the employer and each person responsible for administering benefits under the plan that caused the violation is liable for the tax. The employer can also be held liable for legal costs, court costs, and even medical claims filed by a qualified beneficiary under this act.

Thresholds That Provide Exemptions. The continuation requirement of this statute does not apply to any group health plan for any calendar year offered by an employer that normally employed fewer than 20 employees on a typical business day during 50 percent of the preceding calendar year. Part-time employees are counted as fractions of full-time employees, with the fraction determined by the number of hours worked (29 U.S.C. 1161 [b]).[1]

---

[1]   This statute does not apply to a firm that chooses not to offer a group health plan, regardless of firm size.

Employee Retirement and Income Security Act (P.L. 93-406, 1974)

Intent of Statute. To protect the interests of participants in employee-benefit plans and their beneficiaries by requiring the disclosure and reporting of financial and other information by establishing standards of conduct, responsibility, and obligation for fiduciaries of employee-benefit plans; by improving the equitable character and the soundness of such plans by requiring them to vest the accrued benefits of employees with significant periods of service to meet minimum standards of funding and by requiring plan-termination insurance; and by providing for appropriate remedies, sanctions, and ready access to the federal courts.

Requirements. This statute requires the disclosure and reporting of financial and other information. It also establishes standards of conduct, responsibility, and obligation for fiduciaries of employee-benefit plans by requiring them to meet minimum standards of funding and requiring plan-termination insurance. A summary description of any employee-benefit plan shall be furnished to participants and beneficiaries as provided in 29 U.S.C. 1024(b). The summary description must include the information described in 29 U.S.C. 1022(b), be written in a manner calculated to be understood by the average plan participant, and be sufficiently accurate and comprehensive to reasonably apprise such participants and beneficiaries of their rights and obligations under the plan. An annual report of such a plan must be filed with the U.S. Secretary of Labor and be made available and furnished to participants.

Penalties. Any individual who willfully violates any provision of part 1 of the section addressing disclosure and reporting requirements (see 29 U.S.C. 1021 et seq. for a full description) or any regulation or order issued under any such provision shall, on conviction, be fined not more than $100,000 or imprisoned not more than 10 years or both, except that, in the case of such violation by a corporation or small business enterprise (not an individual), the fine imposed will not exceed $500,000.

Thresholds That Provide Exemptions. Small firms are not exempt from the regulations of this statute because of their size. This statute does not apply if the firm does not have an employee-benefit plan in place; if such plan is maintained solely for the purpose of complying with applicable WC, unemployment-compensation, or disability-insurance laws; or if such plan is an excess-benefit plan (as defined in 29 U.S.C. 1002[36]) and is unfunded (29 U.S.C. 1002[5]).

Occupational Safety and Health Act (P.L. 91-596, 1970)

Intent of Statute. To assure, so far as possible, every working person safe and healthful working conditions, to encourage employers and employees in their efforts to reduce the number of occupational safety and health hazards at their places of employment, and to stimulate employers and employees to institute new and to perfect existing programs for providing safe and healthful working conditions.

Requirements. Each employer

1. must furnish to each of its employees employment and a place of employment that are free from recognized hazards that are causing or are likely to cause death or serious physical harm to its employees
2. must comply with occupational safety and health standards promulgated under this chapter. Each employee must comply with occupational safety and health standards and all rules, regulations, and orders issued pursuant to this chapter that apply to his or her conduct.

Each employer must maintain appropriate records (as determined by the U.S. Secretary of Labor or the U.S. Secretary of Health and Human Services) regarding

1. the causes and prevention of occupational accidents and illnesses
2. work-related deaths
3. employee exposure to volatile chemicals and toxic substances
4. injuries and illnesses other than minor injuries requiring only first-aid treatment and that do not involve medical treatment, loss of consciousness, restriction of work or motion, or transfer to another job.

Furthermore, employers are required to conduct inspections and post information for employees regarding safety and health standards. For a complete description of regulations and standards, see 29 U.S.C. 651 et seq. (OSHA also supports small businesses by providing resources to aid in compliance, such as appropriate regulation descriptions, a free inspection walk-through, and reduced fines based on number of employees. For more detail, see OSHA, 2005.)

Penalties. Any employer that willfully or repeatedly violates the requirements or the standards set forth in this act (in §§654 and 655, respectively) or regulations set forth by OSHA may be assessed a civil penalty of not more than $70,000 for each violation but not less than $5,000 for each willful violation. Each first-time violation that is determined to be a serious violation will result in a civil penalty of up to $7,000.

Failure to correct a violation for which an employer has been cited (within the predetermined timeframe) may be assessed a civil penalty of not more than $7,000 for each day during which such failure or violation continues.

If an employer willfully violates a rule or standard of this act and that violation causes the death of an employee, the employer will (on conviction) be punished by a fine of not more than $10,000 or by imprisonment for not more than six months or by both, except that, if the conviction is for a violation committed after a first conviction, punishment will be by a fine of not more than $20,000 or by imprisonment for not more than one year or by both.

Any employer that violates any of the posting requirements described in this statute will be assessed a civil penalty of up to $7,000 for each violation.[2]

Thresholds That Provide Exemptions. Employers that employ fewer than 11 workers are exempt from most OSHA record-keeping requirements for recording and reporting occupational injuries and illnesses (29 U.S.C. 657[d]). An annual rider on OSHA's appropriation bills, which has been renewed annually for many years, also prohibits

---

[2] For a complete list of civil and criminal penalties, see §666.

OSHA from conducting scheduled inspections of employers with 10 or fewer employees in low-hazard industries.

Age Discrimination in Employment Act (P.L. 90-202, 1967)

Intent of Statute. To promote employment of older people based on their abilities rather than age, to prohibit arbitrary age discrimination in employment, and to help employers and workers find ways of meeting problems arising from the impact of age on employment.[3]

Requirements. Employers may not refuse to hire, discharge, or otherwise discriminate against an individual with respect to terms and conditions of employment because of such individual's age. The EEOC has the power to make investigations and require the keeping of records necessary or appropriate for the administration of this chapter in accordance with the powers and procedures provided in §§209 and 211 of this title.

In particular, employers are forbidden from altering or segregating employee-benefit programs based on age and are required to maintain records demonstrating the contrary. Many of the requirements are specific to benefit-plan type. (For a full description of compliance requirements, see 29 U.S.C. 623.)

Penalties. Action may be brought against an employer either by an individual (who believes that he or she is the victim of age discrimination by an employer) or by a representative of the EEOC. The court may rule on this action, either dismissing the claim or requiring the employer to

1. hire, reinstate, or promote the employee against whom discrimination has occurred
2. compensate the employee in the amounts of unpaid minimum wages or unpaid overtime compensation (relevant to the claim).

Any employer that fails to cooperate in the investigation of a claim (of a violation of guaranteed rights under this statute) may be punished

---

[3] The prohibitions in this chapter are limited to individuals of at least 40 years of age.

by fine of up to $500 or, if the interfering party has been convicted of previous interference, up to one year of imprisonment.

Thresholds That Provide Exemptions. A firm that employs fewer than 20 employees each working day for 32 weeks in the current or preceding year is exempt (29 U.S.C. 630[b]).

Legislative Note. The original draft of this act allowed for a threshold of 50 employees before June 30, 1968. This statute does not prohibit compulsory retirement of any employee who has attained 65 years of age and who, for the two-year period immediately before retirement, is employed in a bona fide executive or high policymaking position, if such employee is entitled to an immediate, nonforfeitable annual retirement benefit from a pension, profit-sharing, savings, or deferred compensation plan, or any combination of such plans, of the employer of such employee, which equals, in the aggregate, at least $44,000.

Civil Rights Act of 1964 (P.L. 88-352, 1964)

Intent of Statute. To ensure equality of employment opportunities by eliminating those practices and other devices that discriminate on basis of race, color, religion, sex, or national origin.

Requirements. It is beyond the scope of this document to list all the act's requirements, but an adequate summary applied with common sense is useful. In particular, it is unlawful for an employer to

1. fail to hire, discharge, or otherwise discriminate against any individual with respect to his or her compensation, terms, conditions, or privileges of employment because of such individual's race, color, religion, sex, or national origin
2. limit, segregate, or classify employees or applicants for employment in any way that would deprive or tend to deprive any individual of employment opportunities or otherwise adversely affect that person's status as an employee because of such individual's race, color, religion, sex, or national origin. (For a complete description of unlawful discriminatory employment practices, see 42 U.S.C. 2000e-2.)

Furthermore, every employer, employment agency, and labor organization must

1. make and keep records for the purpose of defending the firm from accusations of unlawful labor practices
2. preserve these records and make such reports as deemed necessary by the EEOC.

Penalties. The EEOC is responsible for investigating claims of unlawful employment practices. The commission either dismisses the claim or tries to eliminate any such alleged unlawful employment practice.

If the court finds that the respondent has intentionally engaged in an unlawful employment practice, the court may

1. enjoin the respondent from engaging in such unlawful employment practice
2. order the reinstatement or hiring of employees with or without back pay (up to two years, payable by the employer, employment agency, or labor organization) or any other equitable relief as the court deems appropriate.[4]

Thresholds That Provide Exemptions. A firm that employs fewer than 15 employees for more than 32 weeks in each of the prior two calendar years is exempt from record-keeping requirements (42 U.S.C. 2000e[b]).

Fair Labor Standards Act (P.L. 75-718, 1938)

Intent of Statute. To establish a federal minimum wage and overtime requirements and more generally promote a minimum standard of living necessary for health, efficiency, and general well-being of workers.

Requirements. The Fair Labor Standards Act requires employers to pay no less than the federal minimum wage.

---

[4]   Interim earnings or amounts earnable with reasonable diligence by the person or persons discriminated against reduce the back pay otherwise allowable.

The act also requires employers to pay employees at a rate not less than 1.5 times the regular rate for hours worked in excess of 40 hours in a week.

This statute also sets requirements for the use of child labor. (A detailed description is given by 29 U.S.C. 212.)

Penalties. Penalties are as follows;

1. Any individual, corporation, or partnership that willfully violates any of the provisions of §215 of this title will, on conviction thereof, be subject to a fine of not more than $10,000 or (if convicted of previous violations) to imprisonment for not more than six months or both.

2. Any employer that violates the minimum wage or maximum-hours provisions of this title will be liable to the employee or employees affected in the amount of their unpaid minimum wages or their unpaid overtime compensation, as the case may be, and in an additional equal amount as liquidated damages.

3. Any employer that discharges an employee for filing unfair-labor charges will be liable for such legal or equitable relief as may be appropriate, including employment, reinstatement, promotion, and the payment of wages lost and an additional equal amount as liquidated damages.

4. Any employer that violates the provisions of this title relating to child labor or any regulation issued under §212 or §213(c)(5) of this title is subject to a civil penalty of up to $10,000 for each employee who was the subject of such a violation. Any person who repeatedly or willfully violates the minimum-wage or maximum-hours provisions of this title is subject to a civil penalty of up to $1,000 for each such violation.

Thresholds That Provide Exemptions. A firm with gross sales under $500,000 is exempt from the regulations of this act (29 U.S.C. 203[s][1][A]). Minimum-wage and maximum-hour requirements do not apply to the following types of employees:

1. Any employee employed in a bona fide executive, administrative, or professional capacity (including any employee employed in the capacity of academic administrative personnel or teacher in elementary or secondary schools)
2. Any employee employed by an establishment that is an amusement or recreational establishment (excluding skiing companies), organized camp, or religious or nonprofit educational conference center (under certain conditions)
3. Any employee employed in the catching, taking, propagating, harvesting, cultivating, or farming of any kind of fish, shellfish, crustacea, sponges, seaweeds, or other aquatic forms of animal and vegetable life, or in the first processing, canning, or packing of such marine products
4. Any employee employed in agriculture (for the details of this exemption, see 29 U.S.C. 213[a][6])
5. Any employee employed in connection with the publication of any weekly, semiweekly, or daily newspaper with a circulation of less than 4,000, the major part of which circulation is within the county where published or counties contiguous thereto.

Additional categories of employees are exempt from the maximum-hour requirements. (For a comprehensive list of these exemptions, see 29 U.S.C. 213[b]).

Legislative Note. The original law declared that an employee employed by an enterprise subject to this chapter by the Fair Labor Standards Amendments of 1966 (P.L. 89-601) (1) for a workweek longer than 44 hours during the first year from the effective date of the Fair Labor Standards Amendments of 1966, (2) for a workweek longer than 42 hours during the second year from such date, or (3) for a workweek longer than 40 hours after the expiration of the second year from such date must receive compensation for his or her employment in excess of the hours specified at a rate not less than 1.5 times the regular rate at which he or she is employed.

National Labor Relations Act of 1935 (NLRA) (P.L. 74-198, 1935)

Intent of Statute. To provide employees with the right to self-organization; to form, join, or assist labor organizations; to bargain collectively through representatives of their own choosing; and to engage in other concerted activities for the purpose of collective bargaining or other mutual aid or protection, as well as the right to refrain from any or all of such activities except to the extent that such right may be affected by an agreement requiring membership in a labor organization as a condition of employment as authorized in 29 U.S.C. 158(a)(3).

Requirements. The act makes it illegal for employers to engage in unfair labor practices. Such practices are those that

1. interfere with, restrain, or coerce employees in the exercise of the rights guaranteed in 157 of this title
2. dominate or interfere with the formation or administration of any labor organization or contribute financial or other support to it
3. encourage or discourage membership in any labor organization by discrimination in regard to hire or tenure of employment or any term or condition of employment
4. discharge or otherwise discriminate against an employee because he or she has filed charges or given testimony under this subchapter.

Penalties. The National Labor Relations Board (NLRB) or any agent or agency designated by the NLRB for such purposes has the power to issue and cause to be served on such person (corporation, association, business concern, or organized group of individuals) a complaint stating the charges in that respect and containing a notice of hearing before the NLRB or a member thereof or before a designated agent or agency. (Title 29 U.S.C. 160 details the powers of the board and the conditional role of the courts in resolving labor issues covered under this statute.)

When the NLRB finds that an employer has engaged in unfair labor practices in violation of this act, it may order the employer to cease all unfair labor practices and reinstate employees as may be necessary with or without back pay.

Any person who willfully resists, prevents, impedes, or interferes with any member of the board or any of its agents or agencies in the performance of duties pursuant to this subchapter may be punished by a fine of not more than $5,000 or by imprisonment for not more than one year or both.

Thresholds That Provide Exemptions. Any wholly owned government corporation or any state or political subdivision thereof is exempt. Also, any person or enterprise subject to the Railway Labor Act of 1926 (44 Stat. 577) is exempt from the regulations of this act (29 U.S.C. 152[2]).[5]

Environmental Regulations

Most federal environmental regulations do not provide an exemption from these regulations for a business because of its small size. Even when there is an explicit size exemption, such as in the Small Business Liability Relief and Brownfields Revitalization Act of 2001 (P.L. 107-117), the exemption is determined by the volume of material that a firm releases rather than by the size of the firm itself.

The federal government has recognized that compliance with environmental regulations can be particularly costly for small businesses—especially those engaged in manufacturing. Compliance with many regulations carries with it disproportionately large fixed costs, which can be a heavy burden for small firms. Rather than provide exemption from environmental-regulation compliance for small firms, the EPA (the organization responsible for enforcing these regulations) has created a wealth of resources to aid small-business operations with the compliance process.

---

[5] As used in these environmental statutes, the term *person* means an individual, firm, corporation, association, partnership, consortium, joint venture, commercial entity, U.S. government, state, municipality, commission, political subdivision of a state, or any interstate body.

More information about environmental compliance for small businesses can be found in the environmental-assistance resource guide (EPA, 2001).

Comprehensive Environmental Response, Compensation, and Liability Act (P.L. 96-510, 1980)

Intent of Statute. To promote the public health and address other threats posed by sites where hazardous substances have been or may be released into the environment.

Requirements. The EPA administrator issues rules and requires the maintenance of records specifying the identity, characteristics, quantity, origin, or condition (including containerization and previous treatment) of any hazardous substances contained or deposited in a facility.

Beginning with December 11, 1980, for 50 years thereafter or for 50 years after the date of establishment of a record (whichever is later), it is unlawful for anyone knowingly to destroy, mutilate, erase, dispose of, conceal, or otherwise render unavailable or unreadable or to falsify any records required by this act.

Penalties. Penalties are as follows:

1. The owner and operator of a vessel or a facility where hazardous substances were produced or disposed of
2. Any person who arranged for disposal or treatment of hazardous substances at any facility or incineration vessel owned or operated by another party
3. Any person who accepts or accepted any hazardous substances for transport to disposal or treatment facilities, incineration vessels, or sites selected by such person from which there is a release or a threatened release that causes the incurrence of response costs of a hazardous substance

shall be liable for all costs of removal or remedial action incurred by the U.S. government, a state, or a native tribe, including damages for injury to, destruction of, or loss of natural resources (including the reasonable costs of assessing the damage caused by such a release) and the costs of any health assessment or health-effect study carried out under §9604(i).

The liability under this section of a responsible person for each incident involving release of a hazardous substance shall not exceed the total of all costs of response plus $50,000,000 for any damages under this subchapter.

Thresholds That Provide Exemption. Lower limits apply to vessels other than incineration vessels (motor vehicles, aircraft, hazardous-liquid pipeline facility) carrying hazardous substances.

Small Business Liability Relief and Brownfields Revitalization Act (P.L. 107-117, 2002)

Intent of Statute. To amend §107 of CERCLA to provide relief for small-business concerns.

Thresholds That Provide Exemption. There is a conditional exemption from CERCLA for waste generators or transporters that disposed of only very small volumes of materials containing hazardous substances. In particular, firms that disposed of less than 110 gallons of liquid or less than 220 pounds of solid waste or had all or part of disposal treatment (or transport) occur before April 1, 2001, are conditionally exempt. Such generators receive the designation "conditionally exempt small-quantity generators" (CESQG) and are subject to the limited requirements defined for this class (42 U.S.C. 9607[o][1]).

The statute further declares that, under 42 U.S.C. 9607(a)(3), a person shall not be liable with respect to response costs at a facility on the national priorities list for municipal solid waste disposed of at a facility if the person can demonstrate that he or she is a business entity (including a parent, subsidiary, or affiliate of the entity) that, during its three taxable years preceding the date of transmittal of written notification from the President of its potential liability under this section, employed on average not more than 100 full-time individuals or the equivalent thereof and that it is a small-business concern (within the meaning of the Small Business Act [15 U.S.C. 631 et seq.]) from which was generated all of the municipal solid waste attributable to the entity with respect to that facility.

Note that *municipal hazardous waste* is intended to mean waste that contains a relative quantity of hazardous substances no greater than the relative quantity of hazardous substances contained in waste material generated by a typical single-family household.

Legislative Note. The act combined two earlier bills: the Small Business Liability Protection Act and the Brownfields Revitalization and Environmental Restoration Act. These two bills reflect the dual purpose of the act—of providing relief from Superfund liability for small businesses and certain property owners and to promote the revitalization of brownfields, properties where the presence or potential presence of contamination hinders redevelopment. The act clarifies the previous innocent-landowner defense under CERCLA and the new bona fide prospective-purchaser defense to CERCLA liability that the act provides.

Solid Waste Disposal Act of 1965 (P.L. 89-272, 1965)

Intent of Statute. Through financial and technical assistance and leadership in the development, demonstration, and application of new and improved methods and processes, to reduce the amount of waste and unsalvageable materials and to provide for proper and economical solid-waste disposal practices.

Requirements. The act requires firms to follow standards and requirements established by the EPA regarding

1. recordkeeping practices that accurately identify the quantities, constituents, and disposition of hazardous waste
2. labeling practices for any containers used for the storage, transport, or disposal of such waste
3. use of appropriate containers for such waste
4. furnishing of information on the general chemical composition of such waste to those transporting, treating, storing, or disposing of such waste
5. use of a manifest system and any other reasonable means necessary to ensure that all such waste generated is designated for treatment, storage, or disposal and arrives at treatment, storage, or disposal facilities

6. submission of reports to the administrator (or the state agency in any case in which such agency carries out a permit program pursuant to this subchapter) at least once every two years, setting out

    a. the quantities and nature of hazardous waste generated during the year
    b. the disposition of all hazardous waste reported
    c. the efforts undertaken during the year to reduce the volume and toxicity of waste generated
    d. the changes in volume and toxicity of waste actually achieved during the year in question in comparison with previous years, to the extent that such information is available for years prior to November 8, 1984.

For a complete description of hazardous-waste management, see subchapter 3 of chapter 82 of title 42.

Penalties. Whenever, on the basis of any information, the administrator determines that anyone has violated or is in violation of any requirement of this subchapter, the administrator may issue an order assessing a civil penalty for any past or current violation, requiring compliance immediately or within a specified period, or both, or the administrator may commence a civil action in the U.S. district court in the district in which the violation occurred for appropriate relief, including a temporary or permanent injunction. Any order issued pursuant to 42 U.S.C. 6928 (summarized here) may include a suspension or revocation of any permit issued by the administrator or a state. The order will state, with reasonable specificity, the nature of the violation. Any penalty assessed in the order will not exceed $25,000 per day of noncompliance for each violation of a requirement of this subchapter. In assessing such a penalty, the administrator will take into account the seriousness of the violation and any good-faith efforts to comply with applicable requirements.

Furthermore, anyone who knowingly transports hazardous waste without a permit; knowingly generates, treats, stores, or disposes of hazardous waste in violation of this chapter (including inappropriate documentation thereof); or knowingly falsifies records, will, on conviction, be subject to a fine of not more than $50,000 for each day of violation or imprisonment not to exceed two years (five years in the case of a more egregious violation) or both. If the conviction is for a violation committed after a first conviction under this section, the maximum punishment will be doubled with respect to both fine and imprisonment.

Thresholds That Provide Exemptions. None.

Legislative Note. Nothing in this chapter should be construed to apply to (or to authorize any state, interstate, or local authority to regulate) any activity or substance that is subject to the Federal Water Pollution Control Act (P.L. 92-500); the Safe Drinking Water Act (P.L. 93-523); the Marine Protection, Research and Sanctuaries Act of 1972 (P.L. 92 532); or the Atomic Energy Act of 1954 (P.L. 83-703) except to the extent that such application (or regulation) is not inconsistent with the requirements of such acts.

Air Pollution Control Act (P.L. 84-159, 1955)

Intent of Statute. To protect and enhance the quality of the nation's air.

Requirements. The EPA administrator may require anyone who owns or operates any emission source, who manufactures emission-control equipment or process equipment, who the administrator believes may have necessary information regarding emission standards or violations thereof to

1. establish and maintain such records, reporting these to EPA
2. install, use, and maintain such monitoring equipment and use such audit procedures, or methods
3. sample such emissions
4. keep records on control-equipment parameters, production variables, or other indirect data when direct monitoring of emissions is impractical
5. submit compliance certifications
6. provide such other information as the administrator may reasonably require.

For a detailed description of the act's requirements, refer to the subchapter on Air Quality and Emissions Limitations in the U.S. Code.

Penalties. Any person who knowingly

1. makes any false statement or representation (either explicitly or by omission) or alters, conceals, or fails to file or maintain any notice, application, record, report, plan, or other document required to be either filed or maintained
2. fails to notify or report as required under this chapter
3. falsifies, tampers with, renders inaccurate, or fails to install any monitoring device or method required to be maintained or followed

will, on conviction, be punished by a fine pursuant to title 18 (describing legal consequences of specific crimes) or by imprisonment for not more than two years or both.

If a conviction of any person for these violations is a second such conviction, the maximum punishment will be doubled with respect to both the fine and imprisonment.

Thresholds That Provide Exemptions. While there is no explicit exemption based on firm size, the Clean Air Act Amendments of 1990 (P.L. 101-549) provide some exceptions.

Exemptions from Economic Regulation

The federal regulations categorized here as economic regulations tend to utilize size thresholds based on the scale of the specific economic activity being regulated. Thus, the labeling provisions of the Federal Food, Drug, and Cosmetic Act (P.L. 75-717) apply only to companies with an aggregate of consumer sales in excess of $500,000 or consumer food sales in excess of $50,000.

Exemptions from the federal regulation of securities offerings are offered primarily based on the size of the firm making the offer, the size of the offering, the number and sophistication of potential investors, and whether investors are actively solicited.

Food and Drug Administration Modernization Act (P.L. 105-115, 1997)

Intent of Statute. To provide customers with nutritional information about food offered for sale to assist consumers in maintaining healthy dietary practices. This statute also provides guidelines for labeling of drugs and cosmetic products in the interest of consumer safety.

Requirements. A more complete description of labeling requirements appears in 21 U.S.C. 343. The U.S. Secretary of Health and Human Services sets regulations regarding packaging, labeling, nutritional information, quality, and identity of food intended for public consumption. Many of these regulations either vary by type of food (perishable, nonperishable, produce) or pertain to specific foods and often control for things like additives, color enhancement, and chemical residues that may be present. (For a comprehensive description of food regulations, see 21 U.S.C. 341 et seq.)

This act describes standards under which a drug will be considered adulterated (21 U.S.C. 351), misbranded (21 U.S.C. 352), or conditionally exempt from labeling requirements and sale and distribution restrictions (21 U.S.C. 353). It also addresses circumstances under which it is appropriate for a pharmacist to engage in compounding of prescription drugs, setting specific guidelines regarding identification requirements of patients and necessary qualifications to compound a drug, and regulating the quality of substances that are used to compound a drug (21 U.S.C. 353a).

This act regulates new drugs in the following ways:

1. by describing the specific contents and filing procedures of new drug applications
2. by detailing the review and approval process for new drug applications
3. by stating exemption requirements relating to drugs for research and investigational use by scientific experts.

The statute includes an extensive list of prohibited acts and a comprehensive description of drug regulations (see 21 U.S.C. 331 et seq.).

Penalties. These are merely some of the highlights of the section describing penalties. For a complete treatment, see 21 U.S.C. 333.

1. Any person who violates a provision of §331 (an extensive list of prohibited actions regarding food, drugs, and cosmetics) shall be imprisoned for not more than one year or fined not more than $1,000 or both.
2. If any person commits a violation of the provisions in §331 after his or her conviction under this section has become final or commits such a violation with the intent to defraud or mislead, such person shall be imprisoned for not more than three years or fined not more than $10,000 or both.

Any person who violates §331(t) by importing, distributing, purchasing, or trading a prescription drug or drug sample (clearly defined in 21 U.S.C. 331) shall be imprisoned for not more than 10 years or fined not more than $250,000 or both.[6]

Any person that the secretary finds has interfered or is interfering with the U.S. Department of Health and Human Services' discharge of its responsibilities in connection with an abbreviated drug application (through misdirection, bribery, or evidence tampering) shall be liable to the United States for a civil penalty for each such violation in an amount not to exceed $250,000 in the case of an individual and $1,000,000 in the case of any other entity.

Any person who introduces into interstate commerce or delivers for introduction into interstate commerce an article of food that is adulterated within the meaning of §342(a)(2)(B) shall be subject to a civil penalty of not more than $50,000 in the case of an individual and $250,000 in the case of any other person for such introduction or delivery, not to exceed $500,000 for all such violations adjudicated in a single proceeding.

---

[6] Fines for inappropriate distribution of prescription drugs begin at $50,000 for each of the first two violations in a 10-year period, followed by $1,000,000 for each additional violation within that same 10-year period.

Thresholds That Provide Exemptions. A firm with total sales to consumers of not more than $500,000 or sales of food to consumers not more than $50,000 is exempt from these requirements unless the label or labeling of food offered by such person provides nutrition information or makes a nutrition claim (21 U.S.C. 343[q][5][D]).

Subchapter S Revision Act of 1982 (P.L. 97-354, 1982)

Intent of Statute. To ease the tax burden of small businesses. S corporations are domestic corporations that can avoid double taxation by electing to be taxed under subchapter S of the Internal Revenue Code—effectively declaring themselves to be small business corporations for the tax year in question. Any corporation that does not qualify as an S corporation is deemed a C corporation.

Requirements. The taxable income of an S corporation is computed in the same manner as it is for an individual, except for the following:

1. The S corporation separately states items of income (including tax-exempt income), loss, deduction, or credit whose separate treatment could affect the liability for tax of any shareholder.
2. The deductions to which 26 U.S.C. 703(a)(2) refers are not allowed to the S corporation.
3. An S corporation's organizational expenditures may, at the corporation's election, be treated as deferred expenses. In computing taxable income, such deferred expenses are allowed as a deduction ratably over a period of not less than 60 months as the corporation chooses (beginning with the month in which it begins business).
4. If the S corporation (or any predecessor) was a C corporation for any of the three immediately preceding taxable years, 26 U.S.C. 291 applies.

Penalties. In the case of federal income tax, appropriate penalties for general tax evasion apply. However, in the context of this document, it could be considered a violation if an S corporation were forced to change its filing status to that of a C corporation or fail to qualify as an S corporation in the first place. In that case, such a corporation would be subject to the stricter tax requirements imposed on larger corporations. In particular, such a corporation would be subject to the normal taxes and surtaxes imposed by the code.

Thresholds Defining S Corporations. To meet the definition of an S corporation (small business corporation), a firm must meet the following criteria:

- It must not have more than 75 shareholders.
- It must not have as a shareholder an entity that is not an individual.
- It must not have a nonresident alien as a shareholder
- It must not have more than one class of stock.
- It must meet eligibility criteria as defined in 26 U.S.C. 1361(b)(2) (26 U.S.C. 1361[b]).

Furthermore, the statute also provides for specific instances in which the definition of *small business corporation* may be relaxed—in particular with regard to the number of shareholders and which trusts may be legally be shareholders (without changing the status of the corporation).

Legislative Note. Thresholds for subchapter S corporations are less significant with the growing use of LLCs, which also allow investors to avoid double taxation. For LLCs in most states, there are no restrictions on ownership: Members may include individuals, corporations, other LLCs, and foreign entities. There is also typically no maximum number of members in an LLC.

Securities Exchange Act (P.L. 73-291, 1934)

Intent of Statute. To protect investors by requiring that publicly held firms disclose material information about the nature, financial structure, organization, and other material information about the business.

Requirements. A security may be registered on a national securities exchange by the issuer filing an application with the exchange containing such information as the SEC may require as necessary or appropriate in the public interest or for the protection of investors, such as the following:

1. The organization, financial structure, and nature of the business
2. The terms, position, rights, and privileges of the different classes of securities outstanding
3. The terms on which their securities are to be and, during the preceding three years, have been offered to the public or otherwise
4. The directors, officers, and underwriters and each security holder of record holding more than 10 percent of any class of any equity security of the issuer (other than an exempted security)
5. The nature of the holder's relationship with the issuer and any person directly or indirectly controlling or controlled by the issuer
6. Bonus and profit-sharing arrangements
7. Management and service contracts
8. Material contracts not made in the ordinary course of business that are to be executed in whole or in part at or after the filing of the application or that were made not more than two years before such filing
9. Balance sheets for not more than the three preceding fiscal years, certified if required by the SEC by a registered public accounting firm
10. Profit and loss statements for not more than the three preceding fiscal years, certified if required by the rules and regulations of the SEC by a registered public accounting firm
11. Any further financial statements that the SEC may deem necessary or appropriate for the protection of investors.

The SEC may further require copies of articles of incorporation, bylaws, trust indentures, or material contracts.

Penalties. Failure to meet these requirements may cause a security to remain unregistered until all relevant requirements are met to the SEC's satisfaction.

Thresholds That Provide Exemptions. Fewer than 500 stockholders and less than $1 million in assets (15 U.S.C. 78l[g]).

Securities Act (P.L. 73-22, 1933)

Intent of Statute. To protect investors by requiring public firms to disclose material information relevant to the decisions of potential investors.

Requirements. Any security may be registered with the SEC by filing a registration statement in triplicate, at least one copy of which shall be signed by each issuer, its principal executive officers, its principal financial officer, its comptroller or principal accounting officer, and the majority of its board of directors or persons performing similar functions (or, if there is no board of directors or persons performing similar functions, by the majority of the persons or board having the power of management of the issuer).

At the time of filing a registration statement, the applicant pays to the SEC a fee at a rate equal to $92 per $1,000,000 of the maximum aggregate price at which such securities are proposed to be offered, except that, for the years 2003 through 2011, the SEC will, by order, adjust the rate required for such fiscal year to a rate that, when applied to the baseline estimate of the aggregate maximum offering prices for such fiscal year, is reasonably likely to produce aggregate fee collections that are equal to the target offsetting collection amount for such fiscal year. The registration statement will contain the information and be accompanied by the documents specified in 15 U.S.C. 77aa.

Penalties. Any person who violates the provisions of this subchapter or who willfully, in a filed registration statement, makes any untrue statement of material fact (either directly or by omission) will, on conviction, be fined not more than $10,000 or imprisoned not more than five years or both.

Whenever it appears to the SEC that any person has violated any provision of this subchapter or the rules specified by the SEC, it may bring an action in a U.S. district court to seek a civil penalty to be paid by the person who committed such violation. The possible civil penalties are three-tiered:

1. less than or equal to $5,000 for a natural person or $50,000 for any other person
2. less than or equal to $50,000 for a natural person or $250,000 for any other person
3. less than or equal to $100,000 for a natural person or $500,000 for any other person or the gross amount of pecuniary gain to such defendant as a result of the violation for all three tiers, as described in 15 U.S.C. 77t.

Thresholds That Provide Exemptions.

1. Regulation A: Raise up to $5 million every 12 months; can solicit but must also file with the SEC.
2. Regulation D, Rule 504: Raise up to $1 million; can solicit but most investors cannot resell
3. Regulation D, Rule 505: Raise up to $5 million but only accredited investors plus 35 nonaccredited and cannot resell easily
4. Regulation D, Rule 506: No dollar limit but only accredited investors plus 35 sophisticated investors; cannot solicit or resell easily
5. Sales to accredited investors only of less than $5 million (15 U.S.C. 77c[a]).

Legislative Note. Final registration-rate adjustment: For fiscal year 2012 and all succeeding fiscal years, the SEC will, by order, adjust the rate required for all of such fiscal years to a rate that, when applied to the baseline estimate of the aggregate maximum offering prices for fiscal year 2012, is reasonably likely to produce aggregate fee collections in fiscal year 2012 equal to the target offsetting collection amount for fiscal year 2011.

Legislation Supportive of Small Businesses

The federal government has funded various programs to support small-business operations. The most prominent of these is the Small Business

Act of 1953 (P.L. 83-163), which created the SBA. That legislation used a definition of *small business* that was industry- and context-specific, and the majority of federal legislation supporting small-business activity relies on similar, context-specific definitions of *small business*.

Small Business Act (P.L. 83-163, 1953)

Intent of Statute. To aid, counsel, assist, and protect, insofar as is possible, the interests of small-business concerns to preserve free, competitive enterprise; to ensure that a fair proportion of the total purchases and contracts or subcontracts for property and services for the government (including, but not limited to, contracts or subcontracts for maintenance, repair, and construction) be placed with small-business enterprises; and to ensure that a fair proportion of the total sales of government property be made to such enterprises.

Provisions. Title 15, section 633 of the U.S. Code provides for the creation of the SBA, the purpose of which is to carry out the policies declared in this statute. The SBA also oversees small-business loans, provided documentation concerning all previous refused loans from other lenders.

This statute also establishes the Small Business Innovation Research (SBIR) program, under which a portion of a federal agency's research or research and development effort is reserved for award to small-business concerns through a uniform process.

A provision in this statute establishes funding for the creation of state-level small-business development centers. Small-business development centers are authorized to form an association to pursue matters of common concern. Furthermore, on an annual basis, small-business development centers review and coordinate public and private partnerships and cosponsorships with the SBA to more efficiently leverage available resources on a national and a state basis.

Special contracting considerations are also made for small businesses. In particular, priority is given to awarding contracts and placing subcontracts with small-business concerns that perform a substantial proportion of the production on those contracts and subcontracts within areas of concentrated unemployment or underemployment or within labor-surplus areas.

Thresholds That Provide Coverage. A small-business concern is one that is independently owned and operated and that is not dominant in its field of operation. The appropriate standard may use number of employees, dollar volume of business, net worth, net income, a combination thereof, or other appropriate factors, and the administrator ensures that the size standard varies from industry to industry to the extent necessary to reflect the differing characteristics of the various industries and consider other factors deemed to be relevant by the administrator.

According to the SBA (15 U.S.C. 632[a]), the most common (current) size standards (by industry) are

- 500 employees for most manufacturing and mining industries
- 100 employees for all wholesale trade industries
- $5 million for most retail and service industries
- $27.5 million for most general and heavy construction industries
- $11.5 million for all special trade contractors
- $0.75 million for most agricultural industries.

Regulatory Flexibility Act (P.L. 96-354, 1980)

Intent of Statute. To protect small entities from undue burdens created by imposing federal rules by requiring that, for any proposed rule, the relevant agency prepare and make available for public comment an initial regulatory-flexibility analysis that describes the impact of the proposed rule on small entities.

Provisions. Federal agencies are required to prepare and make publicly available an initial regulatory-flexibility analysis before new rulemaking. This analysis describes the impact of the proposed rule on small entities, as well as an estimate of the number of small entities that the proposed rule is likely to affect. Finally, the analysis includes a description of reporting and recordkeeping requirements.

Each initial regulatory-flexibility analysis also contains a description of any significant alternatives to the proposed rule that accomplish the stated objectives of applicable statutes and that minimize any significant economic impact of the proposed rule on small entities. Consistent with the stated objectives of applicable statutes, the analysis discusses significant alternatives such as

1. the establishment of differing compliance or reporting requirements or timetables that take into account the resources available to small entities
2. the clarification, consolidation, or simplification of compliance and reporting requirements for small entities
3. the use of performance rather than design standards
4. an exemption from coverage of the rule or any part thereof for such small entities.

Thresholds That Provide Exemptions. Same as Small Business Act (P.L. 83-163) (5 U.S.C. 601[3]).

Proper Consideration of Small Entities in Agency Rulemaking (Bush, 2002)

Intent of Statute. To require agencies to establish policies and procedures to promote compliance with the RFA (P.L. 96-354).

Provisions. The SBA Office of Advocacy submits a report not less than annually to the OMB director on the extent of agencies' compliance with this order.

Agencies thoroughly review draft rules to assess and take appropriate account of the potential impact on small businesses, small governmental jurisdictions, and small organizations as provided by the RFA. The SBA chief counsel for advocacy is available to advise agencies in performing that review consistently with RFA provisions.

Thresholds That Provide Coverage. Same as Small Business Act (P.L. 83-163) (15 U.S.C. 632[a]).

Small Business Paperwork Relief Act (P.L. 107-198, 2002)

Intent of Statute. Requires OMB and other federal agencies to publish on the Internet a list of the compliance-assistance resources available at federal agencies for small businesses.

Provisions. With respect to the collection of information and the control of paperwork, each agency certifies (and provides a record supporting such certification, including public comments received by the agency) that each collection of information submitted to the OMB director for review under §3507

1. is necessary for the agency to properly perform its functions, including that the information has practical utility
2. is not unnecessarily duplicative of information otherwise reasonably accessible to the agency
3. reduces to the extent practicable and appropriate the burden on persons who provide information to or for the agency, including with respect to small entities, as defined under 5 U.S.C. 601(6), the use of such techniques as
   a. establishing differing compliance or reporting requirements or timetables that take into account the resources available to those who are to respond
   b. the clarification, consolidation, or simplification of compliance and reporting requirements
   c. an exemption from coverage of the collection of information or any part thereof.

Thresholds That Provide Coverage. Firms with fewer than 25 employees are defined as *small businesses*. (Also applies to firms defined as small businesses under the Small Business Act [P.L. 83-163].) (See 44 U.S.C. 3506[c][3].)

Paperwork Reduction Acts (P.L. 96-511, 1980; P.L. 104-13, 1995)

Intent of Statute. Minimize the paperwork burden resulting from the collection of information by or for the federal government for individuals; small businesses; educational and nonprofit institutions; federal contractors; state, local, and tribal governments; and other persons.

Provisions. With respect to the collection of information and the control of paperwork, in addition to the requirements of this chapter regarding the reduction of information-collection burdens for small-business concerns (as defined in §3 of the Small Business Act [P.L. 83-163]), each agency makes efforts to further reduce the information-collection burden for small-business concerns with fewer than 25 employees.

Thresholds That Provide Coverage. Fewer than 25 employees. Also applies to firms defined as *small businesses* under the Small Business Act (P.L. 83-163) (44 U.S.C. 3506[c][4]).

Small Business Regulatory Enforcement Fairness Act (P.L. 104-121, 1996)

Intent of Statute. To ensure federal-agency compliance with the RFA (P.L. 96-354).

Provisions. For each rule or group of related rules for which an agency is required to prepare a final regulatory-flexibility analysis under 5 U.S.C. 604, the agency publishes one or more guides to assist small entities in complying with the rule and designates such publications as small-entity compliance guides. The guides explain the actions that a small entity is required to take to comply with a rule or group of rules. The agency ensures that the guide is written using sufficiently plain language that is likely to be understood by affected small entities.

The SBA ombudsman is granted authority to work with each agency with regulatory authority over small businesses to ensure that small-business concerns that receive or are subject to an audit, on-site inspection, compliance assistance effort, or other enforcement-related communication or contact by agency personnel are provided with a means to comment on the enforcement activity conducted by such personnel.

Thresholds That Provide Coverage. Same as Small Business Act (P.L. 83-163) (15 U.S.C. 632[a]).

Clean Air Act Amendments of 1990 (P.L. 101-549, 1990)

Intent of Statute. To assist small-business stationary sources with pollution prevention and accidental-release detection and prevention, providing information concerning alternative technologies, process changes, products, and methods of operation that help reduce air pollution.

Provisions. After reasonable notice and public hearings, each state adopts and submits to the administrator plans for establishing a small-business stationary-source technical and environmental compliance-assistance program. Programs should include

1. adequate mechanisms for developing, collecting, and coordinating information concerning compliance methods and technologies for small-business stationary sources and programs to encourage lawful cooperation among such sources and other persons to further compliance with this chapter.
2. adequate mechanisms for assisting small-business stationary sources with pollution prevention and accidental-release detection and prevention, including providing information concerning alternative technologies, process changes, products, and methods of operation that help reduce air pollution.
3. a designated state office within the relevant state agency to serve as ombudsman for small-business stationary sources in connection with the implementation of this chapter.
4. a compliance-assistance program for small-business stationary sources that assists small-business stationary sources in determining applicable requirements and in receiving permits under this chapter in a timely and efficient manner.
5. adequate mechanisms to ensure that small-business stationary sources receive notice of their rights under this chapter in such manner and form as to ensure reasonably adequate time for such sources to evaluate compliance methods and any relevant or applicable proposed or final regulation or standard issued under this chapter.
6. adequate mechanisms for informing small-business stationary sources of their obligations under this chapter, including mechanisms for referring such sources to qualified auditors or, at the state's option, for providing audits of the operations of such sources to determine compliance with this chapter.
7. procedures for consideration of requests from a small-business stationary source for modification of
   a. any work practice or technological method of compliance
   b. the schedule of milestones for implementing such work practice or method of compliance preceding any applicable

compliance date based on the technological and financial capability of any such small-business stationary source. No such modification may be granted unless it is in compliance with the applicable requirements of this chapter, including the requirements of the applicable implementation plan.

Thresholds That Provide Coverage. A firm designated as a small-business stationary source must

1. have fewer than 100 employees
2. meet the definition of *small business* under the Small Business Act (P.L. 83-163)
3. not be identified as a major stationary source
4. not emit 50 tons or more per year of any regulated pollutant
5. emit less than 75 tons per year of all regulated pollutants (42 U.S.C. 7661f[c]).

Conclusions

The federal statutes and programs reviewed in this chapter use a variety of criteria to define *small business* for the purpose of determining whether the statute applies. A business that is considered a small business for the purposes of one statute may not be considered small for other purposes. Most workplace regulations provide exemptions for small businesses, but the threshold used to determine whether a business is small for the purpose of such exemption is defined by the number of employees and varies widely from 11 to 100. In general, recently enacted workplace regulations have higher employment thresholds. Environmental regulations do not provide exemptions based on firm size, although the regulatory process often establishes special programs to help small businesses comply with the regulations or establishes different enforcement procedures for smaller businesses. Economic regulations typically exempt or do not apply to small businesses. In the case of economic regulations, the threshold is defined not in terms of the number of employees, but through some measure that reflects the scale of the economic activity being regulated. All programs that are designed to benefit small businesses have thresholds that determine eligibility. Even within this set of programs, there is no single definition of *small business*. Rather, eligibility thresholds are industry- and context-specific.

This review highlights the complexity of the federal regulatory environment facing small businesses and the challenges involved in evaluating the impact of regulations on small businesses. Given the wide range of thresholds that exist under different regulatory regimes, there is no simple answer to the question of how regulation affects small businesses. The review raises an obvious question of how regulatory thresholds are determined and whether the threshold is appropriate or effective.

APPENDIX B

Methodology for Analysis of Small Businesses and Workplace Fatality Risk

John Mendeloff, Christopher Nelson, Kilkon Ko, and Amelia Haviland

In this appendix, we provide a more detailed discussion of our methodology. We begin by describing how fatality rates were derived for our analysis, first for the numerator (the number of deaths) and then for the denominator (exposure to the risk of death). We then describe the regression analyses used to add more control variables to the analysis and the data on violations and injury cause that were used to explore the drivers of the size-fatality risk relationships we observed.

Numerator Data

The data on workplace deaths for this study come from the inspection files in OSHA's IMIS. Data for the IMIS are available from mid-1974. Before 1987, data were often not available from states using their own state plans to guide inspections (i.e., the 21 states where OSHA had delegated enforcement authority to state agencies). By 1991, all states were participating in IMIS. Most of our analyses use only more recent data, including 17,481 fatalities for the years 1992 through 2001.[1] For comparisons with earlier periods, going from 1975 to 2002, we use data only from the OSHA states (which represent a total of 33,391 deaths). To examine whether size-related patterns change with acci-

---

[1] Unlike this study, the work of Mendeloff and Kagey (1990) used fatal accidents rather than individual fatalities as the unit of analysis. Of all deaths in the OSHA file, 84.4 percent occurred in events with a single death.

dent severity, we also studied hospitalization cases. While these are not included in national databases, we used California data in the IMIS, also for the years 1992 through 2001.

OSHA has always had a requirement that employers notify it by telephone within 24 hours (more recently within eight hours) about work-related deaths and catastrophes, defined as events leading to the hospitalization of three or more workers. The OSHA area director is supposed to investigate these incidents unless they fall outside of OSHA jurisdiction (see below). These investigations (labeled FAT/CATs for fatality/catastrophe) rank second only to "imminent dangers" in OSHA's inspection-priority system. Each year, OSHA investigates fewer than 2,000 deaths (including both OSHA and state-plan states).

There are limitations to the OSHA FAT/CATs data. First, there has been some ambiguity about exactly which cases need to be reported to OSHA. In 2001, OSHA clarified that motor-vehicle accidents on a public street or highway do not have to be reported unless they occurred in a construction work zone. Also exempt from reporting were events that involved a commercial airplane, train, subway, or bus. In contrast, heart attacks at work did have to be reported, as did cases of workplace violence; whether OSHA investigated would be determined by the area director and depend on the circumstances (OSHA, 2001). In general, as we show below, OSHA has investigated only a small percentage of heart attacks and deaths due to assaults.

Another concern is that the fatality investigations in IMIS are incomplete, either because an employer failed to report a fatal injury or because OSHA did not investigate a reported fatal injury. No national file is kept for cases that are reported but not investigated; therefore, we cannot know how many cases fell in the second category.

We assessed the completeness of the IMIS data by comparing the number of cases in IMIS with the number in CFOI. We found that the annual number of deaths in CFOI has averaged more than 6,000 per year, far more than the 1,800 or 1,900 in IMIS. About 20 percent of the CFOI deaths occur to nonemployees (e.g., self-employed, volunteers). If we also remove deaths due to highway motor-vehicle accidents and to assaults, the CFOI annual average dips below 3,000.

For the purposes of this research, however, the key issue is not whether IMIS contains a complete set of fatalities (within the OSHA jurisdiction) but whether the reporting and investigating process leads to *biases* with regard to the size of establishments or firms in the data set. We saw in Chapter Four that there is evidence that smaller establishments may underreport injuries. The underreporting appears to decrease with the severity of the injuries; however, there is no reason to believe that it does not extend, to some degree, to fatalities.[2]

A critical feature of the IMIS data is that they include measures of both establishment and firm employment.[3] It is, however, important to realize that these numbers are not validated. Compliance officers typically write down whatever company officials tell them. Moreover, our examination of the data showed that, prior to 1984, the data submitted to IMIS almost always show the same figures for establishment and firm employment. The figures for that earlier period are higher than later establishment-size numbers but much lower than later firm-size numbers. Since 1984, the figures for average establishment and firm size have been stable. So we decided to ignore pre-1984 data in our analyses of fatality data from federal states. Even after 1983, it is plausible that there are errors in these figures, especially for the firm

---

[2]   To gain some insight into nonreporting to OSHA, we did examine data on the cases in which OSHA issued a citation for employers' failures to report fatalities and hospitalizations. In recent years, these have occurred at a rate of about 40 per year. Most of the cases are in manufacturing; however, this does not mean that most of the underreporting is in that sector. Workplaces are much likelier to be inspected in that sector than in any other; as a result, OSHA is likelier to conduct a routine inspection that discovers that a worker was recently killed. A disproportionate number (relative to reported fatalities) of these citations in manufacturing are against establishments with fewer than 100 workers. The number against workplaces with 1 to 19 workers is not high, but this could be because workplaces with 1 to 10 workers are exempt from programmed inspections; thus OSHA would have fewer opportunities to detect underreporting there.

[3]   Variables in IMIS for fatalities include the following: name and address of company, date of injury, number of employees at that establishment, number of employees covered by the inspection, number of employees controlled for employer, union representation (yes or no), industry, nature of injury (e.g., broken leg, contusions), degree of injury (e.g., died, hospitalized, not hospitalized), injury event (e.g., fall from roof), standards cited as related to the accident (if applicable) and the particular standards violated, the severity of each violation, the penalty (if any) for each violation, age, sex, and occupation.

employment, in which OSHA asks for the "number of employees controlled by the employer." In addition, the number of employees can change over the course of a year, so that the numbers provided, even if accurate, may give a misleading estimate of the average employment for the year.

To gain further insight into possible underreporting, we examined data on *serious, nonfatal injuries* from California, which has had a broader telephone-reporting requirement and accident-investigation program than OSHA has. In addition to requiring reporting of amputations and some other specific injury types, California requires employers to report all cases in which a worker is hospitalized for more than 24 hours (other than for observation). Highway motor-vehicle accidents and assaults are exempt from these requirements. There are roughly seven times as many hospitalized workers as fatally injured ones in the California data; however, it is possible that the cases in the file substantially undercount all hospitalizations. A recent Washington study that relied on reports to the state's monopoly WC-insurance fund (for all but the self-insured) found that the number of hospitalizations was 10 times the number of deaths (Alexander, Franklin, and Fulton-Kehoe, 1999).

In our analyses, we examined fatality rates by industry sectors and by some two-digit SICs (using 1987 SICs). We also looked at more detailed categories. For manufacturing, we looked at four-digit SICs; for other industries, we used three-digit SICs.

For these analyses, the criteria for inclusion in the analysis were as follows:

- For the 1992–2001 analysis of establishment size by firm size, the SIC must have at least 70 deaths during that period.
- For the 1984–2002 analysis of OSHA states, the SIC must have at least 150 deaths over the 1975–2002 period.

Denominator Data

Data on the number of workers employed are needed to provide a measure of exposure to risk and the denominator in the fatality-rate calculations. Data for each establishment-size class come from CBP, which provides annual employment by detailed establishment-size categories by industry and state. At our request, the U.S. Census Bureau produced a matrix showing the number of employees for different combinations of establishment sizes and firm sizes (e.g., establishments with 1 to 19 employees that were part of firms with 20 to 49 employees). The table used 1997 data, the last year the Census Bureau used SICs before switching to NAICS. The Census Bureau tabulates data by employment size of enterprise (see U.S. Census Bureau, undated[h]). Ideally, we would also obtain the Census Bureau establishment/firm matrix data for each year to take into account any changes in the distribution of establishments within firms. However, the cost of that would be prohibitive. Moreover, it seems unlikely that the size distribution of establishments within firms would change very much. Therefore, we assume that the distribution of employment from establishments to firms in 1997 remains the same in other years from 1992 through 2001.

One shortcoming of CBP is that it reports annual employment as of the second week in March. (Other data sources provide more accurate annual average employment by industry but do not provide data by establishment size.) Thus, the rates for industries with high seasonal employment variation (e.g., construction) are likely to be misestimated. However, this is a problem for this study only if the errors affect different size classes of establishments or firms differently. If they do, then the relative rates would be biased.

Based on limited evidence, we found that use of March data may somewhat underestimate the true employment denominator and thus overestimate the rates at smaller establishments. Some insight into the possible size of this bias came from BLS's QCEW, which is based on employers' reports to state UI agencies. A published report on these data compared March 2000 with June 2000 (Okolie, 2004). Overall, national employment grew 3.2 percent. However, employment in establishments that had one to four employees in March grew by 16.8

percent; those that had five to nine, by 6.6 percent; 10 to 19, by 4.8 percent; 20 to 49, by 3.6 percent; 50 to 99, by 2.4 percent; 100 to 249, by 1.3 percent; 250 to 499, by 0.2 percent; 500 to 999, by −0.1 percent; and more than 1,000, by 0.2 percent. Okolie reports, "This finding of monotonically declining (not seasonally adjusted) net employment growth rates does not hold for the other quarters in calendar-year 2000" (2004, p. 12, fn. 5).

A more serious problem with using CBP employment data concerns the construction sector. Recall that our numerator data for the number of deaths in each establishment-size category are based on the IMIS data element for how many workers were employed at the worksite. For fixed-site establishments, the definition that OSHA uses conforms to the establishment definition used by CBP. However, the number of workers that an employer has working at a particular construction site (the OSHA definition) will not necessarily conform to the CBP definition. Often, the construction workers on site will be part of a larger establishment by the CBP definition. As a result, the fatality rates we get by dividing the IMIS deaths in each size category (based on workers on site) by the employment in the size category (based on the CBP definition) will overstate the fatality rates in smaller establishments (and in all establishment-size categories except the largest). Because of this difficulty, we do not include construction in our comparison of establishment-size rates.

Regression Analyses

To see whether our conclusions about the effects of firm and establishment size might be biased due to the omission of variables with which they might be correlated, we conducted regression analyses that allowed us to control for the effects of some other variables. The question posed in this analysis is whether individual workers faced a higher risk of a fatal accident in establishments or firms of different sizes. To answer this question, we had to construct a different data set because we wanted to compare the establishments and firms that have fatalities to similar ones that are randomly selected. However, our fatality data come only from establishments that OSHA inspected, and the basis for inspections is not necessarily random (e.g., worker complaints). Fortunately, planned (or programmed) inspections were targeted randomly prior to 1998. These inspections were carried out only in manufacturing and only in industries (four-digit) with average lost-workday injury rates higher than the private-sector average.[4] We identified the fatality investigations that occurred within those industries that were subject to programmed inspections (exempting establishments with fewer than 11 employees) and merged them in a file with the cases for the programmed inspections. (In these cases, we looked at whether there was a fatal accident at the workplace, not the number of fatalities.) Thus, for example, we may have 100 programmed inspections in the meatpacking industry and five fatality investigations. The analysis looks at whether the probability of a fatality differed by establishment or firm size. Both of those size variables are taken from IMIS; the Census Bureau employment figures were not used in this analysis. This analysis was carried out using Poisson regression.

This analysis also included data on whether a union represented workers at the establishment and whether the workplace was located in a metropolitan area. The union variable was taken from IMIS. The metropolitan variable was calculated by merging the county variable from IMIS with the OMB list of standard metropolitan areas. These two variables both appeared to be possible confounders. It seems likely both that occupational fatality rates are higher in rural or nonmetropolitan areas and that workplaces in those areas tended to be smaller. One reason for the higher fatality rates could be that it takes longer to get injured workers to hospitals where they can get high-quality care.[5] Another hypothesis is that smaller establishments in rural areas are at

---

[4] There are some other exemptions: OSHA does not include establishments with fewer than 11 workers in this program, and it does not inspect if the establishment was the subject of a comprehensive inspection within the prior two years.

[5] Susan P. Baker et al. (1982) examined occupational deaths in Maryland in 1978 and found that 68 percent had died at the scene or en route to the hospital. Since only those who die at the scene are definitely beyond the help of an improved EMS, this finding leaves open the possibility that the effect of EMS might be significant.

a special disadvantage in terms of having access to safety information and in supplying safety to their workers.

The expected effects of unions are more ambiguous. Unions are more common at larger establishments within an industry. If unions reduce fatality risks, then failing to include a union variable could lead us to again overestimate the *direct*, causal role of small size in creating hazards. Viscusi (1983) has noted that finding that unionized workplaces often appear less safe than nonunionized workplaces may reflect a tendency for unions to focus their organizing efforts on workers at less safe workplaces. If unionized workplaces are less safe, omitting a union variable could lead us to underestimate the effect of small size on riskiness.

Violation Data

The IMIS data also include a violation file, which reports all violations cited in the course of an inspection, the particular standard cited, the seriousness of the violation, and the penalty. Although some violations cited in the course of an accident investigation may be unrelated to the accident, the great majority are at least alleged to be related. However, the existence of related violations does not necessarily mean that the death would not have occurred in the absence of the violations. For example, the violation might have had a small effect on the likelihood or severity of the injury.

Event-Type Data

The IMIS data include codes, as judged by special OSHA-paid coders, on a number of variables, including the body part affected, the nature of the injury, and the event type. The latter refers to categories such as "falls from heights" and "struck by." As noted, these codes differ from the ones that BLS uses, there are far fewer of them, and they are less specific.

Regression Analysis for Analysis of Small Businesses and Workplace Fatality Risk

John Mendeloff, Christopher Nelson, Kilkon Ko, and Amelia Haviland

We carried out a regression analysis using the Poisson model to see whether adding variables for nonmetropolitan location and unionization affected our estimates of establishment- and firm-size effects. Establishments in nonmetropolitan areas would be farther from trauma centers capable of providing adequate care to seriously injured workers and perhaps would have less access to information about hazards. Union status is linked with larger establishment and firm size and might be associated with higher risks, as other studies (Viscusi, 1983) have found. Although it might be useful to test other variables as well, these two were the only variables available in our data set.[1]

For these analyses, we constructed a new data set for OSHA states. The data set included randomly conducted, planned inspections in manufacturing from 1984 through 1995 and fatality investigations in the same industries during that period. It is important to note that this sample is quite different, even for manufacturing, from the one we examined in the tabular analysis. It includes different years, and it does not include all manufacturing industries. We carried out regressions using the Poisson model, which estimates the risk that an indi-

---

[1] One reviewer did note that we could have included a variable describing the frequency of inspections in each industry and state. This would allow us to test whether a higher probability of inspection was linked to lower fatality rates. Neither the reviewer nor we believed, however, that inclusion of this variable was likely to change the size coefficients. Another possible variable could have characterized each establishment's OSHA-inspection history. However, constructing this variable would have involved a major data-linking exercise, because the OSHA data do not include a unique establishment identifier.

vidual worker will have a fatal accident. The Poisson model was also useful because it smoothes out small effects, reducing the signal-to-noise ratio.

First, we compared the results of analyses with and without the metropolitan and union variables and found that their inclusion did not affect the coefficients for establishment and firm size. Although we cannot be certain that this same conclusion applies to the 1992–2001 data set that we examined in our tabular analysis, it seems likely that it does. Therefore, including those variables would probably not change our results. Second, as in our tabular analysis, the findings were that fatality rates were highest in the smallest establishment-size category (1 to 19 employees).[2] Figure C.1 shows the coefficients.[3]

Third, the analyses indicate that, within a given establishment-size category, fatality risks tend to increase with firm size in a number of sectors, except for the 1,000-or-more-employee firm-size category. The pattern of increases with larger firm size was stronger than the one that appears in the tabular analysis. In particular, in every establishment-size category, the fatality rate for the 1,000-or-more-employee firm size was clearly higher than the rate for the smallest firms; in the tabular analysis, these rates were often similar. Although many of the differences in firm-size effects in the Poisson regression were not statistically significant, this comparison between the 1,000-or-more-employee firm-size category and the smallest firm-size category was.

Metropolitan location by itself reduces the fatality rate by about 40 percent. Finally, our analyses also indicate that fatality risks at non-union workplaces are about 12 percent lower than at unionized workplaces. It is not clear whether this reflects a failing of unions or a tendency for unions to organize at workplaces with higher risks.

---

[2]   As we did with the tabular analysis, we also redid the analysis omitting inspections at plants in the logging industry (results not shown). As in the tabular analysis, the results did decrease the effect of being in the smallest establishment-size category but showed the same basic patterns.

[3]   The actual calculations of risk can be found in Appendix C of Mendeloff et al. (2006).

Figure C.1
**Poisson Regression Coefficients and Their Confidence Intervals, by Each
Size Level**

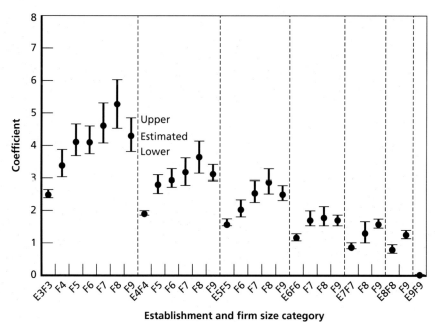

Firms' Reasons to Go Private or Go Dark After Sarbanes-Oxley

Ehud Kamar, Pinar Karaca-Mandic, and Eric Talley

Below, we provide reasons that firms offered for their decision to go private or to go dark after SOX was enacted.

Landair Transport explains the following in a Schedule TO it filed on December 23, 2003, as part of its going private:

> Over the past year, [the CEO and the COO] discussed in general terms the disadvantages faced by Landair as a smaller sized publicly-traded company. In particular, they noted the historically low trading volume for the common stock of Landair that resulted in an illiquid market for Landair's public shareholders; Landair's limited ability to attract institutional investors and equity research analyst coverage; the costs of (and efforts of management required as a result of) being a public company; and the reduced flexibility to focus on long-term business goals, as opposed to the more short-term focus that can result from quarterly earnings releases and filing requirements of the SEC.

> In late September and early October of 2002, [they] concluded that these disadvantages were significantly outweighing the advantages of leaving Landair as a publicly-traded company controlled by [the CEO]. A factor contributing to this conclusion . . . was the enactment of the Sarbanes-Oxley Act of 2002 and the adoption of related rule proposals by the [National Association of Securities Dealers]. As a result of these developments and the current environment relating to the regulation of public companies, [they] anticipated significant increased costs in operat-

ing as a public company. They also believed that such increased regulation would place additional burdens on management that would further distract them from managing the business operations of Landair. (Tweed, Landair Acquisition Corporation, and Niswonger, 2002)

Similarly, Coast Dental Services explains its reasoning in a Schedule TO it filed on March 4, 2003, as part of its going dark:

> The Board of Directors of Coast Dental (the "Board") believes that the public market has not shown much interest in Coast Dental Shares the past few year and that Coast Dental has been unable to realize the principal benefits of being a publicly-traded company. Coast Dental shares are very thinly traded and provide little, if any, liquidity for shareholders, particularly those shareholders with larger equity positions in Coast Dental. During the twelve months prior to February 1, 2003, the average daily trading volume of our shares has been less than 2,000 and on approximately 27 percent of the trading days there were no shares traded. In addition, it is unlikely that Coast Dental could issue additional shares to obtain financing because of the low trading price, low trading volume and illiquidity of the shares.

> The Board also believes that there are considerable costs and detriments in remaining a publicly-traded company. In addition to the substantial time expended by Coast Dental management, the legal, auditing, accounting and other expenses involved in the preparation, filing and dissemination of annual and other periodic reports are considerable and will likely increase significantly in the future as a result of the Sarbanes-Oxley Act of 2002. Additionally, management believes that required public disclosures under the Exchange Act give its competitors, some of which are not publicly-traded companies, certain information and insights about us that may help such competitors in competing against us. (Coast Dental Services, 2003)

References

Abowd, John, John Haltiwanger, Julia Lane, and Kristin Sandusky, *Within and Between Firm Changes in Human Capital, Technology, and Productivity*, Washington, D.C.: U.S. Census Bureau, October 6, 2001. As of July 27, 2007: http://lehd.dsd.census.gov/led/library/misc/hcpaper.pdf

Abowd, John M., John Haltiwanger, Ron Jarmin, Julia Lane, Paul Lengermann, Kristin McCue, Kevin McKinney, and Kristin Sandusky, *The Relation Among Human Capital, Productivity and Market Value: Building Up from Micro Evidence*, paper presented at April 2002 National Bureau of Economic Research Conference on Research in Income and Wealth, December 6, 2002. As of July 27, 2007: http://instruct1.cit.cornell.edu/~jma7/nbercriw_20021206.pdf

Acs, Zoltan J., and Catherine Armington, *Job Flow Dynamics in the Service Sector*, Washington, D.C.: Center for Economic Studies, U.S. Department of Commerce, Bureau of the Census, 1999.

Agency for Healthcare Research and Quality, *Medical Expenditure Panel Survey*, 2000. As of August 9, 2007: http://www.meps.ahrq.gov/mepsweb/index.jsp

———, *Medical Expenditure Panel Survey*, 2003. As of August 9, 2007: http://www.meps.ahrq.gov/mepsweb/index.jsp

Agesa, Jacqueline, Richard U. Agesa, and Gary A. Hoover, "Market Structure and Racial Earnings: Evidence from Job-Changers.," *American Economic Review*, Vol. 91, No. 2, May 2001, pp. 169–173.

AHIP—*see* America's Health Insurance Plans.

AHRQ—*see* Agency for Healthcare Research and Quality.

Alexander, Bruce H., Gary M. Franklin, and Deborah Fulton-Kehoe, "Comparison of Fatal and Severe Nonfatal Traumatic Work-Related Injuries in Washington State," *American Journal of Industrial Medicine*, Vol. 36, No. 2, August 1999, pp. 317–325.

America's Health Insurance Plans, "Health Savings Accounts Off to Fast Start, New AHIP Study Shows," press release, January 12, 2005. As of July 12, 2007: http://www.ahip.org/content/pressrelease.aspx?docid=7303

———, "January 2006 Census Shows 3.2 Million People Covered by HSA Plans," 2006. As of July 12, 2007: http://www.ahipresearch.org/pdfs/HSAHDHPReportJanuary2006.pdf

American Chemistry Council, "Responsible Care®," undated Web page. As of July 5, 2007: http://www.americanchemistry.com/s_responsiblecare/ sec.asp?CID=1298&DID=4841

Antos, Joseph R., "Union Effects on White-Collar Compensation," *Industrial and Labor Relations Review*, Vol. 36, No. 3, April 1983, pp. 461–479.

Armington, Catherine, and Zoltan J. Acs, "Job Creation and Persistence in Services and Manufacturing," *Journal of Evolutionary Economics*, Vol. 14, No. 3, July 2004, pp. 309–325.

Armington, Catherine, and Alicia Robb, *Mergers and Acquisitions in the United States: 1990–1994*, Washington, D.C.: Center for Economic Studies, U.S. Department of Commerce, Bureau of the Census, 1998.

Arthur Andersen and Company, and National Small Business United, *Survey of Small and Mid-Sized Businesses: Trends for 1994*, St. Louis, Mo.: Arthur Andersen Enterprise Group, 1994.

Asthana, Sharad, Steven Balsam, and Sungsoo Kim, *The Effect of Enron, Andersen, and Sarbanes-Oxley on the Market for Audit Services*, June 2004.

Austin, Jeannette L., "The Rise of Citizen-Suit Enforcement of Environmental Law: Reconciling Private and Public Attorneys General," *Northwestern University Law Review*, Vol. 81, No. 2, 1986–1987, pp. 220–262.

Baker, George P., and Rachel Parkin, "Changing Structure of the Legal Services Industry and the Careers of Lawyers," *North Carolina Law Review*, Vol. 84, No. 5, June 2006, pp. 1635–1682.

Baker, George P., and Karen H. Wruck, "Organizational Changes and Value Creation in Leveraged Buyouts: The Case of the O. M. Scott and Sons Company," *Journal of Financial Economics*, Vol. 25, No. 2, December 1989, pp. 163–190.

Baker, Scott, and Kimberly D. Krawiec, "The Economics of Limited Liability: An Empirical Study of New York Law Firms," *University of Illinois Law Review*, Vol. 2005, No. 1, 2005, pp. 107–170.

Baker, Susan P., Judith S. Samkoff, Russell S. Fisher, and Carol B. Van Buren, "Fatal Occupational Injuries," *Journal of the American Medical Association*, Vol. 248, No. 6, August 13, 1982, pp. 692–697.

Barsky, Carl B., "Incidence Benefits Measures in the National Compensation Survey," *Monthly Labor Review*, Vol. 127, No. 8, August 2004, pp. 21–28. As of July 27, 2007:
http://stats.bls.gov/opub/mlr/2004/08/art3full.pdf

Bartel, Ann P., and Lacy Glenn Thomas, "Predation Through Regulation: The Wage and Profit Effects of the Occupational Safety and Health Administration and the Environmental Protection Agency," *Journal of Law and Economics*, Vol. 30, No. 2, October 1987, pp. 239–264.

Bates, Timothy, *Small Businesses Do Appear to Benefit from State-Local Government Economic Development Assistance*, Washington, D.C.: Bureau of the Census, Center for Economic Studies discussion paper 95-2, February 1995.

Baumol, William J., Robert E. Litan, and Carl J. Schramm, *Good Capitalism, Bad Capitalism, and the Economics of Growth and Prosperity*, New Haven, Conn.: Yale University Press, 2007.

Becker, Randy, and J. Vernon Henderson, *Effects of Air Quality Regulation on Decisions of Firms in Polluting Industries*, Cambridge, Mass.: National Bureau of Economic Research, W6160, 1997.

Belman, Dale, and David I. Levine, "Size, Skill, and Sorting," *Labour: Review of Labour Economics and Industrial Relations*, Vol. 18, No. 4, December 2004, pp. 515–561.

Bennett, James D., and David L. Passmore, "Unions and Coal Mine Safety: The Effect of Unionization on Safety in Bituminous Deep Mines," *Journal of Labor Research*, Vol. 6, No. 2, Spring 1985, pp. 211–216.

Benninga, Simon, Mark Helmantel, and Oded Sarig, "The Timing of Initial Public Offerings," *Journal of Financial Economics*, Vol. 75, No. 1, January 2005, pp. 115–132.

Berger, Mark C., Dan A. Black, Frank A. Scott, and Steven N. Allen, *Distribution of Low-Wage Workers by Firm Size in the U.S.: Final Report*, Lexington, Ky.: Carolyn Looff and Associates, December 9, 1999. As of July 27, 2007:
http://www.sba.gov/advo/research/rs196tot.pdf

Berkeley Planning Associates, and U.S. Small Business Administration, *Labor Turnover and Worker Mobility in Small and Large Firms: Evidence from the SIPP (Survey of Income and Program Participation)*, Berkeley, Va.: Berkeley Planning Associates, 1988.

Bernstein, Jared, and Maury Gittleman, "Exploring Low-Wage Labor with the National Compensation Survey," *Monthly Labor Review*, Vol. 126, Nos. 11–12, November–December 2003, pp. 3–12. As of July 27, 2007:
http://stats.bls.gov/opub/mlr/2003/11/art1full.pdf

Bitler, Marianne P., *Small Businesses and Computers: Adoption and Performance*, San Francisco, Calif.: Federal Reserve Bank of San Francisco, working paper 2001-15, 2001. As of July 27, 2007:
http://www.frbsf.org/publications/economics/papers/2001/wp01-15bk.pdf

Bitler, Marianne P., Alicia M. Robb, and John D. Wolken, "Financial Services Used by Small Businesses: Evidence from the 1998 Survey of Small Business Finances," *Federal Reserve Bulletin*, Vol. 87, No. 4, April 2001, pp. 183–205. As of July 27, 2007:
http://www.federalreserve.gov/pubs/bulletin/2001/0401lead.pdf

Block, Stanley B., "The Latest Movement to Going Private: An Empirical Study," *Journal of Applied Finance*, Vol. 14, No. 1, Spring–Summer 2004, pp. 36–44.

BLS—*see* U.S. Bureau of Labor Statistics.

Blumberg, Linda J., and Len M. Nichols, *Health Insurance Market Reforms: What They Can and Cannot Do*, Washington, D.C.: Urban Institute, 1995.

———, "First, Do No Harm: Developing Health Insurance Market Reform Packages," *Health Affairs*, Vol. 15, No. 3, Fall 1996, pp. 35–53.

Boden, Richard J., Jr., *Establishment Employment Change and Survival, 1992–1996: Analyses Based on a New, Longitudinal Database with Special Focus on Information Technology Industries*, Washington, D.C.: U.S. Small Business Administration, February 2000a. As of July 27, 2007:
http://www.sba.gov/advo/research/rs200tot.pdf

———, *Analyses of Business Dissolution by Demographic Category of Business Ownership*, Washington, D.C.: U.S. Small Business Administration, December 2000b. As of July 27, 2007:
http://www.sba.gov/advo/research/rs204tot.pdf

Bowlus, Audra J., Nicholas M. Kiefer, and George R. Neumann, "Estimation of Equilibrium Wage Distributions with Heterogeneity," *Journal of Applied Econometrics*, Vol. 10, Special Issue: *The Microeconometrics of Dynamic Decision Making*, December 1995, pp. S119–S131.

Bradford, Steven C., "Does Size Matter? An Economic Analysis of Small Business Exemptions from Regulation," *Journal of Small and Emerging Business Law*, Vol. 8, No. 1, Spring 2004, pp. 1–38.

Brock, Kathy, "LifeWise Edges Back into Small-Group Market," *Portland Business Journal*, January 23, 1998. As of July 10, 2007:
http://www.bizjournals.com/portland/stories/1998/01/26/newscolumn2.html

Bromberg, Alan R., and Larry E. Ribstein, *Bromberg and Ribstein on Limited Liability Partnerships, the Revised Uniform Partnership Act, and the Uniform Limited Partnership Act (2001)*, Frederick, Md.: Aspen Law and Business, 2003.

Brown, Charles, James Hamilton, and James L. Medoff, *Employers Large and Small*, Cambridge, Mass.: Harvard University Press, 1990.

Brown, Charles, and James Medoff, "The Employer Size-Wage Effect," *Journal of Political Economy*, Vol. 97, No. 5, October 1989, pp. 1027–1059.

Brown, Clair, John C. Haltiwanger, and Julia I. Lane, *Economic Turbulence: Is a Volatile Economy Good for America?* Chicago, Ill.: University of Chicago Press, 2006.

Buchmueller, Thomas, and John DiNardo, "Did Community Rating Induce an Adverse Selection Death Spiral? Evidence from New York, Pennsylvania, and Connecticut," *American Economic Review*, Vol. 92, No. 1, March 2002, pp. 280–294.

Buchmueller, Thomas C., and Gail A. Jensen, "Small Group Reform in a Competitive Managed Care Market: The Case of California, 1993 to 1995," *Inquiry*, Vol. 34, No. 3, 1997, pp. 249–263.

Buntin, Melinda Beeuwkes, Cheryl Damberg, Amelia Haviland, Kanika Kapur, Nicole Lurie, Roland McDevitt, and M. Susan Marquis, "Consumer-Directed Health Care: Early Evidence About Effects on Cost and Quality," *Health Affairs*, Web Exclusive, Vol. 25, No. 6, November–December 2006, pp. w516–w530.

Bush, George W., "Proper Consideration of Small Entities in Agency Rulemaking," executive order 13272, *Federal Register*, Vol. 67, No. 159, August 13, 2002, pp. 53461–53462. As of July 5, 2007:
http://www1.va.gov/orpm/docs/EO_13272_Bush_Aug13_02.pdf

Butani, Shail J., Richard L. Clayton, Vinod Kapani, James R. Spletzer, David M. Talan, and George S. Werking Jr., "Business Employment Dynamics: Tabulations by Employer Size," *Monthly Labor Review*, Vol. 129, No. 2, February 2006, pp. 3–22. As of July 27, 2007:
http://stats.bls.gov/opub/mlr/2006/02/art1full.pdf

Card, David, "The Effect of Unions on the Structure of Wages: A Longitudinal Analysis," *Econometrica*, Vol. 64, No. 4, July 1996, pp. 957–979.

Carney, William J., "The Costs of Being Public After Sarbanes-Oxley: The Irony of Going Private," *Emory Law Journal*, Vol. 55, No. 1, 2006, pp. 141–160.

Carr, Jack, and Frank Mathewson, "The Economics of Law Firms: A Study in the Legal Organization of the Firm," *Journal of Law and Economics*, Vol. 33, No. 2, October 1990, pp. 307–330.

Carrington, William J., Kristin McCue, and Brooks Pierce, "The Role of Employer/Employee Interactions in Labor Market Cycles: Evidence from the Self-Employed," *Journal of Labor Economics*, Vol. 14, No. 4, October 1996, pp. 571–602.

———, "Using Establishment Size to Measure the Impact of Title VII and Affirmative Action," *Journal of Human Resources*, Vol. 35, No. 3, Summer 2000, pp. 503–523.

CDC—*see* Centers for Disease Control and Prevention.

CDMR—*see* Consumer Driven Market Report.

Centers for Disease Control and Prevention, "National Center for Health Statistics—National Employer Health Insurance Survey (NEHIS) Available Through the NCHS Research Data Center," last reviewed January 11, 2007a. As of July 27, 2007:
http://www.cdc.gov/nchs/about/major/nehis/pudf.htm

———, "National Center for Health Statistics—National Employer Health Insurance Survey," last reviewed May 24, 2007b. As of July 27, 2007:
http://www.cdc.gov/nchs/about/major/nehis/nehis.htm

Chandra, Amitabh, Shantanu Nundy, and Seth A. Seabury, "The Growth of Medical Malpractice Payments: Evidence from the National Practitioner Data Bank," *Health Affairs*, Web exclusive, May 31, 2005.

Charette, Aimee, *Fifty State Profiles: Health Care Reform, 1995*, 4th ed., Washington, D.C.: Intergovernmental Health Policy Project at The George Washington University, 1995.

Chhaochharia, Vidhi, and Yaniv Grinstein, *Corporate Governance and Firm Value—The Impact of the 2002 Governance Rules*, August 2005.

Chollet, Deborah J., *Community Rating: Issues and Experience*, Washington, D.C.: Alpha Center, 1994.

Ciccotello, Conrad S., and C. Terry Grant, "LLCs and LLPs: Organizing to Deliver Professional Services," *Business Horizons*, Vol. 42, No. 2, March–April 1999, pp. 85–91.

Claxton, Gary, Jon Gabel, Isadora Gil, Jeremy Pickreign, Heidi Whitmore, Benjamin Finder, Shada Rouhani, Samantha Hawkins, and Diane Rowland, "What High-Deductible Plans Look Like: Findings from a National Survey of Employers, 2005," *Health Affairs*, Web Exclusive, September 14, 2005.

Coast Dental Services, Inc., *Schedule Tender Offer–I/A, Coast Dental Services, Inc., et al.*, SEC files 5-50731 (SC 13E3) and 5-50731, March 12, 2003. As of August 9, 2007:
http://www.secinfo.com/dsVsf.22U1.htm#1stPage

Coates, John C., IV, "The Goals and Promise of the Sarbanes-Oxley Act," *Journal of Economic Perspectives*, Vol. 21, No. 1, 2007, pp. 91–116.

Coglianese, Cary, and Laurie K. Allen, *Building Sector-Based Consensus: A Review of the EPA's Common Sense Initiative*, Cambridge, Mass.: John F. Kennedy School of Government, Harvard University, 2003. As of July 6, 2007:
http://ksgnotes1.harvard.edu/research/wpaper.nsf/rwp/RWP03-037/$File/rwp03%5F037%5Fcoglianese.pdf

Coglianese, Cary, and Jennifer Nash, *Leveraging the Private Sector: Management-Based Strategies for Improving Environmental Performance*, Washington, D.C.: Resources for the Future, 2006.

Coleman, Susan, "The Borrowing Experience of Black and Hispanic-Owned Small Firms: Evidence from the 1998 Survey of Small Business Finances," *Academy of Entrepreneurship Journal*, Vol. 8, No. 1, 2002a, pp. 1–20.

———, "Characteristics and Borrowing Behavior of Small, Women-Owned Firms: Evidence from the 1998 Survey of Small Business Finances," *Journal of Small Business and Entrepreneurship*, Vol. 14, No. 2, April 2002b, pp. 151–166.

———, "Borrowing Patterns for Small Firms: A Comparison by Race and Ethnicity," *Journal of Entrepreneurial Finance and Business Ventures*, Vol. 7, No. 3, 2003, pp. 87–108.

Commonwealth of Massachusetts, "Chapter 58 of the Acts of 2006," April 12, 2006, certain sections overridden May 4, 2006. As of July 5, 2007: http://www.mass.gov/legis/laws/seslaw06/sl060058.htm

Compact Library Publishers, "Bankruptcy Reform Act: A Comprehensive Summary of the Bankruptcy Reform Act of 2005," undated Web page. As of August 25, 2005: http://ws5.com/bankruptcy

Consumer Driven Market Report, "Full Integration of HSAs and HDHPs Coming," email news alert, March 23, 2005.

Coustan, Harvey, Linda M. Leinicke, W. Max Rexroad, and Joyce A. Ostrosky, "Sarbanes-Oxley: What It Means to the Marketplace," *Journal of Accountancy*, Vol. 197, February 2004, pp. 43–47. As of July 24, 2007: http://www.aicpa.org/pubs/jofa/feb2004/coustan.htm

CRA—*see* CRA International.

CRA International, *Sarbanes-Oxley Section 404 Costs and Implementation Issues: Survey Update*, Washington, D.C.: CRA International, December 8, 2005.

———, *Sarbanes-Oxley Section 404 Costs and Implementation Issues: Spring 2006 Survey Update*, Washington, D.C.: CRA International, April 17, 2006.

Cunningham, Lawrence A., "The Sarbanes-Oxley Yawn: Heavy Rhetoric, Light Reform (and It Just Might Work)," *Connecticut Law Review*, Vol. 35, No. 3, Spring 2003, pp. 915–988.

Cutler, David M., *Market Failure in Small Group Health Insurance*, Cambridge, Mass.: National Bureau of Economic Research, working paper 4879, 1994.

Cutler, David M., and Brigitte C. Madrian, "Labor Market Responses to Rising Health Insurance Costs: Evidence on Hours Worked," *RAND Journal of Economics*, Vol. 29, No. 3, Autumn 1998, pp. 509–530.

Daines, Robert, "Does Delaware Law Improve Firm Value?" *Journal of Financial Economics*, Vol. 62, No. 3, December 2001, pp. 525–558.

Davidoff, Amy, Linda Blumberg, and Len Nichols, "State Health Insurance Market Reforms and Access to Insurance for High-Risk Employees," *Journal of Health Economics*, Vol. 24, No. 4, July 2005, pp. 725–750.

Davis, Steven J., John Haltiwanger, Ron S. Jarmin, C. J. Krizan, Javier Miranda, Alfred Nucci, and Kristin Sandusky, *Measuring the Dynamics of Young and Small Businesses: Integrating the Employer and Nonemployer Universes*, Washington, D.C.: Bureau of the Census, February 2006.

Dean, Thomas J., Robert L. Brown, and Victor Stango, "Environmental Regulation as a Barrier to the Formation of Small Manufacturing Establishments: A Longitudinal Examination," *Journal of Environmental Economics and Management*, Vol. 40, No. 1, July 2000, pp. 56–75.

de la Fuente v. DCI Telecomms., Inc., 206 F.R.D. 369, S.D.N.Y., March 4, 2003.

Dietz, Elizabeth, "Trends in Employer-Provided Prescription-Drug Coverage," *Monthly Labor Review*, Vol. 127, No. 8, August 2004, pp. 37–45. As of July 27, 2007:
http://stats.bls.gov/opub/mlr/2004/08/art5full.pdf

Dixon, Lloyd, *The Financial Implications of Releasing Small Firms and Small-Volume Contributors from Superfund Liability*, Santa Monica, Calif.: RAND Corporation, MR-1171-EPA, 2000. As of July 6, 2007:
http://www.rand.org/pubs/monograph_reports/MR1171/

DOJ—*see* U.S. Department of Justice.

DOL—*see* U.S. Department of Labor.

Donn, Allan G., "Limited Liability Entities for Law Firms—10 Years Later," *Journal of Passthrough Entities*, July–August 2004, pp. 19–27.

Doyle, Jeffrey, Weili Ge, and Sarah McVay, *Determinants of Weaknesses in Internal Control Over Financial Reporting and the Implications for Earnings Quality*, March 1, 2005.

The Economist, "The Case for Going Private," January 25, 2003a, pp. 57–58.

———, "A (Going) Private Matter," March 22, 2003b, p. 74.

Eldridge, Susan W., and Burch T. Kealey, *SOX Costs: Auditor Attestation Under Section 404*, June 13, 2005.

Engel, Ellen, Rachel M. Hayes, and Xue Wang, *The Sarbanes-Oxley Act and Firms' Going-Private Decisions*, May 6, 2004.

EPA—*see* U.S. Environmental Protection Agency.

Epstein, Richard Allen, *Antidiscrimination in Health Care: Community Ratings and Preexisting Conditions*, Oakland, Calif.: Independent Institute, 1996.

Evans, David S., *An Analysis of the Differential Impact of EPA and OSHA Regulations Across Firm and Establishment Size in the Manufacturing Industries*, Old Greenwich, Conn.: Brock and Evans, Inc., 1985.

Evans, David S., and Linda S. Leighton, "Some Empirical Aspects of Entrepreneurship," *American Economic Review*, Vol. 79, No. 3, June 1989, pp. 519–535.

Even, William E., and David A. Macpherson, "Employer Size and Labor Turnover: The Role of Pensions," *Industrial and Labor Relations Review*, Vol. 49, No. 4, July 1996, pp. 707–728.

Faberman, R. Jason, "Job Creation and Destruction Within Washington and Baltimore," *Monthly Labor Review*, Vol. 124, No. 9, September 2001, pp. 24–31. As of July 27, 2007:
http://stats.bls.gov/opub/mlr/2001/09/art3full.pdf

———, "Job Flows and Labor Dynamics in the U.S. Rust Belt," *Monthly Labor Review*, Vol. 125, No. 9, September 2002, pp. 3–10. As of July 27, 2007:
http://stats.bls.gov/opub/mlr/2002/09/art1full.pdf

———, *Gross Job Flows Over the Past Two Business Cycles: Not All "Recoveries" Are Created Equal*, Washington, D.C.: U.S. Bureau of Labor Statistics, working paper 372, June 2004. As of July 27, 2007:
http://www.bls.gov/ore/pdf/ec040020.pdf

Fairlie, Robert, *Technology and Entrepreneurship: A Cross-Industry Analysis of Access to Computers and Self-Employment*, U.S. Small Business Administration, Office of Advocacy, research summary 259, June 2005. As of July 27, 2007:
http://www.sba.gov/advo/research/rs259tot.pdf

Fairlie, Robert W., and Alicia M. Robb, *Families, Human Capital, and Small Business: Evidence from the Characteristics of Business Owners Survey*, Washingon, D.C.: Bureau of the Census, June 2005a.

———, *Why Are Black Businesses Less Successful Than White-Owned Businesses? The Role of Families, Inheritances, and Business Human Capital*, Washington, D.C.: Bureau of the Census, June 2005b.

Fallick, Bruce, Charles A. Fleischman, and James B. Rebitzer, "Job-Hopping in Silicon Valley: Some Evidence Concerning the Microfoundations of a High-Technology Cluster," *Review of Economics and Statistics*, Vol. 88, No. 3, August 2006, pp. 472–481.

Fan, Wei, and Michelle J. White, "Personal Bankruptcy and the Level of Entrepreneurial Activity," *Journal of Law and Economics*, Vol. 46, No. 2, October 2003, pp. 543–567.

FDA—*see* U.S. Food and Drug Administration.

Federal Register, "Small Business Size Regulations; Size Standards and the North American Industry Classification System; Proposed Rule," Vol. 64, No. 204, October 22, 1999, pp. 57187–57286.

Federal Reserve Board, "Abstracts and Bibliography: Survey of Small Business Finances," last updated November 1, 2006. As of July 27, 2007: http://www.federalreserve.gov/pubs/oss/oss3/abstract.html

FEI—*see* Financial Executives International.

Fenn, Paul, and Simon Ashby, *Workplace Risk, Establishment Size, and Union Density: New Evidence,* Nottingham, UK: University of Nottingham, Centre for Risk and Insurance Studies, no. 2001.I, December 17, 2001. As of July 13, 2007: http://www.nottingham.ac.uk/business/cris/papers/2001-1.pdf

Financial Executives International, *FEI Special Survey on Sarbanes-Oxley Section 404 Implementation,* Florham Park, N.J.: Financial Executives International, 2005.

———, *FEI Survey: Compliance Costs for Section 404,* Florham Park, N.J.: Financial Executives International, March 2006.

———, *FEI Survey on Sarbanes-Oxley Section 404 Implementation,* Florham Park, N.J.: Financial Executives International, May 2007.

Finto, Kevin J., "Regulation by Information Through EPCRA," *Natural Resources and Environment,* Vol. 4, No. 3, Winter 1990, pp. 13–15.

Foss v. Bear, Stearns and Co., Inc., 394 F.3d 540, 7th Cir., January 11, 2005.

Foster, Lucia, *Establishment and Employment Dynamics in Appalachia: Evidence from the Longitudinal Business Database,* Washington, D.C.: U.S. Census Bureau, December 2003.

Fronstin, Paul, and Ruth Helman, *Small Employers and Health Benefits: Findings from the 2000 Small Employer Health Benefits Survey,* Washington, D.C.: Employee Benefit Research Institute, issue brief 226, special report SR35, October 2000.

Gabel, Jon, Larry Levitt, Erin Holve, Jeremy Pickreign, Heidi Whitmore, Kelley Dhont, Samantha Hawkins, and Diane Rowland, "Job-Based Health Benefits in 2002: Some Important Trends," *Health Affairs,* Vol. 21, No. 5, September–October 2002, pp. 143–151.

GAO—*see* U.S. Government Accountability Office.

Garibaldi, Pietro, Lia Pacelli, and Andrea Borgarello, "Employment Protection Legislation and the Size of Firms," *Giornale degli Economisti e Annali di Economia,* Vol. 63, No. 1, 2004, pp. 33–68.

Garicano, Luis, and Thomas N. Hubbard, *Learning About the Nature of Production from Equilibrium Assignment Patterns*, Chicago, Ill.: University of Chicago Graduate School of Business, April 25, 2005a. As of July 27, 2007:
http://www.kellogg.northwestern.edu/faculty/hubbard/htm/research/papers/humancapital42005.pdf

———, *Specialization, Firms, and Markets: The Division of Labor Within and Between Law Firms*, May 2005b. As of July 27, 2007:
http://www.kellogg.northwestern.edu/faculty/hubbard/htm/research/papers/boundaries%20051705.pdf

———, *Managerial Leverage Is Limited by the Extent of the Market: Hierarchies, Specialization and the Utilization of Lawyers' Human Capital*, September 2005c. As of July 27, 2007:
http://www.kellogg.northwestern.edu/faculty/hubbard/htm/research/papers/hierarchies905.pdf

Gilson, Ronald J., "Unlimited Liability and Law Firm Organization: Tax Factors and the Direction of Causation," *Journal of Political Economy*, Vol. 99, No. 2, April 1991, pp. 420–425.

Ginsburg, Marjorie, "Rearranging the Deck Chairs," *Health Affairs*, Web Exclusive, Vol. 25, No. 6, November–December 2006, pp. w537–w539.

Glaeser, Edward L., and Andrei Shleifer, "The Rise of the Regulatory State," *Journal of Economic Literature*, Vol. 41, No. 2, June 2003, pp. 401–425.

Glanzer, Judith E., Joleen Borgerding, Jan T. Lowery, Jessica Bondy, Kathryn L. Mueller, and Kathleen Kreiss, "Construction Injury Rates May Exceed National Estimates: Evidence from the Construction of Denver International Airport," *American Journal of Industrial Medicine*, Vol. 34, No. 2, August 1998, pp. 105–112.

Glaser v. Enzo Biochem, 126 Fed. Appx. 593, 4th Cir., March 21, 2005.

Goldman, Dana P., Joan L. Buchanan, and Emmett B. Keeler, "Simulating the Impact of Medical Savings Accounts on Small Business," *Health Services Research*, Vol. 35, No. 1, Part 1, April 2000, pp. 53–75.

Gordon, Jeffrey N., "Governance Failures of the Enron Board and the New Information Order of Sarbanes-Oxley," *Connecticut Law Review*, Vol. 35, No. 3, Spring 2003, pp. 1125–1144.

Gray, Wayne B., and John M. Mendeloff, "Declining Effects of OSHA Inspections on Manufacturing Injuries, 1979–1998," *Industrial and Labor Relations Review*, Vol. 58, No. 4, July 2005, pp. 571–587.

Gresenz, Carole Roan, Jeannette Rogowski, and José J. Escarce, *Health Care Markets, the Safety Net and Access to Care Among the Uninsured*, Santa Monica, Calif.: RAND Corporation, WR-215, 2005. As of July 27, 2007:
http://www.rand.org/pubs/working_papers/WR215/

Greve, Michael S., "Environmentalism and Bounty Hunting," *Public Interest,* Vol. 97, Fall 1989, pp. 15–29.

Gruber, Jonathan, "The Incidence of Mandated Maternity Benefits," *American Economic Review,* Vol. 84, No. 3, June 1994a, pp. 622–641.

———, "State-Mandated Benefits and Employer-Provided Insurance," *Journal of Public Economics,* Vol. 55, No. 3, November 1994b, pp. 433–464.

Gruber, Jonathan, and Brigitte C. Madrian, "Health Insurance and Job Mobility: The Effects of Public Policy on Job-Lock," *Industrial and Labor Relations Review,* Vol. 48, No. 1, October 1994, pp. 86–102.

Gruber, Jonathan, and James Poterba, "Tax Incentives and the Decision to Purchase Health Insurance: Evidence from the Self-Employed," *Quarterly Journal of Economics,* Vol. 109, No. 3, August 1994, pp. 701–733.

Haberstroh, Chadwick J., "Administration of Safety in the Steel Industry," *Management Science,* Vol. 7, No. 4, July 1961, pp. 436–444.

Hall, Mark A., "The Structure and Enforcement of Health Insurance Rating Reforms," *Inquiry,* Vol. 37, No. 4, 2000, pp. 376–388.

Haltiwanger, John C., Lisa M. Lynch, and Christopher D. Mackie, *Understanding Business Dynamics: An Integrated Data System for America's Future,* Washington, D.C.: National Academies Press, 2007.

Harhoff, Dietmar, Konrad Stahl, and Michael Woywode, "Legal Form, Growth and Exit of West German Firms—Empirical Results for Manufacturing, Construction, Trade and Service Industries," *Journal of Industrial Economics,* Vol. 46, No. 4, December 1998, pp. 453–488.

Hartman, Thomas E., *The Cost of Being Public in the Era of Sarbanes-Oxley,* Chicago, Ill.: Foley and Lardner, June 16, 2005.

———, *The Cost of Being Public in the Era of Sarbanes-Oxley,* Chicago, Ill.: Foley and Lardner, June 15, 2006. As of July 24, 2007:
http://www.foley.com/files/tbl_s31Publications/FileUpload137/3420/ndi%202006%20public%20study%20FINAL.pdf

Hatch, Julie, "Employment in the Public Sector: Two Recessions' Impact on Jobs," *Monthly Labor Review,* Vol. 127, No. 10, October 2004, pp. 38–47. As of July 27, 2007:
http://stats.bls.gov/opub/mlr/2004/10/art3full.pdf

Haviland, Amelia, and Bogdan Savych, *A Description and Analysis of Evolving Data Resources on Small Business,* Santa Monica, Calif.: RAND Corporation, WR-293, 2005. As of August 9, 2007:
http://www.rand.org/pubs/working_papers/WR293/

Headd, Brian, "The Characteristics of Small-Business Employees," *Monthly Labor Review*, Vol. 123, No. 4, April 2000, pp. 13–18. As of July 10, 2007: http://stats.bls.gov/opub/mlr/2000/04/art3full.pdf

―――, *Business Success: Factors Leading to Surviving and Closing Successfully*, Washington, D.C.: Center for Economic Studies, U.S. Department of Commerce, Bureau of the Census, CES-WP-01-01, 2001.

Helwege, Jean, and Frank Packer, *The Decision to Go Public: Evidence from Mandatory SEC Filings of Private Firms*, Columbus, Ohio: Fisher College of Business, Ohio State University, working paper 2003-18, 2003.

Henry J. Kaiser Family Foundation, "Health Care Marketplace: Blue Cross Blue Shield Announces Plans to Offer Health Savings Accounts Nationwide by 2006," *Daily Health Policy Report*, November 19, 2004. As of July 12, 2007: http://www.kaisernetwork.org/daily_reports/rep_index. cfm?hint=3&DR_ID=26836

Henry J. Kaiser Family Foundation, and Health Research and Educational Trust, *Employee Health Benefits: 2003 Annual Survey*, Menlo Park, Calif.: Henry J. Kaiser Family Foundation, 2003. As of July 12, 2007: http://www.kff.org/insurance/ehbs2003-abstract.cfm

―――, *Employer Health Benefits: 2004 Annual Survey*, Menlo Park, Calif.: Henry J. Kaiser Family Foundation, 2004. As of July 12, 2007: http://www.kff.org/insurance/7148.cfm

―――, *Employer Health Benefits: 2005 Annual Survey*, Menlo Park, Calif.: Henry J. Kaiser Family Foundation, 2005. As of July 12, 2007: http://www.kff.org/insurance/7315.cfm

―――, *Employer Health Benefits: 2006 Annual Survey*, Menlo Park, Calif.: Henry J. Kaiser Family Foundation, 2006. As of July 12, 2007: http://www.kff.org/insurance/7527/index.cfm

Hetrick, Ron L., "Analyzing the Recent Upward Surge in Overtime Hours," *Monthly Labor Review*, Vol. 123, No. 2, February 2000, pp. 30–33. As of July 27, 2007: http://stats.bls.gov/opub/mlr/2000/02/art3full.pdf

HHS—*see* U.S. Department of Health and Human Services.

Hillman, Robert W., "Organizational Choices of Professional Service Firms: An Empirical Study," *Business Lawyer*, Vol. 58, No. 4, August 2003, pp. 1387–1412.

Hing, Esther, and Gail A. Jensen, "Health Insurance Portability and Accountability Act of 1996: Lessons from the States," *Medical Care*, Vol. 37, No. 7, 1999, pp. 692–705.

Hirsch, Barry T., and Edward J. Schumacher, "Unions, Wages, and Skills," *Journal of Human Resources*, Vol. 33, No. 1, Winter 1998, pp. 201–219.

Hirsch, Barry T., David A. Macpherson, and J. Michael DuMond, "Workers' Compensation Recipiency in Union and Nonunion Workplaces," *Industrial and Labor Relations Review*, Vol. 50, No. 2, January 1997, pp. 213–236.

Holman, Keith W., "The Regulatory Flexibility Act at 25: Is the Law Achieving Its Goal?" *Fordham Urban Law Journal*, Vol. 33, May 2006, pp. 1119–1137.

Holmes, Thomas J., and James Andrew Schmitz, *On the Turnover of Business Firms and Business Managers*, Washington, D.C.: Bureau of the Census, Center for Economic Studies discussion paper 92-6, July 1992.

Holstein, William J., "The Very Big Business of Private Equity," *New York Times*, May 23, 2004, p. C11.

Hopkins, Thomas D., *A Survey of Regulatory Burdens: Report to the U.S. Small Business Administration Prepared Under Contract with Diversified Research, Inc.*, Irvington, N.Y.: Diversified Research, Inc., 1995.

Idson, Todd L., and Daniel J. Feaster, "A Selectivity Model of Employer-Size Wage Differentials," *Journal of Labor Economics*, Vol. 8, No. 1, Part 1, January 1990, pp. 99–122.

In re Enterprise Mortgage Acceptance Co., LLC, Securities Litigation, Aetna Life Insurance Company and Great Southern Life Insurance Company v. Enterprise Mortgage Acceptance Company, LLC, Jeffrey J. Knyal, Kenneth A. Saverin, Charlene S. Chai, Sean A. Stalfort, Koch Industries, Inc., Koch Capital Services, Inc. and Jeffrey R. Thompson, 391 F.3d 401, 2d Cir., December 6, 2004.

Jain, Pankaj K., and Zabihollah Rezaee, "The Sarbanes-Oxley Act of 2002 and Capital-Market Behavior: Early Evidence," *Contemporary Accounting Research*, Vol. 23, No. 3, Fall 2006, pp. 629–654.

Jarmin, Ron S., Shawn D. Klimek, and Javier Miranda, *Firm Entry and Exit in the U.S. Retail Sector, 1977–1997*, Washington, D.C.: U.S. Census Bureau, October 2004.

Jensen, Gail A., and Michael A. Morrisey, "Research Papers: Small Group Reform and Insurance Provision by Small Firms, 1989–1995," *Inquiry*, Vol. 36, No. 2, 1999, pp. 176–187.

Jensen, Gail A., Michael A. Morrisey, and R. J. Morlock, "The Effects of State Initiatives in the Small Group Insurance Market," paper presented at "The Rapidly Changing Insurance Market: Policy and Market Forces" conference, sponsored by the Robert Wood Johnson Foundation, 1995.

Jensen, Michael C., "Eclipse of the Public Corporation," *Harvard Business Review*, Vol. 67, No. 4, September–October 1989, pp. 61–74.

Kaestner, Robert, and Kosali Ilayperuma Simon, "Labor Market Consequences of State Health Insurance Regulation," *Industrial and Labor Relations Review*, Vol. 56, No. 1, October 2002, pp. 136–159.

Kamar, Ehud, Pinar Karaca-Mandic, and Eric Talley, *Going-Private Decisions and the Sarbanes-Oxley Act of 2002: A Cross-Country Analysis*, Santa Monica, Calif.: RAND Corporation, WR-300-1-ICJ, 2006. As of July 25, 2007: http://www.rand.org/pubs/working_papers/WR300-1/

Kaplan, Steven, "Management Buyouts: Evidence on Taxes as a Source of Value," *The Journal of Finance*, Vol. 44, No. 3, *Papers and Proceedings of the Forty-Eighth Annual Meeting of the American Finance Association, New York, New York, December 28–30, 1988*, July 1989a, pp. 611–632.

———, "The Effects of Management Buyouts on Operating Performance and Value," *Journal of Financial Economics*, Vol. 24, No. 2, October 1989b, pp. 217–254.

Kapur, Kanika, "Labor Market Implications of State Small Group Health Insurance Reform," *Public Finance Review*, Vol. 31, No. 6, November 2003, pp. 571–600.

———, "The Impact of the Health Insurance Market on Small Firm Employment," *Journal of Risk and Insurance*, Vol. 71, No. 1, 2004, pp. 63–90.

———, *Where Do the Sick Go? Health Insurance and Employment in Large and Small Firms*, Dublin: University College Dublin, Department of Economics, 2006.

Kapur, Kanika, Pinar Karaca-Mandic, Susan M. Gates, and Brent D. Fulton, *Do Small Group Health Insurance Regulations Influence Small Business Growth?* Santa Monica, Calif.: RAND Corporation, WR-351-ICJ, 2006. As of July 10, 2007: http://www.rand.org/pubs/working_papers/WR351/

Kapur, Kanika, and M. Susan Marquis, "Health Insurance for Workers Who Lose Jobs: Implications for Various Subsidy Schemes," *Health Affairs*, Vol. 22, No. 3, May–June 2003, pp. 202–213.

Karoly, Lynn A., and Julie Zissimopoulos, *Self-Employment Trends and Patterns Among Older U.S. Workers*, Santa Monica, Calif.: RAND Corporation, WR-136, 2004. As of July 27, 2007: http://www.rand.org/pubs/working_papers/WR136/

Keefe, Ryan, Susan M. Gates, and Eric Talley, *Criteria Used to Define a Small Business in Determining Thresholds for the Application of Federal Statutes*, Santa Monica, Calif.: RAND Corporation, WR-292-ICJ, 2005. As of July 27, 2007: http://www.rand.org/pubs/working_papers/WR292/

KFF—*see* Henry J. Kaiser Family Foundation.

KFF/HRET—*see* Henry J. Kaiser Family Foundation and Health Research and Educational Trust.

Kirkland, Katie, "On the Decline in Average Weekly Hours Worked," *Monthly Labor Review*, Vol. 123, No. 7, July 2000, pp. 26–31. As of July 27, 2007: http://stats.bls.gov/opub/mlr/2000/07/art3full.pdf

Klingsberg, Ethan, and Marie Noble, "SOX 404-Mania: Y2K Déjà Vu, Myths, Risks and What It All Means for M&A," *M&A Lawyer*, September 2004, pp. 1–7.

Kolko, Gabriel, *Railroads and Regulation, 1877–1916*, New York: Norton, 1970.

Konigsberg, Sheryl, David Talan, and Richard Clayton, *The Geospatial Distribution of Employment: Examples from the Bureau of Labor Statistics Quarterly Census of Employment and Wages Program*, Washington, D.C.: Federal Committee on Statistical Methodology, 2005. As of July 27, 2007:
http://www.fcsm.gov/05papers/Konigsberg_Talan_Clayton_VC.pdf

Krantz, Rachel, "Employment in Business Services: A Year of Unprecedented Decline," *Monthly Labor Review*, Vol. 125, No. 4, April 2002, pp. 17–24. As of July 27, 2007:
http://stats.bls.gov/opub/mlr/2002/04/art2full.pdf

Kropf, Jurgen, and Patricia Getz, "Noneconomic Fluctuations in Hours and Earnings Data," *Monthly Labor Review*, Vol. 122, No. 8, August 1999, pp. 20–27. As of July 27, 2007:
http://stats.bls.gov/opub/mlr/1999/08/art4full.pdf

Laffont, Jean-Jacques, and Jean Tirole, "The Politics of Government Decision-Making: A Theory of Regulatory Capture," *Quarterly Journal of Economics*, Vol. 106, No. 4, November 1991, pp. 1089–1127.

Laing, JoAnn, "The HSA Option for Small Business Health Care," *About.com: Small Business Information*, undated Web page. As of June 2006:
http://sbinformation.about.com/od/insurance/a/ucHSA.htm

Lee, D. Scott, "Management Buyout Proposals and Inside Information," *Journal of Finance*, Vol. 47, No. 3, *Papers and Proceedings of the Fifty-Second Annual Meeting of the American Finance Association, New Orleans, Louisiana January 3–5, 1992*, July 1992, pp. 1061–1079.

Lee, Peter, and Emma Hoo, "Beyond Consumer-Driven Health Care: Purchasers' Expectations of All Plans," *Health Affairs*, Web Exclusive, Vol. 25, No. 6, November–December 2006, pp. w544–w548.

Leigh, J. Paul, James P. Marcin, and Ted R. Miller, "An Estimate of the U.S. Government's Undercount of Nonfatal Occupational Injuries," *Journal of Occupational and Environmental Medicine*, Vol. 46, No. 1, January 2004, pp. 10–18.

Lel, Ugur, and Gregory F. Udell, *Financial Constraints, Start-Up Firms and Personal Commitments*, Bloomington, In.: Indiana University Kelley School of Business, 2002.

Leonard, Arne R., "When Should an Administrative Enforcement Action Preclude a Citizen Suit Under the Clean Water Act?" *Natural Resources Journal*, Vol. 35, No. 3, Summer 1995, pp. 555–624.

Lerner, Joshua, "Venture Capitalists and the Decision to Go Public," *Journal of Financial Economics*, Vol. 35, No. 3, June 1994, pp. 293–316.

Leuz, Christian, Alexander J. Triantis, and Tracy Yue Wang, *Why Do Firms Go Dark? Causes and Economic Consequences of Voluntary SEC Deregistrations*, March 2006.

Li, Haidan, Morton Pincus, and Sonja O. Rego, "Market Reaction to Events Surrounding the Sarbanes-Oxley Act of 2002," *Journal of Law and Economics*, forthcoming.

Lichtenberg, Frank R., and Donald Siegel, "The Effect of Leveraged Buyouts on Productivity and Related Aspects of Firm Behavior," *Journal of Financial Economics*, Vol. 27, No. 1, September 1990, pp. 165–194.

Linck, James S., Jeffry M. Netter, and Tina Yang, *The Effects and Unintended Consequences of the Sarbanes-Oxley Act, and Its Era, on the Supply and Demand for Directors*, February 14, 2007.

Litvak, Kate, *The Effect of the Sarbanes-Oxley Act on Non-US Companies Cross-Listed in the US*, University of Texas Law School research paper 55, May 2005.

———, "The Effect of the Sarbanes-Oxley Act on Non-US Companies Cross-Listed in the US," *Journal of Corporate Finance*, Vol. 13, Nos. 2–3, June 2007a, pp. 195–228.

———, "Sarbanes-Oxley and the Cross-Listing Premium," *Michigan Law Review*, Vol. 105, No. 8, June 2007b, pp. 1857–1898.

Loewenstein, Mark A., and James R. Spletzer, "Delayed Formal On-the-Job Training," *Industrial and Labor Relations Review*, Vol. 51, No. 1, October 1997, pp. 82–99.

Long, Stephen H., and M. Susan Marquis, "Pooled Purchasing: Who Are the Players?" *Health Affairs*, Vol. 18, No. 4, July–August 1999, pp. 105–111.

Loomis, Tamara, "Beware Delaware," *New York Law Journal*, May 15, 2003, p. 5.

Lublin, Joann S., "IRS Is Cracking Down on Abuse of Executive-Bonus Tax Breaks," *Wall Street Journal*, June 18, 2004, p. B5.

MacFadyen, Ken, "Long Awaited Deal Flood Hits in Q3," *Buyouts*, October 7, 2002, p. 1.

———, "Deal Flow Surges Forward with Q4 Splash: Fourth Quarter Deals Push Year-End Volume to $42 Billion," *Buyouts*, January 6, 2003, p. 1.

———, "The Deals Just Keep Coming and Coming," *Buyouts*, July 12, 2004, p. 1.

Macpherson, David A., and Barry T. Hirsch, "Wages and Gender Composition: Why Do Women's Jobs Pay Less?" *Journal of Labor Economics*, Vol. 13, No. 3, July 1995, pp. 426–471.

Management Research and Planning Corporation, *Analysis of State Efforts to Mitigate Regulatory Burdens on Small Businesses*, Raleigh, N.C.: U.S. Small Business Administration, June 1, 2002. As of July 5, 2007:
http://www.sba.gov/advo/research/rs219tot.pdf

Marcus, David, "Reform Fever Hits Delaware," *Corporate Control Alert*, February 23, 2003, p. 16.

Marquis, M. Susan, and Stephen H. Long, "Effects of 'Second Generation' Small Group Health Insurance Market Reforms, 1993 to 1997," *Inquiry*, Vol. 38, No. 4, 2001, pp. 365–380.

Martindale-Hubbell Law Directory, Inc., Martindale-Hubbell, Inc., and Martindale-Hubbell, *The Martindale-Hubbell Law Directory*, New York: Martindale-Hubbell Law Directory, Inc., annually since 1931. As of July 27, 2007:
http://www.martindale.com

———, "About Martindale-Hubbell," undated Web page. As of August 9, 2007:
http://www.martindale.com/xp/legal/About_Martindale/about_martindale.xml

Maupin, Rebekah J., Clinton M. Bidwell, and Alan K. Ortegren, "An Empirical Investigation of Publicly-Quoted Corporations Which Change to Closely-Held Ownership Through Management Buyouts," *Journal of Business Finance and Accounting*, Vol. 11, No. 4, Winter 1984, pp. 435–450.

McCubbins, Mathew D., Roger G. Noll, and Barry R. Weingast, "Administrative Procedures as Instruments of Political Control," *Journal of Law, Economics, and Organization*, Vol. 3, No. 2, Autumn 1987, pp. 243–277.

———, "Structure and Process, Politics and Policy: Administrative Arrangements and the Political Control of Agencies," *Virginia Law Review*, Vol. 75, No. 2, Symposium on the Law and Economics of Bargaining, March 1989, pp. 431–482.

McCue, Kristin, and Alice M. Zawacki, *Using Census Business Data to Augment the MEPS-IC*, Washington, D.C.: Bureau of the Census, Center for Economic Studies discussion paper 05-26, 2005.

McFadden, Daniel, "Conditional Logit Analysis of Qualitative Choice Behaviour," in Paul Zarembka, ed., *Frontiers in Econometrics*, New York: Academic Press, 1974, pp. 105–142.

McKinnon, John D., "IRS Inspects Executives' Returns, as It Shifts Focus to Well-to-Do," *Wall Street Journal*, March 2, 2005, p. A2.

McLaughlin, Catherine G., "The Dilemma of Affordability: Health Insurance for Small Businesses," in Robert B. Helms, ed., *American Health Policy: Critical Issues for Reform*, Washington, D.C.: AEI Press, 1993, pp. 152–163.

McWilliams, Martin C., Jr., "Who Bears the Costs of Lawyers' Mistakes? Against Limited Liability," *Arizona State Law Journal*, Vol. 36, No. 3, Fall 2004, pp. 885–952.

Meason, James E., "Environmental Audits, Privileges from Disclosure, and Small Business Penalty Policies," *Northern Illinois University Law Review*, Vol. 18, No. 3, Summer 1998, pp. 497–518.

Mellow, Wesley, "Employer Size and Wages," *Review of Economics and Statistics*, Vol. 64, No. 3, August 1982, pp. 495–501.

Mendeloff, John, and Wayne Gray, *An Evaluation of the OSHA Consultation Program*, Washington, D.C.: Occupational Safety and Health Administration, 2001.

Mendeloff, John, and Betsy Kagey, "Using Occupational Safety and Health Administration Accident Investigations to Study Patterns in Work Fatalities," *Journal of Occupational Medicine*, Vol. 32, No. 11, November 1990, pp. 1117–1123.

Mendeloff, John, Christopher Nelson, Kilkon Ko, and Amelia Haviland, *Small Businesses and Workplace Fatality Risk: An Exploratory Analysis*, Santa Monica, Calif.: RAND Corporation, TR-371-ICJ, 2006. As of July 9, 2007: http://www.rand.org/pubs/technical_reports/TR371/

Miller, Carol J., "LLPs: How Limited Is Limited Liability?" *Journal of the Missouri Bar*, Vol. 53, No. 3, May–June 1997, p. 154.

Monheit, Alan C., and Joel C. Cantor, *State Health Insurance Market Reform: Toward Inclusive and Sustainable Health Insurance Markets*, London and New York: Routledge, 2004.

Monheit, Alan C., and Barbara Steinberg Schone, "How Has Small Group Market Reform Affected Employee Health Insurance Coverage?" *Journal of Public Economics*, Vol. 88, No. 1, January 2004, pp. 237–254.

Monheit, Alan C., and Jessica P. Vistnes, "Implicit Pooling of Workers from Large and Small Firms," *Health Affairs*, Vol. 13 No. 1, Spring 1994, pp. 301–314.

———, "Health Insurance Availability at the Workplace: How Important Are Worker Preferences?" *Journal of Human Resources*, Vol. 34, No. 4, Autumn 1999, pp. 770–785.

———, *Health Insurance Enrollment Decisions: Preferences for Coverage, Working Sorting, and Insurance Take Up*, Cambridge, Mass.: National Bureau of Economic Research, working paper 12429, August 2006. As of June 2006: http://www.nber.org/papers/w12429

Morse, Tim, Charles Dillon, Joseph Weber, Nick Warren, Heather Bruneau, and Rongwei Fu, "Prevalence and Reporting of Occupational Illness by Company Size: Population Trends and Regulatory Implications," *American Journal of Industrial Medicine*, Vol. 45, No. 4, April 2004, pp. 361–370.

MRP—*see* Management Research and Planning Corporation.

National Center for Policy Analysis, "Community Rating: Excerpted from: State Briefing Book on Health Care," September 23, 1994. As of August 9, 2007:
http://www.ncpa.org/w/w37.html

National Federation of Independent Business, "NFIB Research Foundation," undated Web page. As of July 10, 2007:
http://www.nfib.com/page/researchFoundation

———, "2004 in Review: Health Insurance Costs: A 'Critical' Problem for Small Business," December 23, 2004. As of June 2006:
http://www.nfib.com/object/IO_19339.html

National Institute for Occupational Safety and Health, *Identifying High-Risk Small Business Industries: The Basis for Preventing Occupational Injury, Illness, and Fatality: NIOSH Special Hazard Review*, Rockville, Md.: U.S. Department of Health and Human Services, Public Health Service, Centers for Disease Control and Prevention, National Institute for Occupational Safety and Health, 99-107, 1999. As of July 13, 2007:
http://purl.access.gpo.gov/GPO/LPS48029

NCPA—*see* National Center for Policy Analysis.

NFIB—*see* National Federation of Independent Business.

Nichols, Theo, Amanda Dennis, and Will Guy, "Size of Employment Unit and Injury Rate in British Manufacturing: A Secondary Analysis of WIRS 1990 Data," *Industrial Relations Journal*, Vol. 26, No. 1, 1995, pp. 45–56.

Nijman, Jennifer T., "Supreme Court Should Limit Rule on Vicarious Liability of Illinois Lawyers," *CBA Record*, Vol. 17, 2003, p. 12.

NIOSH—*see* National Institute for Occupational Safety and Health.

Nixon, Richard, "Reorganization Plan No. 3 of 1970," *United States Code Congressional and Administrative News*, 91st Congress, 2nd Session, 1970. As of July 5, 2007:
http://www.epa.gov/history/org/origins/reorg.htm

OECD—*see* Organisation for Economic Co-Operation and Development

Ofek, Eli, "Efficiency Gains in Unsuccessful Management Buyouts," *Journal of Finance*, Vol. 49, No. 2, June 1994, pp. 637–654.

Okolie, Cordelia, "Why Size Class Methodology Matters in Analyses of Net and Gross Job Flows," *Monthly Labor Review*, Vol. 127, No. 7, July 2004, pp. 3–12. As of July 27, 2007:
http://stats.bls.gov/opub/mlr/2004/07/art1full.pdf

Oleinick, Arthur, J. V. Gluck, and K. E. Guire, "Establishment Size and Risk of Occupational Injury," *American Journal of Industrial Medicine*, Vol. 28, No. 1, July 1995, pp. 1–21.

Olson, Mancur, *The Logic of Collective Action: Public Goods and the Theory of Groups*, Cambridge, Mass.: Harvard University Press, 1965.

Organisation for Economic Co-Operation and Development, *The Use of Voluntary Agreements in the United States: An Initial Survey*, Environment Directorate and Environment Policy Committee, ENV/EPOC/GEEI(98)27/FINAL, December 8, 1998. As of July 5, 2007:
http://www.olis.oecd.org/olis/1998doc.
nsf/LinkTo/ENV-EPOC-GEEI(98)27-FINAL

OSHA—*see* U.S. Occupational Safety and Health Administration.

Oyer, Paul, and Scott Schaefer, "Sorting, Quotas, and the Civil Rights Act of 1991: Who Hires When It's Hard to Fire?" *Journal of Law and Economics*, Vol. 45, No. 1, April 2002, pp. 41–68.

Pagano, Marco, and Ailsa Roell, "The Choice of Stock Ownership Structures: Agency Costs, Monitoring, and the Decision to Go Public," *Quarterly Journal of Economics*, Vol. 113, No. 1, February 1998, pp. 187–225.

Pagano, Marco, Fabio Panetta, and Luigi Zingales, "Why Do Companies Go Public? An Empirical Analysis," *Journal of Finance*, Vol. 53, No. 1, February 1998, pp. 27–64.

Pashigian, B. Peter, "The Effect of Environmental Regulation on Optimal Plant Size and Factor Shares," *Journal of Law and Economics*, Vol. 27, No. 1, April 1984, pp. 1–28.

Pearce, James E., "Tenure, Unions, and the Relationship Between Employer Size and Wages," *Journal of Labor Economics*, Vol. 8, No. 2, April 1990, pp. 251–269.

Pedersen, David H., and William Karl Sieber, *National Occupational Exposure Survey*, Vol. III: *Analysis of Management Interview Responses*, Cincinnati, Ohio: U.S. Department of Health and Human Services, Public Health Service, Centers for Disease Control, National Institute for Occupational Safety and Health, Division of Surveillance, Hazard Evalations, and Field Studies, 1989.

Peek-Asa, Corinne, Rosemary Erickson, and Jess F. Kraus, "Traumatic Occupational Fatalities in the Retail Industry, United States 1992–1996," *American Journal of Industrial Medicine*, Vol. 35, No. 2, January 1999, pp. 186–191.

Peltzman, Sam, "Toward a More General Theory of Regulation," *Journal of Law and Economics*, Vol. 19, No. 2, August 1976, pp. 211–240.

Pendell, Judyth W., and Paul Hinton, *Tort Liability Costs for Small Businesses*, National Economic Research Associates, May 17, 2007. As of August 9, 2007:
http://www.nera.com/publication.asp?p_ID=3146

Peracchi, Franco, and Finis Welch, "Trends in Labor Force Transitions of Older Men and Women," *Journal of Labor Economics*, Vol. 12, No. 2, April 1994, pp. 210–242.

Peterson, Mark A., Robert T. Reville, Rachel Kaganoff Stern, and Peter S. Barth, *Compensating Permanent Workplace Injuries: A Study of the California System*, Santa Monica, Calif.: RAND Corporation, MR-920-ICJ, 1998. As of August 9, 2007: http://www.rand.org/pubs/monograph_reports/MR920/

Phillips, Bruce D., *Small Business Problems and Priorities*, Washington, D.C.: National Federation of Independent Business Research Foundation, June 2004. As of July 25, 2007: http://www.nfib.com/object/IO_16191.html

Pittman, Russell W., "Issue in Pollution Control: Interplant Cost Differences and Economies of Scale," *Land Economics*, Vol. 57, No. 1, February 1981, pp. 1–17.

Proposition 65, Safe Drinking Water and Toxic Enforcement Act of 1986, November 1986.

Public Law 49-41, Interstate Commerce Act, February 4, 1887.

Public Law 59-384, Pure Food and Drug Act of 1906, June 30, 1906.

Public Law 73-22, Securities Act of 1933, May 27, 1933.

Public Law 73-291, Securities Exchange Act of 1934, June 6, 1934.

Public Law 74-198, National Labor Relations Act of 1935, July 5, 1935.

Public Law 74-271, Social Security Act of 1935, August 14, 1935.

Public Law 75-717, Federal Food, Drug, and Cosmetic Act of 1938, June 25, 1938.

Public Law 75-718, Fair Labor Standards Act of 1938, June 25, 1938.

Public Law 80-104, Federal Insecticide, Fungicide, and Rodenticide Act of 1947, June 25, 1947.

Public Law 83-163, Small Business Act of 1953, July 30, 1953.

Public Law 83-703, Atomic Energy Act of 1954, August 30, 1954.

Public Law 84-159, Air Pollution Control Act of 1955, July 14, 1955.

Public Law 88-38, Equal Pay Act of 1963, June 10, 1963.

Public Law 88-352, Civil Rights Act of 1964, July 2, 1964.

Public Law 89-272, Solid Waste Disposal Act of 1965, October 20, 1965.

Public Law 89-601, Fair Labor Standards Amendments of 1966, November 13, 1966.

Public Law 90-148, Air Quality Act of 1967, November 21, 1967.

Public Law 90-202, Age Discrimination in Employment Act of 1967, December 15, 1967.

Public Law 91-190, National Environmental Policy Act, January 1, 1970.

Public Law 91-596, Occupational Safety and Health Act of 1970, December 29, 1970, as amended through January 1, 2004. As of July 5, 2007: http://www.osha.gov/pls/oshaweb/owadisp.show_document?p_table=OSHACT&p_id=2743

Public Law 91-604, Clean Air Act Extension of 1970, January 1, 1970.

Public Law 92-500, Federal Water Pollution Control Act Amendments of 1972, October 18, 1972.

Public Law 92-532, Marine Protection, Research and Sanctuaries Act of 1972, October 23, 1972.

Public Law 93-406, Employment Retirement and Income Security Act of 1974, September 2, 1974.

Public Law 93-523, Safe Drinking Water Act of 1974, December 12, 1974.

Public Law 94-469, Toxic Substances Control Act of 1976, October 11, 1976.

Public Law 94-580, Resource Recovery and Conservation Act of 1976, October 21, 1976.

Public Law 95-213, Foreign Corrupt Practices Act of 1977, December 19, 1977.

Public Law 95-217, Clean Water Act of 1977, December 28, 1977.

Public Law 95-555, Pregnancy Discrimination Act of 1978, October 31, 1978.

Public Law 96-354, Regulatory Flexibility Act of 1980, September 19, 1980.

Public Law 96-510, Comprehensive Environmental Response, Compensation, and Liability Act of 1980, December 11, 1980.

Public Law 96-511, Paperwork Reduction Act of 1980, December 11, 1980.

Public Law 97-354, Subchapter S Revision Act of 1982, October 19, 1982.

Public Law 99-272, Consolidated Omnibus Budget Reconciliation Act, April 7, 1986.

Public Law 99-499, Superfund Amendments and Reauthorization Act of 1986, October 17, 1986.

Public Law 99-603, Immigration Reform and Control Act of 1986, November 6, 1986.

Public Law 100-379, Worker Adjustment and Retraining Notification Act of 1988, August 4, 1988.

Public Law 100-647, Technical and Miscellaneous Revenue Act of 1988, November 10, 1988.

Public Law 101-336, Americans with Disabilities Act of 1990, July 26, 1990.

Public Law 101-508, Pollution Prevention Act of 1990, November 6, 1990.

Public Law 101-549, Clean Air Act Amendments of 1990, November 15, 1990.

Public Law 103-3, Family and Medical Leave Act of 1993, February 5, 1993.

Public Law 104-13, Paperwork Reduction Act of 1995, May 22, 1995.

Public Law 104-121, Small Business Regulatory Enforcement Fairness Act of 1996, March 29, 1996.

Public Law 104-191, Health Insurance Portability and Accountability Act of 1996, August 21, 1996.

Public Law 104-204, Mental Health Parity Act of 1996, September 26, 1996.

Public Law 104-204, Newborns' and Mothers' Health Protection Act of 1996, September 26, 1996.

Public Law 105-115, Food and Drug Administration Modernization Act of 1997, November 21, 1997.

Public Law 105-277, Women's Health and Cancer Rights Act of 1998, October 21, 1998.

Public Law 107-117, Small Business Liability Relief and Brownfields Revitalization Act of 2001, January 11, 2002.

Public Law 107-198, Small Business Paperwork Relief Act of 2002, June 28, 2002.

Public Law 107-204, Sarbanes-Oxley Act of 2002, January 23, 2002. As of July 5, 2007:
http://frwebgate.access.gpo.gov/cgi-bin/getdoc.cgi?dbname=107_cong_bills&docid=f:h3763enr.txt.pdf

Public Law 108-173, Medicare Prescription Drug, Improvement, and Modernization Act of 2003, December 8, 2003.

Public Law 109-8, Bankruptcy Abuse Prevention and Consumer Protection Act of 2005, April 20, 2005.

Ramos, Manuel R., "Legal Malpractice: No Lawyer or Client Is Safe," *Florida Law Review*, Vol. 47, No. 1, January 1995, pp. 1–62.

Reed, Kristin, "The EPA's Environmental Audit Policy: Are Small Firms Disadvantaged?" *Dickinson Journal of Environmental Law and Policy*, Vol. 8, Fall 1999, pp. 299–324.

Reuben, Richard C., "Added Protection: Law Firms Are Discovering That Limited Liability Business Structures Can Shield Them from Devastating Malpractice Awards and Double Taxation," *ABA Journal*, Vol. 80, September 1994, p. 54.

Reville, Robert T., Suzanne Polich, Seth A. Seabury, and Elizabeth Giddens, *Permanent Disability at Private, Self-Insured Firms: A Study of Earnings Loss, Replacement, and Return to Work for Workers' Compensation Claimants*, Santa Monica, Calif.: RAND Corporation, MR-1268-ICJ, 2001. As of August 9, 2007: http://www.rand.org/pubs/monograph_reports/MR1268/

Ribstein, Larry E., "Ethical Rules, Agency Costs, and Law Firm Structure," *Virginia Law Review*, Vol. 84, No. 8, November 1998, pp. 1707–1759.

———, "Ethical Rules, Law Firm Structure and Choice of Law," *University of Cincinnati Law Review*, Vol. 69, No. 4, Summer 2001, pp. 1161–1204.

———, "Market vs. Regulatory Responses to Corporate Fraud: A Critique of the Sarbanes-Oxley Act of 2002," *Journal of Corporation Law*, Vol. 28, No. 1, Fall 2002, pp. 1–68.

———, *Unincorporated Business Entities*, 3rd ed., Newark, N.J.: LexisNexis, 2004.

Ribstein, Larry E., and Robert R. Keatinge, *Ribstein and Keatinge on Limited Liability Companies*, Vol. I, Colorado Springs, Colo.: Shepard's/McGraw-Hill, 2003.

Ringleb, Al H., and Steven N. Wiggins, "Liability and Large-Scale, Long-Term Hazards," *Journal of Political Economy*, Vol. 98, No. 3, June 1990, pp. 574–595.

Robb, Alicia, "Small Business Financing: Differences Between Young and Old Firms," *Journal of Entrepreneurial Finance and Business Ventures*, Vol. 1, No. 2, December 2002.

Roberts v. Dean Witter Reynolds, Inc., 2003 WL 1936116, M.D. Fla., March 31, 2003.

Robinson, James C., "Hospital Tiers in Health Insurance: Balancing Consumer Choice with Financial Motives," *Health Affairs*, Web exclusive, March 19, 2003.

Robinson, James C., and Glenn M. Shor, "Business-Cycle Influences on Work-Related Disability in Construction and Manufacturing," *Milbank Quarterly*, Vol. 67, Supp. 2, Part 1, *Disability Policy: Restoring Socioeconomic Independence*, 1989, pp. 92–113.

Rogers, David, "Senate Committee Gives Approval to a Record Budget for the SEC," *Wall Street Journal*, July 17, 2002, p. A2.

Romano, Roberta, "The Sarbanes-Oxley Act and the Making of Quack Corporate Governance," *Yale Law Journal*, Vol. 114, No. 7, May 2005, pp. 1521–1612.

Romley, John A., and Eric Talley, *Uncorporated Professionals*, Santa Monica, Calif.: RAND Corporation, WR-302-ICJ, 2005. As of July 25, 2007: http://www.rand.org/pubs/working_papers/WR302/

SBA—*see* U.S. Small Business Administration.

Schieber, S. J., *Why Coordination of Health Care Spending and Savings Accounts Is Important*, Washington, D.C.: Watson Wyatt Worldwide, July 2004.

Schivardi, Fabiano, and Roberto Torrini, *Threshold Effects and Firm Size: The Case of Firing Costs*, London: Centre for Economic Performance, London School of Economics and Political Science, discussion paper 633, 2004. As of July 10, 2007: http://cep.lse.ac.uk/pubs/download/dp0633.pdf

Schwartz, Charles W., and Lewis C. Sutherland, "Class Certification for Environmental and Toxic Tort Claims," *Tulane Environmental Law Journal*, Vol. 10, No. 2, Summer 1997, pp. 187–232.

SEC—*see* U.S. Securities and Exchange Commission.

Seligman, Paul J., William Karl Sieber, David H. Pedersen, David S. Sundin, and Todd M. Frazier, "Compliance with OSHA Recordkeeping Requirements," *American Journal of Public Health*, Vol. 78, No. 9, September 1988, pp. 1218–1219.

Shaller, Leon C., Patrick J. McNulty, and Karen R. Chinander, "Impact of Hazardous Substances Regulations on Small Firms in Delaware and New Jersey," *Risk Analysis*, Vol. 18, No. 2, April 1998, pp. 181–189.

Simon, Kosali Ilayperuma, "Adverse Selection in Health Insurance Markets? Evidence from State Small-Group Health Insurance Reforms," *Journal of Public Economics*, Vol. 89, Nos. 9–10, September 2005, pp. 1865–1877.

Sloan, Frank A., and Christopher J. Conover, "Research Papers: Effects of State Reforms on Health Insurance Coverage of Adults," *Inquiry*, Vol. 35, No. 3, 1998, pp. 280–293.

"Small Business Not So Small," *OMB Watch*, April 17, 2002. As of August 9, 2007: http://www.ombwatch.org/article/articleview/687

Smith, Abbie J., "Corporate Ownership Structure and Performance: The Case of Management Buyouts," *Journal of Financial Economics*, Vol. 27, No. 1, September 1990, pp. 143–164.

Smith, Gordon S., Mark A. Veazie, and Katy L. Benjamin, "The Use of Sentinel Injury Deaths to Evaluate the Quality of Multiple Source Reporting for Occupational Injuries," *Annals of Epidemiology*, Vol. 15, No. 3, March 2005, pp. 219–227.

Solomon, Deborah, and Cassell Bryan-Low, "Companies Complain About Cost of Corporate-Governance Rules," *Wall Street Journal*, February 10, 2004, p. A1.

Sorensen, Elaine, "The Crowding Hypothesis and Comparable Worth," *Journal of Human Resources*, Vol. 25, No. 1, Winter 1990, pp. 55–89.

Stigler, George, "The Theory of Economic Regulation," *Bell Journal of Economics*, Vol. 2, No. 1, 1971, pp. 3–21.

Stinson, Martha, *Estimating the Relationship Between Employer-Provided Health Insurance, Worker Mobility, and Wages*, Washington, D.C.: U.S. Census Bureau, Longitudinal Employer-Household Dynamics technical paper TP-2002-23, June 2003. As of July 27, 2007:
http://lehd.dsd.census.gov/led/library/techpapers/tp-2002-23.pdf

Strine, Leo E., Jr., "Derivative Impact—Some Early Reflections on the Corporation Law Implications of the Enron Debacle," *Business Lawyer*, Vol. 57, No. 4, August 2002, pp. 1371–1402.

Strople, Michael H., "From Supermarkets to Supercenters: Employment Shifts to the One-Stop Shop," *Monthly Labor Review*, Vol. 129, No. 2, February 2006, pp. 39–46. As of July 27, 2007:
http://stats.bls.gov/opub/mlr/2006/02/art3full.pdf

Subramanian, Guhan, "Bargaining in the Shadow of Takeover Defenses," *Yale Law Journal*, Vol. 113, No. 3, December 2003, pp. 621–686.

Thomas, P., "Safety in Smaller Manufacturing Establishments," *Employment Gazette*, Vol. 99, No. 1, 1991, pp. 20–26.

Thompson, James L., "Citizen Suits and Civil Penalties Under the Clean Water Act," *Michigan Law Review*, Vol. 85, No. 7, June 1987, pp. 1656–1680.

Thompson, Robert B., "Piercing the Corporate Veil: An Empirical Study," *Cornell Law Review*, Vol. 76, No. 5, 1990–1991, pp. 1036–1074.

Thompson, Roger, "States Take Lead in Health Reform," *Nation's Business*, Vol. 80, No. 4, April 1992, pp. 18–26.

Trejo, Stephen J., "Why Do Mexican Americans Earn Low Wages?" *Journal of Political Economy*, Vol. 105, No. 6, December 1997, pp. 1235–1268.

Tweed, John A., Landair Acquisition Corporation, and Scott M. Niswonger, Schedule Tender Offer–T, Landair Corporation, SEC file 5-54679, December 23, 2002. As of August 9, 2007:
http://www.secinfo.com/dsVsf.3CM1.htm#1stPage

Uccello, Cori E., *Firms' Health Insurance Decisions: The Relative Effects of Firm Characteristics and State Insurance Regulations*, Washington, D.C.: Urban Institute, 1996.

United States v. Bestfoods et al., 524 U.S. 51, 118 S. Ct. 1876, 141 L. Ed. 2d 43, June 8, 1998.

U.S. Bureau of Labor Statistics, "Employment, Hours, and Earnings from the Current Employment Statistics Survey (National)," undated Web page (a). As of July 27, 2007:
http://www.bls.gov/ces/

———, "Quarterly Census of Employment and Wages," undated Web page (b). As of July 27, 2007:
http://www.bls.gov/cew/

———, *Census of Fatal Occupational Injuries*, Washington, D.C.: U.S. Department of Labor, Bureau of Labor Statistics, since 1993. As of July 13, 2007:
http://purl.access.gpo.gov/GPO/LPS6189

———, *BLS Handbook of Methods*, Washington, D.C.: U.S. Bureau of Labor Statistics, 1997.

———, "Mission Statement," October 16, 2001. As of July 27, 2007:
http://www.bls.gov/bls/blsmissn.htm

———, "Researcher Access to Confidential Data Files at the Bureau of Labor Statistics," last modified June 27, 2007. As of July 27, 2007:
http://www.bls.gov/bls/blsresda.htm

U.S. Census Bureau, "Research Program," undated Web page (a). As of August 9, 2007:
http://www.ces.census.gov/index.php/ces/1.00/researchprogram

———, "Statistics of U.S. Businesses: Tabulations by Enterprise Size: Introductory Text," undated Web page (b). As of July 13, 2007:
http://www.census.gov/epcd/susb/introusb.htm

———, *Census of Manufactures*, Washington, D.C.: U.S. Department of Commerce, Social and Economic Statistics Administration, and U.S. Bureau of the Census, quinquennially since 1947.

———, *1992 Census of Service Industries: Subject Series: Establishment and Firm Size (Including Legal Form of Organization)*, Washington, D.C.: U.S. Department of Commerce, Economics and Statistics Administration, and Bureau of the Census, 1995. As of May 8, 2006:
http://purl.access.gpo.gov/GPO/LPS29353

———, "Standard Industrial Classification (1994–1997)," Web page searching county business patterns for 1994 through 1997. As of July 23, 2007:
http://censtats.census.gov/cbpsic/cbpsic.shtml

———, "Establishment and Employment Changes from Births, Deaths, Expansions, and Contractions by Employment Size of the Enterprise for the United States, Industries (to 3 digit SIC): 1995–1996," spreadsheet, c. 1996. As of August 9, 2007:
http://www.census.gov/csd/susb/us3d95_96.xls

———, *1997 Economic Census: Health Care and Social Assistance*, Washington, D.C.: U.S. Census Bureau, 2000a. As of April 12, 2006:
http://purl.access.gpo.gov/GPO/LPS11908

————, *1997 Economic Census: Subject Series: Professional, Scientific, and Technical Services: Establishment and Firm Size (Including Legal Form of Organization)*, Washington, D.C.: U.S. Department of Commerce, Economics and Statistics Administration, and U.S. Census Bureau, 2000b. As of April 12, 2006: http://www.census.gov/prod/ec97/97s54-sz.pdf

————, "Technical Papers," last revised April 18, 2007a. As of August 9, 2007: http://lehd.did.census.gov/led/library/techpapers.html

————, "Statistics About Business Size (Including Small Business) from the U.S. Census Bureau," Web page, last modified April 25, 2007b. As of July 5, 2007: http://www.census.gov/epcd/www/smallbus.html

U.S. Chamber of Commerce, "Just the Facts: Small Business Health Plans," undated Web page. As of July 12, 2007: http://www.uschamber.com/issues/index/health/0306_ahps_facts.htm

U.S. Congress, Office of Technology Assessment, *Medical Testing and Health Insurance*, Washington, D.C.: Congress of the United States, Office of Technology Assessment, OTA-H-384, 1988. As of July 10, 2007: http://purl.access.gpo.gov/GPO/LPS27731

U.S. Department of Health and Human Services, "Agency for Healthcare Research and Quality: Medical Expenditure Panel Survey," undated Web page. As of July 27, 2007: http://www.meps.ahrq.gov/mepsweb/

————, "Office for Civil Rights—HIPAA," Web page, last revised June 29, 2007. As of July 10, 2007: http://www.hhs.gov/ocr/hipaa/

U.S. Department of Justice, *A Guide to Disability Rights Laws*, Washington, D.C.: U.S. Department of Justice, Civil Rights Division, Disability Rights Section, 2005. As of July 10, 2007: http://purl.access.gpo.gov/GPO/LPS70015

U.S. Department of Labor, "Compliance Assistance: Fair Labor Standards Act (FLSA)," undated Web page (a). As of July 9, 2007: http://www.dol.gov/esa/whd/flsa/

————, "State Workers' Compensation Laws," undated Web page (b). As of August 9, 2007: http://www.dol.gov/esa/regs/statutes/owcp/stwclaw/stwclaw.htm

————, "Consultation Program," Web page, last updated February 20, 2007. As of July 9, 2007: http://www.osha.gov/dcsp/smallbusiness/consult.html

U.S. Environmental Protection Agency, *33/50 Program: The Final Record*, Washington, D.C.: U.S. Environmental Protection Agency, EPA-745-R-99-004, March 1999. As of July 5, 2007:
http://www.epa.gov/opptintr/3350/

———, "Small Business Compliance Policy," May 11, 2000. As of July 6, 2007:
http://www.epa.gov/compliance/resources/policies/incentives/smallbusiness/sbcomppolicy.pdf

———, Office of Policy, Economics, and Innovation, *Environmental Assistance Services for Small Business: A Resource Guide*, Washington, D.C.: U.S. Environmental Protection Agency, Office of Policy, Economics, and Innovation, August 2001. As of September 17, 2007:
http://purl.access.gpo.gov/GPO/LPS12599

———, "Project XL," Web page, last updated March 2, 2006a. As of July 5, 2007:
http://www.epa.gov/projctxl/

———, "Compliance Incentives and Auditing," last updated March 23, 2006b. As of August 9, 2007:
http://www.epa.gov/compliance/incentives/smallbusiness/index.html

———, "National Environmental Performance Track," Web page, last updated June 25, 2007. As of July 5, 2007:
http://www.epa.gov/perftrac/

U.S. Food and Drug Administration, "The Food Label," backgrounder 99-5, updated May 17, 1999. As of July 5, 2007:
http://www.fda.gov/opacom/backgrounders/foodlabel/newlabel.html

U.S. General Accounting Office, *Health Insurance Regulation: Variation in Recent State Small Employer Health Insurance Reforms: Fact Sheet for the Chairman, Subcommittee on Employer-Employee Relations, Committee on Economic and Educational Opportunities, House of Representatives*, Washington, D.C.: U.S. General Accounting Office, GAO/HEHS-95-161FS, 1995. As of July 10, 2007:
http://purl.access.gpo.gov/GPO/LPS11369

———, *Regulatory Burden: Measurement Challenges and Concerns Raised By Selected Companies: Report to Congressional Requesters*, Washington, D.C.: U.S. General Accounting Office, GAO/GGD-97-2, 1996. As of July 5, 2007:
http://purl.access.gpo.gov/GPO/LPS12784

———, *Private Health Insurance: Small Employers Continue to Face Challenges in Providing Coverage*, Washington, D.C.: U.S. General Accounting Office, GAO-02-8, 2001. As of July 10, 2007:
http://purl.access.gpo.gov/GPO/LPS46078

—————, *Private Health Insurance: Federal and State Requirements Affecting Coverage Offered by Small Businesses*, Washington, D.C.: U.S. General Accounting Office, GAO-03-1133, 2003a. As of July 10, 2007:
http://purl.access.gpo.gov/GPO/LPS38118

—————, *Securities and Exchange Commission: Management's Report on Internal Control Over Financial Reporting and Certification of Disclosure in Exchange Act Periodic Reports*, Washington, D.C.: U.S. General Accounting Office, GAO-03-933R, 2003b. As of July 24, 2007:
http://purl.access.gpo.gov/GPO/LPS37472

U.S. Government Accountability Office, and U.S. Senate Committee on Small Business and Entrepreneurship, *Sarbanes-Oxley Act: Consideration of Key Principles Needed in Addressing Implementation for Smaller Public Companies: Report to the Committee on Small Business and Entrepreneurship, U.S. Senate*, Washington, D.C.: U.S. Government Accountability Office, GAO-06-361, 2006. As of July 10, 2007:
http://purl.access.gpo.gov/GPO/LPS70554

U.S. House of Representatives, Committee on the Judiciary, *Bankruptcy Abuse Prevention and Consumer Protection Act of 2005: Report of the Committee on the Judiciary to Accompany S.256 Together with Dissenting, Additional Dissenting, and Additional Minority Views*, Washington, D.C.: U.S. Government Printing Office, 2005. As of July 5, 2007:
http://purl.access.gpo.gov/GPO/LPS61612

U.S. Occupational Safety and Health Administration, "Occupational Injury and Illness Recording and Reporting Requirements," undated Web page. As of August 9, 2007:
http://www.osha.gov/pls/oshaweb/owadisp.show_document?p_table=FEDERAL_REGISTER&p_id=16919

—————, *Small Business Handbook*, Washington, D.C.: U.S. Occupational Safety and Health Administration, 2005. As of July 28, 2007:
http://purl.access.gpo.gov/GPO/LPS61356

—————, "State Occupational Safety and Health Plans," last updated December 27, 2006. As of August 9, 2007:
http://www.osha.gov/dcsp/osp/index.html

U.S. Securities and Exchange Commission, "Conditional Small Issues Exemption from Registration Under the Securities Act of 1933," December 10, 2001. As of July 5, 2007:
http://www.sec.gov/divisions/corpfin/forms/smallbus.shtml

—————, "Pitt Seeks Review of Corporate Governance, Conduct Codes," press release, February 13, 2002a. As of July 25, 2007:
http://www.sec.gov/news/press/2002-23.txt

———, "Order Requiring the Filing of Sworn Statements Pursuant to Section 21(a)(1) of the Securities Exchange Act of 1934," file 4-460, June 27, 2002b. As of July 24, 2007:
http://www.sec.gov/rules/other/4-460.htm

———, "Ownership Reports and Trading by Officers, Directors and Principal Security Holders," releases 34-4621 and 35-27563, August 27, 2002c. As of July 24, 2007:
http://www.sec.gov/rules/final/34-46421.htm

———, "Certification of Disclosure in Companies' Quarterly and Annual Reports," releases 33-8124 and 34-46427, August 28, 2002d. As of July 24, 2007:
http://www.sec.gov/rules/final/33-8124.htm

———, "Insider Trades During Pension Fund Blackout Periods," release 34-47225, January 22, 2003a. As of July 24, 2007:
http://www.sec.gov/rules/final/34-47225.htm

———, "Disclosure Required by Sections 406 and 407 of the Sarbanes-Oxley Act of 2002; Correction," releases 33-8177A and 34-47235A, March 26, 2003b. As of July 24, 2007:
http://www.sec.gov/rules/final/33-8177a.htm

———, "Strengthening the Commission's Requirements Regarding Auditor Independence," release 33-8183, March 27, 2003c. As of August 24, 2007:
http://www.sec.gov/rules/final/33-8183.htm

———, "Standards Relating to Listed Company Audit Committees," releases 33-8220 and 34-47654, April 9, 2003d. As of July 24, 2007:
http://www.sec.gov/rules/final/33-8220.htm

———, "Final Rule: Mandated Electronic Filing and Website Posting for Forms 3, 4 and 5," Releases 33-8230, 34-47809, and 35-27674, May 7, 2003e. As of July 24, 2007:
http://www.sec.gov/rules/final/33-8230.htm

———, "Self-Regulatory Organizations; New York Stock Exchange, Inc. and National Association of Securities Dealers, Inc.; Order Approving Proposed Rule Changes (SR-NYSE-2002-33 and SR-NASD-2002-141) and Amendments No. 1 Thereto; Order Approving Proposed Rule Changes (SR-NASD-2002-77, SR-NASD-2002-80, SR-NASD-2002-138 and SR-NASD-2002-139) and Amendments No. 1 to SR-NASD-2002-80 and SR-NASD-2002-139; and Notice of Filing and Order Granting Accelerated Approval of Amendment Nos. 2 and 3 to SR-NYSE-2002-33, Amendment Nos. 2, 3, 4 and 5 to SR-NASD-2002-141, Amendment Nos. 2 and 3 to SR-NASD-2002-80, Amendment Nos. 1, 2, and 3 to SR-NASD-2002-138, and Amendment No. 2 to SR-NASD-2002-139, Relating to Corporate Governance," release 34-48745, November 4, 2003f. As of July 25, 2007:
http://www.sec.gov/rules/sro/34-48745.htm

————, "Self-Regulatory Organizations; Order Granting Approval of Proposed Rule Change by the American Stock, Exchange LLC and Notice of Filing and Order Granting Accelerated Approval of Amendment No. 2 Relating to Enhanced Corporate Governance Requirements Applicable to Listed Companies," release 34-48863, December 1, 2003g.

————, "Final Rule: Management's Report on Internal Control Over Financial Reporting and Certification of Disclosure in Exchange Act Periodic Reports," release 33-8392, February 24, 2004a. As of July 24, 2007: http://www.sec.gov/rules/final/33-8392.htm

————, "Public Company Accounting Oversight Board; Order Approving Proposed Auditing Standard No. 2, *An Audit of Internal Control Over Financial Reporting Performed in Conjunction with an Audit of Financial Statements* ('Auditing Standard No. 2')," release 34-49884, June 17, 2004b. As of July 24, 2007: http://www.sec.gov/rules/pcaob/34-49884.htm

————, "Order Under Section 36 of the Securities Exchange Act of 1934 Granting an Execmption from Specified Provisions of Exchange Act Rules 13a-1 and 15d-1," release 34-50754, November 30, 2004c. As of July 24, 2007: http://www.sec.gov/rules/exorders/34-50754.htm

————, "Management's Report on Internal Control Over Financial Reporting and Certification of Disclosure in Exchange Act Periodic Reports of Non-Accelerated Filers and Foreign Private Issuers," release 33-8545, March 2, 2005a. As of July 24, 2007: http://www.sec.gov/rules/final/33-8545.htm

————, "Management's Report on Internal Control Over Financial Reporting and Certification of Disclosure in Exchange Act Periodic Reports of Companies That Are Not Accelerated Filers," release 33-8618 and 34-52492, September 22, 2005b. As of July 24, 2007: http://www.sec.gov/rules/final/33-8618.pdf

————, *Final Report of the Advisory Committee on Smaller Public Companies to the United States Securities and Exchange Commission*, Washington, D.C.: Advisory Committee on Smaller Public Companies to the U.S. Securities and Exchange Commission, April 23, 2006a. As of July 24, 2007: http://sec.gov/info/smallbus/acspc/acspc-finalreport.pdf

————, "Q&A: Small Business and the SEC," Web page, last modified May 24, 2006b. As of September 1, 2005: http://www.sec.gov/info/smallbus/qasbsec.htm

————, "Internal Control Over Financial Reporting in Exchange Act Periodic Reports of Non-Accelerated Filers and Newly Public Companies," releases 33-8760 and 34-54942, December 15, 2006c. As of July 24, 2007: http://www.sec.gov/rules/final/2006/33-8760.pdf

————, "Registration Statement Under the Securities Act of 1933," form SB-1, March 2007a. As of July 5, 2007:
http://www.sec.gov/about/forms/formsb-1.pdf

————, "Registration Statement Under the Securities Act of 1933," form SB-2, March 2007b. As of July 5, 2007:
http://www.sec.gov/about/forms/formsb-2.pdf

U.S. Sentencing Commission, *Guidelines Manual*, Washington, D.C.: U.S. Sentencing Commission, November 2004. As of July 25, 2007:
http://www.ussc.gov/2004guid/TABCON04.htm

U.S. Small Business Administration, "Size Standards," undated Web page (a). As of July 27, 2007:
http://www.sba.gov/services/contractingopportunities/sizestandardstopics/

————, Office of the Chief Counsel for Advocacy, "Small Business Law Library," undated Web page (b). As of July 5, 2007:
http://www.sba.gov/advo/laws/law_lib.html

————, *The Changing Burden of Regulation, Paperwork, and Tax Compliance on Small Business: A Report to Congress*, rev. ed., Washington, D.C.: U.S. Small Business Administration, Office of the Chief Counsel for Advocacy, 1995. As of July 5, 2007:
http://purl.access.gpo.gov/GPO/LPS4194

U.S. Small Business Administration, and Government Contracting Institute, *Small Business Administration Small Business Size Standards Under the New North American Industry Classification System (NAICS): Effective October 1, 2000*, Rockville, Md.: Government Contracting Institute, 2000.

U.S. Statutes, Title 26, Section 209, Sherman Act, July 2, 1890.

————, Title 38, Section 717, Federal Trade Commission Act, September 26, 1914.

————, Title 44, Section 577, Railway Labor Act of 1926, May 20, 1926.

Verick, Sher, *Threshold Effects of Dismissal Protection Legislation in Germany*, Bonn: Institute for the Study of Labor, discussion paper 991, January 2004. As of July 10, 2007:
http://www.iza.org/index_html?lang=en&mainframe=http%3A//www.iza.org/en/webcontent/publications/papers/viewAbstract%3Fdp_id%3D991&topSelect=publications&subSelect=papers

Verkuil, Paul R., "A Critical Guide to the Regulatory Flexibility Act," *Duke Law Journal*, Vol. 1982, No. 2, April 1982, pp. 213–276.

Viscusi, W. Kip, *Risk by Choice: Regulating Health and Safety in the Workplace*, Cambridge, Mass.: Harvard University Press, 1983.

Vock, Daniel C., 'High Court OKs Rules to Widen LLC Protections," *Chicago Daily Law Bulletin*, April 1, 2003, p. 1.

Wagner, Stephen, and Lee Dittmar, "The Unexpected Benefits of Sarbanes-Oxley," *Harvard Business Review*, April 2006, pp. 133–141.

Walker, Tom, "Commentary: Bankruptcy Law Gift to Credit-Card Firms," *Providence (Rhode Island) Journal*, July 6, 2005, p. B4.

Weiss, Andrew, and Henry J. Landau, "Wages, Hiring Standards, and Firm Size," *Journal of Labor Economics*, Vol. 2, No. 4, October 1984, pp. 477–499.

White, Lawrence J., "Trends in Aggregate Concentration in the United States," *Journal of Economic Perspectives*, Vol. 16, No. 4, Autumn 2002, pp. 137–160.

Williams, Claudia, *A Snapshot of State Experience Implementing Premium Assistance Programs*, Portland, Me.: National Academy for State Health Policy, 2003. As of July 10, 2007:
http://www.statecoverage.net/statereports/multi19.pdf

Wilson, James Q., *Bureaucracy: What Government Agencies Do and Why They Do It*, New York: Basic Books, 1989.

Wintoki, M. Babajide, "Corporate Boards and Regulation: The Effect of the Sarbanes-Oxley Act and the Exchange Listing Requirements on Firm Value," *Journal of Corporate Finance*, Vol. 13, Nos. 2–3, June 2007, pp. 229–250.

Wolkoff, Neal, "Sarbanes-Oxley Is a Curse for Small-Cap Companies," *Wall Street Journal*, August 15, 2005, p. A13.

Wooldridge, Jeffrey M., *Econometric Analysis of Cross Section and Panel Data*, Cambridge, Mass.: MIT Press, 2002.

Yeager, P. C., "Structural Bias in Regulatory Law Enforcement: The Case of the U.S. Environmental Protection Agency," *Social Problems*, Vol. 34, No. 4, 1987, pp. 330–344.

Zawacki, Alice M., and Amy K. Taylor, *Contributions to Health Insurance Premiums: When Does the Employer Pay 100 Percent?* Washington, D.C.: Bureau of the Census, Center for Economic Studies discussion paper 05-27, 2005.

Zeckhauser, Richard, "Medical Insurance: A Case Study of the Tradeoff Between Risk Spreading and Appropriate Incentives," *Journal of Economic Theory*, Vol. 2, No. 1, March 1970, pp. 10–26.

Zhang, Ivy Xiying, *Economic Consequences of the Sarbanes-Oxley Act of 2002*, doctoral thesis, University of Rochester, 2005.

Zuckerman, Stephen, and Shruti Rajan, "Research Papers: An Alternative Approach to Measuring the Effects of Insurance Market Reforms," *Inquiry*, Vol. 36, No. 1, 1999, pp. 44–56.